DYNAMIC ASSET ALLOCATION WITH FORWARDS AND FUTURES

DYNAMIC ASSET ALLOCATION WITH FORWARDS AND FUTURES

By

ABRAHAM LIOUI
Bar Ilan University, Israel

and

PATRICE PONCET
University of Paris I Pantheon-Sorbonne, France
and
ESSEC Business School, France

Springer

Library of Congress Cataloging-in-Publication Data

Lioui, Abraham.
Dynamic asset allocation with forwards and futures / by Abraham Lioui and Patrice Poncet
p.cm.
Includes bibliographical references and index.
1.Capital assets pricing model. 2. Hedging (Finance) 3. Equilibrium (Economics) I. Poncet, Patrice. II. Title.

HG4515.2.L56 2005
332.64'524—dc22 2004065099

ISBN 0-387-24107-8 e-ISBN 0-387-24106-X Printed on acid-free paper.

Printed in the United States of America.

9 8 7 6 5 4 3 2 1 SPIN 11050636

springeronline.com

To Osnat, Itzhak and Yair

To Marie, Agnès, Caroline and Sophie

TABLE OF CONTENTS

Preface

This book is an advanced text on the theory of forward and futures markets which aims at providing readers with a comprehensive knowledge of how prices are established and evolve in time, what optimal strategies one can expect the participants to follow, whether they pertain to arbitrage, speculation or hedging, what characterizes such markets and what major theoretical and practical differences distinguish futures from forward contracts. It should be of interest to students (MBAs majoring in finance with quantitative skills and PhDs in finance and financial economics), academics (both theoreticians and empiricists), practitioners, and regulators.

Standard textbooks dealing with forward and futures markets generally focus on the description of the contracts, institutional details, and the effective (as opposed to theoretically optimal) use of these instruments by practitioners. The theoretical analysis is often reduced to the (undoubtedly important) cash-and-carry relationship and the computation of the simple, static, minimum variance hedge ratio. This book proposes an alternative approach of these markets from the perspective of dynamic asset allocation and asset pricing theory within an inter-temporal framework that is in line with what has been done many years ago for options markets.

The main ingredients of this recipe are those of modern finance, namely the assumed absence of frictions and arbitrage opportunities in financial and real markets, the uniqueness of the economic general equilibrium (when the no-arbitrage assumption is not powerful enough and such an equilibrium is required), and the tools of continuous time finance, namely martingale theory and stochastic dynamic programming (to keep developments tractable, we will assume that all stochastic processes are diffusion processes). Therefore, tribute must be paid to the pioneers of the relevant fields or techniques: Merton (who introduced continuous time in finance and whose numerous articles during the seventies dealt with all the major topics in that field, such as optimal investment and consumption decisions, contingent claim analysis (an extension of the celebrated Black-Scholes formula (1973)), and inter-temporal asset pricing), Sharpe (1964), Lintner (1965) and Breeden (1979) for capital asset pricing models (CAPM), Harrison and Kreps (1979) and Harrison and Pliska (1981) for the complete structure of asset pricing theory, Cox, Ingersoll and Ross (1985a) for their stochastic production economy and their work on the yield curve, Karatzas, Lehoczky and Shreve (1987) and Cox and Huang (1989, 1991) who showed under what conditions a dynamic optimisation problem reduces to a simpler, static, one, and Heath, Jarrow and Morton (1992) for their pioneering model of stochastic interest rates. Although we will provide a refresher on these concepts, approaches and models before using them extensively, the reader should have preferably a basic knowledge of these materials.

The book is neither a streamlined course text nor a research monograph, but rather stands between the two, as it is the natural extension of one of our common fields of published research. The reader is referred to Kolb (2002), Rendleman (2002) or Hull (2003) for very pedagogical textbooks and to Duffie (1989) for a somewhat more advanced text. The scope of this book is essentially theoretical. Although technicalities are unavoidable, they are kept at the lowest possible level (beyond which some substance is lost). Emphasis is on economic meaning and financial interpretation rather than on mathematical rigor. No attempts are made at estimating or testing the empirical validity of the various models that we or others have developed. It is only by incidence that empirical evidence will be mentioned or discussed. However, simulations will at times be performed when important insights can be delivered or when it is important to assess the practical relevance of some theoretical results. Also, as to the use of forwards and futures for investment and/or hedging, focus is on optimal strategies rather than on actual practice. Finally, potentially important aspects of these derivatives markets are ignored: transaction and information costs, borrowing constraints, legal and tax considerations, issues (such as liquidity) that are best analyzed by means of microstructure theory, differences between forwards and futures other than the marking-to-market mechanism, and so on. On the other hand, differences due to the nature of the underlying asset (be it a commodity, a currency, an interest rate, a bond, a stock or stock index, or an non-tradable asset such as the Consumer Price Index) are discussed when relevant.

The book is structured as follows. Part I offers a general presentation of forward and futures markets and should be read first. Chapter 1 presents the basic economic analysis of forward and futures contracts, some essential institutional details, such as the marking-to-market mechanism that characterizes futures, various data as to the size and scope of the relevant markets, and empirical evidence as to the use and expansion of such instruments, their price relationships and the usefulness of some institutional features. Chapter 2 is essential to the understanding of the sequel as it provides the basic valuation methodology and price formulas we have at our disposal under both deterministic and stochastic interest rates. Throughout the remainder of the book, interest rates will obey stochastic processes.

Parts II and III can be read in any order, although it is more logical to read them in the proposed order. Part II consists of 6 chapters of, very roughly, increasing generality. In each of them, optimal strategies using futures are compared to strategies using the forward counterparts. Chapter 3 deals with a pure hedging problem, as this seems to be a main motivation for market participants. Chapter 4 is more general as it solves the optimal portfolio problem of an investor endowed with a non-traded cash position. Chapter 5 is concerned by investment (or speculation) alone, but in an incomplete (rather than complete as in the previous two chapters) setting. Chapter 6 is specific to exchange risk. It uses a different methodology and tackles the problem of a foreign investor who faces a currency risk in addition to the risks associated with his/her investment abroad and both domestic and foreign random interest rates. Chapter 7 deals with the optimality of using a spread (a long position in one contract and a short one in an other contract of different maturity) and provides the characteristics of the optimal spread. Chapter 8 finally examines the issue of stochastic dividend or convenience yield. Although we retain a complete market setting, this feature alone invalidates most of the results regarding equilibrium prices and optimal strategies valid when these yields are deterministic.

Part III is about general equilibrium pricing. When forward or futures contracts are not redundant instruments, their introduction completes the financial market. Therefore, the usual no-arbitrage arguments are not sufficient to price them and a general equilibrium exercise must be performed. Chapter 9 is set in a pure exchange economy and shows how the various CAPMs must be amended to take properly into account this introduction, which modifies all portfolio allocations and all asset prices. In particular, traditional results regarding the mean-variance efficiency of the market portfolio become invalid. Chapter 10 extends the analysis to the case of a production economy a la Cox, Ingersoll and Ross (1985a), which reshapes the form of the various CAPMs. Also, it is shown that the cash-and-carry relationship does not hold in general and, when it does, must be grounded on equilibrium, not absence of arbitrage, considerations. Finally, Chapter 11 presents the most general framework of all. To the production economy of the previous chapter, we add a monetary sector in which the money supply by the Central Bank is an exogenous stochastic process, so that a genuine monetary economy is obtained. The stochastic process followed by the Consumer Price Index, CPI, is derived in an endogenous manner and then the prices of forward and futures contracts written on it. Since the CPI is not a traded asset, general equilibrium analysis is required.

Acknowledgements

We are grateful to many people, in particular the researchers who have developed the theories and techniques outlined above, as well as the editors and anonymous referees whose comments, remarks and criticisms have often improved substantially the quality of our published work. We also have a long standing intellectual debt towards Florin Aftalion, Bernard Dumas, and, especially, Roland Portait. We have benefited from useful communications and discussions with Darrell Duffie and Oldrich Vasicek, and a joint work in a related area with Pascal Nguyen Duc Trong. We have also benefited from stimulating discussions during workshops and seminars with our respective colleagues at Bar Ilan, the Sorbonne and the ESSEC Business School, and attendants to various international conferences or seminars. As is almost always the case, teaching to our respective students part of the materials that this book is made of was both a challenge and a reward.

Special thanks are due to David Cella for initiating this project and Judith Pforr for continuous assistance during the process.

Finally, we cannot be grateful enough to our wives and children who have had to suffer from often too long intellectual or physical absences and have nonetheless given us their love and patience without parsimony.

Naturally, we alone assume full responsibility for any errors that would have escaped our attention. Readers are welcome to let us know about any of them as well as to send comments. Our respective email addresses are liouia@mail.biu.ac.il and poncet@essec.fr

NOTATIONS

Standard definitions and notations that are used throughout the book are listed below.

- P (t, T) is the price at time t of a zero-coupon (or pure discount) bond maturing at time $T \geq t$, the bond paying \$1 at time T and nothing before. By definition P(T,T) =1.

- r(t) is the (instantaneous) spot rate prevailing at date t. It is the continuously compounded rate on a zero-coupon bond with infinitesimal residual maturity. Hence:

$$r(t) = \left. \frac{-\partial \ln P(t,T)}{\partial T} \right|_{T=t} \tag{1}$$

- f(t, s, T) is the forward rate that prevails at date t, starting at date s>t and with maturity date T>s. It is the continuously compounded yield of the pure discount bond of maturity T traded forward. It is defined as:

$$f(t,s,T) = \frac{\ln P(t,s) - \ln P(t,T)}{T-s} \tag{2}$$

- f(t, s) is the instantaneous forward rate (sometimes misleadingly called "spot" forward rate) prevailing at time t and starting at date s. It is the limit of f(t, s, T) as (T-s) goes to zero:

$$f(t,s) = \lim_{T \to s} f(t,s,T) = \lim_{h \to 0} \left(-\frac{P(t,s+h) - P(t,s)}{h.P(t,s)} \right) = -\frac{\partial \ln P(t,s)}{\partial s} \tag{3}$$

- Thus the spot rate r(t) is the limit of the instantaneous forward rate f(t,s) when (s-t) tends to zero:

$$r(t) = f(t,t) \tag{4}$$

As a general proposition, a spot rate or spot price can always be viewed as a particular case of a forward rate or forward price.

- The locally riskless asset, or money market account, the value of which starts at \$1 at date t=0, is worth at time t:

$$B(t) = \exp\left[\int_0^t r(s) ds \right] \tag{5}$$

- The bond price and the instantaneous forward rates are linked by the following relationship:

$$P(t,T) = \exp\left[-\int_t^T f(t,s)ds\right] \quad (6)$$

which obtains from integrating (3) from t to T.

- S(t) is the spot price of an asset at date t, typically a stock, a stock index, a commodity, or, occasionally and when no confusion can occur, an exchange rate.

- G(t) is the forward price of an asset, and is a short notation for G(t,T), T (> t) being the maturity date of the forward contract, or for $G(t,T,T_P)$ in the case of a contract written on a pure discount bond of maturity $T_P > T$. Sometimes, though, to avoid confusion, we will keep the full notation G(t,T) or $G(t, T,T_P)$.

- H(t), similarly, is the futures price of an asset and is short for either H(t,T) or $H(t,T, T_P)$.

- W(t) is an economic agent's wealth at date t.

- U(W(t)) is an economic agent's Von Neuman - Morgenstern utility function, which is state independent and exhibits risk aversion $(U'>0,\ U'(0) = +\infty,\ U''<0)$.

- J(t, W(t), .) is the economic agent's value (indirect utility) function at time t, defined by $J(.) \equiv E\left[U(W(T)) \middle| F_t\right]$, where T is the agent's horizon, $E[.\,|\,F_t]$ is the conditional expectation operator, conditional on the information (filtration) F_t available at date t (>T).

- a(t) denotes a hedge ratio, for instance the value of an agent's forward or futures position divided by his/her wealth, and A(t) is the number of units of the forward or futures held at time t.

- Z(t) and **Z**(t) are a one-dimensional and a K-dimensional Brownian motion, respectively, defined on a complete probability space. Generally, vectors and matrices are written in bold face while scalars are not.

- $\mu(.)$ is the drift term of a diffusion process, and $\boldsymbol{\mu}(.)$ a vector of drifts.

- $\sigma(.)$ is the diffusion coefficient of a diffusion process and $\Sigma(.)$ is a vector or a matrix of diffusion coefficients.

- $\mathbf{X}(t)$ or $\mathbf{Y}(t)$ is a vector of state variables affecting the investment opportunity set available to the economic agents.

- A lower-case subscript d (respectively, f) denotes a domestic (resp., foreign) variable. For instance, in a two-country economy, $r_d(t)$ and $r_f(t)$ are the relevant spot rates.

PART I

THE BASICS

A basic understanding of the way forward and futures markets work and can be used is required to apprehend the ideas and results developed in parts II and III.

Chapter 1 presents the economic analysis of forward and futures contracts, the necessary institutional details, such as quotations, delivery, margin calls and the marking-to-market mechanism. In addition, since we will not cover these topics except by incidence, we provide a set of data regarding the size and scope of the derivatives markets (including options for comparison with futures and forwards) measured by both volumes and open interests. In addition, a rather large body of empirical evidence is reported, relative to the use and usefulness of forward and futures contracts, their price relationships that link their prices and the underlying spot prices, and the efficiency of some institutional arrangements.

Chapter 2 provides the standard methodology and results regarding the valuation of forward and futures instruments under both deterministic and stochastic interest rates and with and without deterministic dividend or convenience yield. In this book, interest rates will be stochastic and obey various diffusion processes.

CHAPTER 1: FORWARD AND FUTURES MARKETS

The overall outburst of volatility of interest rates, exchanges rate, stocks and commodities that has plagued recurrently most economies, in particular in the West and in South-East Asia, since the late seventies has accelerated the need for and the creation of new speculative and hedging instruments. Among them, swaps, forward and futures contracts play a major role. This phenomenon has also elicited important developments in investment concepts and techniques. This book examines the general issue of optimal portfolio strategy in a multi-period context where investors maximizing expected utility of consumption and/or terminal wealth face all kinds of risks. More precisely, it offers to contribute to the investment and hedging literature in the rather general case where the value of traded and non-traded assets depends on stochastic processes. All economic agents, in particular financial institutions, non financial firms and individuals are in this situation.

The economic significance of forward and futures instruments is not disputable. They have known so huge a development they have dwarfed primitive cash markets both in terms of liquidity and volume of transactions. In particular, most market makers on interest and exchange rate products traded over-the-counter and most major corporations worldwide use all kinds of forwards and futures for hedging purposes. Many such instruments are written on tradable financial assets or storable commodities, which implies that they are fundamentally redundant instruments. However, the proportion of contracts that cannot be considered as redundant, even as a first approximation, is increasing. Some of these are or will shortly be written on non-tradable economic variables. A representative example is the futures contracts on a Consumer Price Index that could be launched in the near future by various Central Banks. Comparable contracts could be expanded to other macro-economic aggregates, such as the Gross National Product and monetary aggregates. Other famous examples are weather or, more generally, nature-linked derivatives. Another category includes forward contracts written on non-storable commodities (such as electricity), which have recently attracted much attention. On-going projects include non-redundant forwards written on computer memory storage capacity, on emission credits and on bank credits. These propositions largely (but not exclusively) focus on forward or futures contracts. Since this book aims to be an advanced text, it provides only the information sufficient to grasp the financial and economic underpinnings of these contracts. We refer the reader to standard textbooks for more institutional details and conventions, the exact characteristics of the contracts and the way to trade them in practice[1]. Also, the list of the main mathematical definitions and notations is provided at the beginning of the book.

1.1. DEFINITIONS

A *forward* or a *futures* contract is an agreement between two parties made on a date t to buy (for the long position holder) and to sell (for the short position holder) a specified amount of an underlying asset (or good or rate) on a future date T (the *delivery date*) and at a given price G(t, T) (*forward price*) or H(t,T) (*futures price*). The price is set such that the *value* of the contract is *nil* for each party at the initial date t. At date T, the seller delivers the underlying asset to the buyer against the agreed price, so that, depending on the actual *spot,* or *cash, price* S(T) of the asset on the market, one of them gains what the other loses (a contract, as any other derivative, is a zero-sum game). For instance, adopting the buyer's standpoint who receives the asset against the agreed price of the contract, the profit-and-loss (P&L) statement writes, at time T:

$$S(T) - G(t,T) \quad \text{or} \quad \approx S(T) - H(t,T) \qquad (1)$$

which can be positive, negative or zero, and where S(T) is a random variable viewed from date t[2]. Hence, the buyer (seller) expects, takes a bet on, or fears a price increase (decrease) of the underlying asset.

Forward contracts are OTC (over-the-counter) instruments that are *customized* to the needs or requirements of the two parties. Futures are *standardized* instruments created and traded on official exchanges which are legal entities endowed with their own characteristics, regulation, supervisory body, and equity capital (to guarantee the safety of deals to all market participants).

Futures and forward contracts are traded all over the world and are written on practically all financial primitive assets and too numerous non-financial goods to mention. Following the lead of the Chicago Board of Trade, established in 1848 to trade agricultural grains, many exchange-traded markets have been created since the 1980's. Table 1.1 provides a list of major US and international futures exchanges.

Table 1.1. Major US and International Futures Exchanges

Name and address	Main contracts
US exchanges	
Chicago Board of Trade (CBOT) www.cbot.com	Treasury Bonds and notes, agricultural grains
Chicago Mercantile Exchange (CME) www.cme.com	S&P 500 Index, Eurodollars, currencies, livestock
New York Mercantile Exchange (NYMEX) www.nymex.com	Metals, crude oil, natural gas
International exchanges	
LIFFE (London) www.liffe.com	European stock indices (e.g. FTSE 100), 3-month Euribor, other European interest rates
EUREX (Francfurt, Zurich, Geneva) www.eurexchange.com	European government bonds (e.g. EURO -BOBL and EURO -BUND, European stock indices (e.g. Dow Jones EURO STOXX and STOXX)
MATIF (Paris) www.matif.fr	EURO-based fixed income instruments, European stock indices (e.g. French CAC 40) commodities
SIMEX (Singapore) www.simex.com.sg	Asian interest rates and equities
TIFFE (Tokyo) www.tiffe.or.jp	Currency and interest rates
BM&F (Brazil) www.bmf.com.br	Gold, stock index, interest and exchange rates
SFE (Sydney) www.sfe.com.au	Interest rates, equities and stock index, commodities

1.2. CONVENTIONS, QUOTATIONS AND DELIVERY

The underlying asset may exist, as is the case for currencies, bills, equities, and commodities or not, as for bonds. In the latter case, the exchange posts a (short) list of the government bonds that can be delivered by sellers to buyers in lieu of the fictitious bond. Since the bonds in the list have not exactly the same value, the actual bond that will be given to the buyer is called the "*cheapest to deliver*". We will not take that feature into account and implicitly assume that the futures or forward is written on a single specific bond. Similarly, when the underlying is a commodity, the *grades* of the goods that can be delivered are specified beforehand. We will also consider implicitly that a single grade is deliverable.

The contract *size* corresponds to the *notional* amount of the underlying asset, such as $1 million for the CME 13-week T-bill contract. The *delivery month* is the month when the contract expires.

The futures (or forward) price is *quoted* differently according to the nature of its underlying asset. The quote may be dollars (or amounts of any other relevant currency), as in the case of commodities or exchange rates, a pure number, as in the case of a stock index, a percentage of the nominal value of the underlying asset (with two decimals) as in the case of bonds, or 100 minus the interest rate (with three decimals) when the underlying asset is an interest rate. The *tick* is the minimum price fluctuation between two successive quotes.

Sometimes the exchanges impose *daily price limits* that can occasionally be complex. Whether these are justified on economic grounds is still the subject of much debate; the current trend is towards liberalization, and the typical price limits in financial futures are more liberal than those in agricultural commodities.

Most contracts allow for the possibility of *physical delivery* of the underlying (commodities, metals, currencies, stocks, bonds and bills). However, *cash settlement* is an alternative, sometimes required because physical delivery is impossible (such as a large stock index, a short term interest rate, a weather or catastrophe index, the Consumer Price Index). In financial terms, *physical delivery* and *cash settlement* are theoretically equivalent and will be treated as such in this book. In other words, possible frictions such as time delay, quality, and location of delivery will be ignored, although they may be relevant in practice.

1.3. MARGIN CALLS AND MARKING-TO-MARKET

Forward and futures contracts differ essentially by two features, one that can (and will) be neglected and one that is crucial and will give rise to important discrepancies between strategies involving either futures or forwards. Both aim at eliminating the risk of default from the party who is losing money on the contract(s) bought or sold. Consider the case of a forward contract. At date T (which can be far away from the initial date t), the price of the spot asset S(T) may be much smaller or much larger than the agreed upon price G(t,T). Consequently, the losing party may be unable to honor his commitment and thus defaults. The other party then sustains a real (opportunity) loss, which could itself provoke her own default under some circumstances.

The first feature is the *initial margin* (or *deposit*) which is the dollar amount per contract that must be deposited by both the buyer and the seller to be allowed to take position on a futures. As the deposit is but a small fraction (typically from 1,5 to 5%) of the value of the futures position, such a position involves substantial *leverage*. Since, however, this margin can (and will) be deposited under the form of a security (a *collateral*) such as a T-bill or T-bond, rather than cash, no opportunity gain is lost in fact by the parties (the interests accrue to the owner of the security). This is the reason why it can and will be ignored in the analysis.

The second feature is the *variation margin*, which can be positive or negative. At the end of each trading day (or, exceptionally, when a price limit has been reached), the clearing house of the exchange fictitiously closes the positions of all participants and cash settles them as follows. Suppose first the trade has taken place the same day. The clearing house computes the gain or loss for the buyer and the seller by subtracting the agreed price from the closing price of the contract. The gain is cashed in by the winner and cashed out by the loser: unlike the initial deposit, the variation margin must be in *cash*. If the losing party is unable to meet his margin call, his position is canceled and taken over by the clearing house who then uses the initial deposit to recoup its loss. If the trade has taken place before the present day (and no canceling position has been taken), the clearing house computes the difference between the closing price of the contract and the closing price of the previous day and, again, the gain is cashed in by the winner and cashed out by the loser.

This important mechanism is known as *marking-to-market* the position. Consequently, for a trader who maintains her position from date t to delivery date T, the final gain or loss is ±(S(T) – H(t,T)), according to formula (1). Indeed, all the intermediate prices H(t', T), for t' = t+1, ..., T-1, cancel out in the summation of margins over time, *provided we ignore as a first approximation the interest factor in daily gains and losses*. We will argue throughout the book that, when interest rates are assumed to be deterministic, this approximation, which leads to no material difference between forwards and futures, is harmless but, when interest rates are stochastic (which they really are), the difference between the two kinds of contracts is substantial strategy-wise. Note also that, as our economies are set in continuous time, our futures contracts will be marked to market *continuously*, as opposed to daily.

Another important difference between forwards and futures that derives from the margin calls mechanism that characterizes futures is the *value* of the contracts. Upon entering a forward or a futures contract, no cash is exchanged between the buyer and the seller and, therefore, the value of the contract is *zero* at its inception. Since a futures contract is continuously marked to the market, its value *remains zero* at any point of time. It is obviously *not* the case for a forward: since no adjustment is made to the initial price G(t,T) although the spot price of the underlying asset changes constantly, the value of the contract at date t' (> t) is ±(G(t',T) – G(t,T)), which in general, except by chance, is not zero. Incidentally, this is precisely the reason why the risk of default may be large in forward markets.

1.4. TRADING ACTIVITY

As previously stated, activity in forwards and futures is huge by any measure. Tables 1.2 to 1.7 provide estimates of the evolution of derivatives from mid-1998 to the end of 2003. Table 1.2 presents the notional amounts outstanding of *most* OTC derivatives (swaps, forwards and options). Although these are admittedly rough estimates (after all, an OTC trade is a private matter), and some activity is lost (e.g. gold), some numbers are nothing but staggering. The notional amount outstanding as of the end of 2003 was equivalent to 171,324 billions of US dollars! This represents an annualized growth rate of 20% during the 5.5 year period under coverage (the figure for June 1998 was 62,619). The bulk of the activity is in interest rates (an obvious demonstration that financial institutions are the major players), roughly 83% of the total, in particular swaps (65%). The reader will recall that a "plain vanilla" swap (the exchange of a stream of fixed cash-flows for a stream of variable ones), by far the most traded of all swaps, can be analyzed simply as a succession of forward contracts written on an interest rate. So the statistics regarding those swaps are relevant to our subject. Foreign exchange contracts represent 14.3% and equity-linked contracts a mere 2.2%. Commodities contracts (without gold) are an almost negligible 0.62%, because the overwhelming activity in this area is in futures. Furthermore, it is interesting to note that options represent 17.3% only of the overall OTC activity.

Table 1.3 tells roughly the same story in terms of the gross market value outstanding of OTC derivatives. It is obtained by aggregation of all the gains (or losses, the two figures must be equal by construction) registered in the books of the market participants, computed for each contract. This gross market value is estimated at US$ 5,903 billions as of the end of 2003, which also represents an annualized growth rate of 20% over the considered period. By this measure, interest rate contracts (73.3%) lose some ground to foreign exchange contracts (22%).

Table 1.2. Notional amounts outstanding of OTC derivatives (US $ billions)

	June 1998	Dec. 1999	Dec. 2000	Dec. 2001	Dec. 2002	Dec. 2003
TOTAL CONTRACTS	62619	76549	82670	96564	123035	171324
Foreign exchange contracts	**29.89%**	**18.74%**	**18.95%**	**17.34%**	**15.00%**	**14.29%**
Outright forwards and forex swaps	19.40%	12.53%	12.26%	10.70%	8.71%	7.23%
Currency swaps	3.11%	3.19%	3.86%	4.08%	3.66%	3.72%
Options	7.38%	3.01%	2.83%	2.56%	2.63%	3.34%
Interest rate contracts	**67.66%**	**78.50%**	**78.22%**	**80.33%**	**82.63%**	**82.88%**
Forward rate agreements	8.22%	8.85%	7.77%	8.01%	7.15%	6.29%
Interest rate swaps	46.89%	57.40%	58.99%	60.99%	64.31%	64.91%
Options	12.55%	12.25%	11.46%	11.32%	11.17%	11.68%
Equity-linked contracts	**2.03%**	**2.36%**	**2.29%**	**1.95%**	**1.88%**	**2.21%**
Forwards and swaps	0.25%	0.37%	0.41%	0.33%	0.30%	0.35%
Options	1.79%	1.99%	1.88%	1.62%	1.58%	1.86%
Commodities Contracts Without Gold	**0.41%**	**0.40%**	**0.54%**	**0.38%**	**0.49%**	**0.62%**
Forwards and swaps	0.24%	0.21%	0.30%	0.22%	0.33%	0.25%
Options	0.17%	0.19%	0.24%	0.16%	0.17%	0.37%

Table 1.3. Gross Market Value of outstanding OTC derivatives (US $ billions)

	June 1998	Dec. 1999	Dec. 2000	Dec. 2001	Dec. 2002	Dec. 2003
TOTAL CONTRACTS	2149	2325	2564	3194	5402	5903
Foreign exchange contracts	**37.18%**	**28.47%**	**33.11%**	**24.39%**	**16.31%**	**22.04%**
Outright forwards and forex swaps	22.15%	15.14%	18.29%	11.71%	8.66%	10.28%
Currency swaps	9.68%	10.75%	12.21%	10.49%	6.24%	9.44%
Options	5.35%	2.58%	2.61%	2.19%	1.41%	2.30%
Interest rate contracts	**53.98%**	**56.09%**	**55.62%**	**69.19%**	**78.97%**	**73.32%**
Forward rate agreements	1.54%	0.52%	0.47%	0.59%	0.41%	0.32%
Interest rate swaps	47.37%	49.46%	49.14%	61.65%	71.53%	66.37%
Options	5.03%	6.06%	6.01%	6.95%	7.05%	6.62%
Equity-linked contracts	**8.84%**	**15.44%**	**11.27%**	**6.42%**	**4.72%**	**4.64%**
Forwards and swaps	0.93%	3.05%	2.38%	1.82%	1.13%	0.97%
Options	7.91%	12.39%	8.93%	4.60%	3.59%	3.68%

Tables 1.4 to 1.7 refer to futures contracts only. In principle, the reported figures are exact numbers, not estimates as above, as they emanate from official exchanges. Tables 1.4 and 1.5 report volumes of trading ("turnover") in terms of notional amounts and of number of contracts, respectively, the latter volumes being less meaningful economically since the size of a contract can be relatively small or large. Again, figures are staggering. For the quarter ending on December 31, 2003, the volume of trading reported in Table 1.4 represented US$ 152,980 billions in notional amounts, i.e. twice the volume traded during the second quarter of 1998. Here again, and even more markedly, interest rate futures are an overwhelming 93.5% of the total, equity indices representing a mere 5.8% and currencies almost nothing. This

repartition is roughly the same across geographical regions. As to the relative importance of futures vis-à-vis options, the ratio is 2.8 for 2003-Q4 (it was 5.0 for 1998-Q2), which confirms the relatively minor (but increasing) role played by options.

Table 1.4. Turnover (notional amount) of Futures (US $ billions)

	1998-Q2	1999-Q4	2000-Q4	2001-Q4	2002-Q4	2003-Q4
All markets	**77207.9**	**61989.7**	**72694.6**	**117537.7**	**120026.6**	**152980.3**
Interest rate	92.85%	89.91%	91.69%	94.56%	93.72%	93.46%
Currency	0.87%	0.98%	0.76%	0.57%	0.51%	0.72%
Equity index	6.28%	9.12%	7.55%	4.87%	5.77%	5.82%
North America	**46.16%**	**47.01%**	**51.03%**	**55.41%**	**51.83%**	**48.56%**
Interest rate	42.14%	41.56%	46.25%	52.43%	48.23%	45.08%
Currency	0.78%	0.84%	0.52%	0.42%	0.46%	0.66%
Equity index	3.24%	4.61%	4.26%	2.56%	3.14%	2.82%
Europe	**36.44%**	**34.85%**	**32.77%**	**34.37%**	**40.25%**	**43.00%**
Interest rate	34.29%	32.11%	30.62%	32.85%	38.55%	41.17%
Currency	0.00%	0.01%	0.00%	0.00%	0.00%	0.00%
Equity index	2.14%	2.73%	2.15%	1.52%	1.69%	1.82%
Asia and Pacific	**16.19%**	**17.23%**	**15.02%**	**8.69%**	**7.51%**	**7.70%**
Interest rate	15.43%	15.50%	13.89%	7.94%	6.58%	6.58%
Currency	0.00%	0.01%	0.03%	0.01%	0.02%	0.01%
Equity index	0.76%	1.72%	1.11%	0.73%	0.91%	1.11%
Other Markets	**1.21%**	**0.91%**	**1.18%**	**1.53%**	**0.42%**	**0.74%**
Interest rate	0.99%	0.73%	0.94%	1.33%	0.36%	0.63%
Currency	0.09%	0.12%	0.21%	0.14%	0.04%	0.05%
Equity index	0.14%	0.05%	0.04%	0.06%	0.02%	0.07%
FUTURES /OPTIONS	504.24%	443.45%	425.77%	255.04%	239.78%	280.65%

Table 1.5. Turnover (number of contracts) of Futures (millions)

	1998-Q2	1999-Q4	2000-Q4	2001-Q4	2002-Q4	2003-Q4
All markets	**245.9**	**206.6**	**253.6**	**404**	**445.5**	**577.1**
Interest rate	77.15%	71.59%	70.58%	71.98%	61.80%	65.57%
Currency	6.67%	4.26%	4.46%	3.69%	2.29%	2.65%
Equity index	16.19%	24.15%	24.96%	24.31%	35.91%	31.78%
North America	**35.10%**	**33.64%**	**33.20%**	**32.97%**	**40.81%**	**44.07%**
Interest rate	27.82%	25.17%	24.13%	23.74%	23.19%	29.47%
Currency	2.97%	2.57%	1.74%	1.39%	1.32%	1.56%
Equity index	4.31%	5.91%	7.37%	7.85%	16.30%	13.03%
Europe	**40.38%**	**45.64%**	**45.03%**	**44.18%**	**44.74%**	**39.25%**
Interest rate	34.12%	34.56%	34.70%	34.18%	31.92%	28.19%
Currency	0.98%	0.24%	0.24%	0.15%	0.11%	0.29%
Equity index	5.25%	10.84%	10.09%	9.85%	12.70%	10.78%
Asia and Pacific	**13.42%**	**12.58%**	**12.54%**	**10.20%**	**9.99%**	**10.02%**
Interest rate	8.70%	6.82%	6.39%	4.98%	3.75%	3.52%
Currency	0.00%	0.05%	0.20%	0.07%	0.09%	0.07%
Equity index	4.72%	5.66%	5.95%	5.12%	6.15%	6.43%
Other Markets	**11.10%**	**8.13%**	**9.23%**	**12.65%**	**4.47%**	**6.67%**
Interest rate	6.51%	4.99%	5.36%	9.08%	2.96%	4.38%
Currency	2.72%	1.40%	2.29%	2.10%	0.76%	0.75%
Equity index	1.87%	1.74%	1.58%	1.49%	0.76%	1.54%
FUTURES /OPTIONS	325.26%	168.10%	142.87%	80.46%	56.57%	59.32%

Table 1.5 reports the number of contracts traded during a quarter and confirms the doubling of activity over the period under scrutiny (from 246 millions to 577). There are, however, two differences with results of Table 1.4. First, the relative size of the interest rate futures market is "only" 65.6% (for 2003-Q4), and that of equity indices is now 31.8%. This implies that the notional amount of an interest rate contract is on average sizably larger than that of an equity index contract. Second, the futures/options ratio (which decreased from 3.3 in 1998-Q2 to 0.6 in 2003-Q4) is now smaller than one, which implies that the average notional amount of a futures contract is much larger than the average value of the option underlying assets.

Finally, Tables 1.6 and 1.7 report the *open interest* in futures as of the end of a given month. This is an important statistics that reflects the total number of long positions outstanding at the end of a given trading day in a futures (or option) contract. This number is of course equal to that of the short positions. If, when a futures is traded, neither the buyer nor the seller is offsetting an existing position, the open interest increases by one contract. If one investor is offsetting an existing position but the other is not, the open interest stays the same. If both are offsetting existing positions, the open interest decreases by one contract. In relation to daily volume of trading, open interest thus measures the propensity of market participants to close their positions rapidly or not. Table 1.6 reports open interest in terms of notional amounts while Table 1.7 reports it in terms of number of contracts. The Tables tell roughly the same story as the previous two ones. Open interest steadily increases through time, although at a more leisurely pace than volume of trading. It is equal to US$ 13,705 billions in notional amounts and to 62.9 millions contracts as of the end of 2003 (9,240 billions and 28.5 millions were the respective figures as of mid-1998). Here again, interest rate futures are overwhelming, although less so in (less significant) terms of number of contracts, and currency futures have a very small share.

Table 1.6. Open interest (notional amount) in Futures (US $ billions)

	June 1998	Dec. 1999	Dec. 2000	Dec. 2001	Dec. 2002	Dec. 2003
All markets	**9240.5**	**8301.8**	**8353.7**	**9669**	**10328.1**	**13705**
Interest rate	96.43%	95.46%	94.66%	95.87%	96.39%	95.75%
Currency	0.53%	0.44%	0.89%	0.68%	0.46%	0.58%
Equity index	3.03%	4.10%	4.45%	3.45%	3.15%	3.66%
North America	**41.68%**	**42.80%**	**51.27%**	**61.13%**	**56.84%**	**56.18%**
Interest rate	39.88%	40.45%	48.52%	58.96%	54.80%	53.88%
Currency	0.49%	0.39%	0.43%	0.37%	0.43%	0.48%
Equity index	1.31%	1.96%	2.33%	1.80%	1.61%	1.83%
Europe	**34.97%**	**28.62%**	**27.74%**	**25.21%**	**31.70%**	**31.83%**
Interest rate	33.95%	27.39%	26.36%	24.04%	30.63%	30.64%
Currency	0.02%	0.01%	0.00%	0.00%	0.00%	0.00%
Equity index	1.00%	1.22%	1.37%	1.16%	1.07%	1.18%
Asia and Pacific	**21.74%**	**26.03%**	**17.99%**	**12.83%**	**10.50%**	**10.83%**
Interest rate	21.05%	25.13%	16.86%	12.11%	10.04%	10.18%
Currency	0.00%	0.01%	0.41%	0.25%	0.00%	0.02%
Equity index	0.69%	0.89%	0.71%	0.47%	0.46%	0.62%
Other Markets	**1.61%**	**2.55%**	**3.00%**	**0.83%**	**0.96%**	**1.16%**
Interest rate	1.56%	2.49%	2.92%	0.75%	0.92%	1.05%
Currency	0.02%	0.04%	0.05%	0.06%	0.02%	0.08%
Equity index	0.03%	0.03%	0.03%	0.02%	0.02%	0.03%
FUTURES /OPTIONS	166.46%	156.99%	141.49%	68.60%	76.58%	59.51%

Table 1.7. Open Interest (number of contracts) in Futures (millions)

	June 1998	Dec. 1999	Dec. 2000	Dec. 2001	Dec. 2002	Dec. 2003
All markets	**28.5**	**21.3**	**25.4**	**21.4**	**28.2**	**62.9**
Interest rate	81.40%	82.16%	77.95%	71.50%	54.96%	63.75%
Currency	9.82%	3.29%	5.91%	6.07%	2.84%	4.13%
Equity index	8.77%	14.55%	15.75%	22.43%	42.55%	31.96%
North America	**22.46%**	**25.35%**	**24.41%**	**35.05%**	**50.35%**	**69.79%**
Interest rate	18.60%	21.13%	20.08%	29.44%	22.34%	45.15%
Currency	2.11%	1.41%	1.57%	1.87%	1.77%	0.95%
Equity index	1.75%	2.82%	2.76%	3.74%	26.24%	23.69%
Europe	**31.23%**	**25.82%**	**25.98%**	**35.98%**	**31.56%**	**16.06%**
Interest rate	21.75%	16.90%	16.54%	21.03%	18.79%	9.70%
Currency	7.37%	0.94%	1.18%	0.93%	0.71%	0.48%
Equity index	2.46%	7.51%	8.66%	14.02%	12.06%	5.88%
Asia and Pacific	**15.44%**	**15.49%**	**14.96%**	**19.63%**	**9.22%**	**5.41%**
Interest rate	11.58%	11.74%	9.06%	13.55%	6.03%	3.34%
Currency	0.00%	0.00%	2.76%	2.34%	0.00%	0.16%
Equity index	3.86%	3.29%	3.15%	3.74%	3.19%	1.91%
Other Markets	**30.88%**	**33.33%**	**34.25%**	**9.81%**	**8.87%**	**8.74%**
Interest rate	29.47%	31.92%	32.68%	7.48%	7.80%	5.56%
Currency	0.70%	0.47%	0.79%	0.93%	0.71%	2.70%
Equity index	0.70%	0.94%	1.18%	0.93%	0.71%	0.32%
FUTURES /OPTIONS	145.41%	78.60%	91.70%	39.93%	51.09%	102.95%

1.5. EMPIRICAL EVIDENCE

Although this book is about theory, some empirical evidence as to, for instance, the behavior of prices, the difference between forward and futures prices, the impact of introducing non-redundant contracts or the way the various market participants use forward and futures contracts may help to give our theoretical results some additional perspective. Since the literature is immense, we must be (rather arbitrarily) selective and essentially mention recent research only. The interested reader will find in the quoted papers the references on earlier works.

Price relationships. Two standard theories are available as to the level of forward and futures prices relative to the underlying spot prices. The first one is the *cost-of-carry*, which directly derives from the no-arbitrage condition and applies to forwards only, not futures (unless interest rates are deterministic!), and only when the underlying asset is tradable, its return is deterministic, *and* there is no convenience yield attached to the possession of the underlying [see Chapter 2]. According to the *cash-and-carry* formula, the forward price is equal to the spot price plus the cost of carrying the spot asset minus the return on the spot asset. It works well for foreign exchange (FX) and interest rates forward contracts [see for instance Chow et al. (2000)]. The second one is the *risk premium*, which applies to all the other situations. Two approaches can be distinguished, which for convenience we will call here the "traditional" and the "modern".

The "traditional" route treats futures and forward contracts in isolation. Futures and forward prices obviously depend on the market expectations about the future spot price of the underlying asset. Thus, since the foreseeable trend in the spot price is incorporated in the current contract price, expected moves of the spot price cannot be a source of return for buyers or sellers of the contract. Only unexpected deviations from the expected future spot price can deliver a return but these are by definition unpredictable and should average out to zero. Consequently, the expected return on an investment in these contracts must be *zero* if the forward or futures price (neglecting for the moment the difference between the two) is equal to the *expected future spot price*. In other words, only if the forward or futures price includes a risk premium (i.e. is set *below* the expected future spot price) will the buyer (seller) earns (loses) money on average, the opposite being true if the risk premium is negative. The theory of a positive risk premium accruing to buyers is called *normal backwardation* [see Keynes (1930) or Hicks (1939)]. This theory, which originated in the commodity sector, postulates that most sellers of the contracts are producers or merchants who will be long in the commodity at some future date and who want to hedge the risk of a declining spot price. Most buyers are risk averse speculators who provide this insurance to the sellers and thus assume the risk of price fluctuations in exchange for a positive risk premium. This is achieved by "backwardating" the futures or forward price relative to the expected future spot price. The opposite situation where the futures price is set *above* the expected future spot price (a negative risk premium) is called *contango*. This could happen in markets where the speculators' positions are large vis-à-vis those of hedgers.

The "modern" route is plain portfolio theory where at market equilibrium all risky asset returns, therefore returns on forward or futures contracts, command positive or negative risk premiums according to the sign of their betas, i.e. of their correlation with the market portfolio.

Whether normal backwardation or contango prevails thus is an empirical issue and will in general depend on the nature of the underlying asset, the time period under investigation, liquidity conditions and so on. Notice beforehand that these two terms are often used by practitioners in commodity futures markets to describe the level of the futures price relative to the *current spot* price, normal backwardation then meaning $H(t,T) < S(t)$ and contango $H(t,T) > S(t)$. This is probably because the expected future spot price, $E(S(T))$, is not observable. However, these definitions have no meaning and are misleading, in particular because a futures price may satisfy simultaneously the normal backwardation theoretically correct definition and the contango practitioner definition, or the other way around. As to commodity futures, recent empirical evidence [see Telser (2000) and Gorton and Rouwenhorst (2004)] strongly suggests that the risk premium is positive and generally large, in accordance with the normal backwardation theory. Historically (for the 1959-2004 period) the premium for commodity futures considered as an asset class is 5% according to the estimation by Gorton and Rouwenhorst, a figure comparable to that for equities and twice as large as that for bonds. Since returns on fully-collateralized futures are negatively correlated with those on stocks and bonds, and positively correlated with both inflation and unexpected inflation, this class of instruments is deemed an attractive additional investment in a diversified portfolio. As to financial forward and futures, the evidence [see Chernenko et al. (2004) for a recent study] also points at positive risk premiums, in particular in foreign exchange (FX) rates and long term interest rates.

Empirical differences between forward and futures prices. As argued above, forwards and futures contracts differ mainly by the marking-to-market mechanism. Theoretically, forward and futures prices should differ because i) interest rates evolve randomly over time [see chapter 2] and ii) default risk is negligible for futures but generally not for forwards. The question of whether forward and futures price differences are statistically significant has been rather extensively investigated by empirical researchers. In general, the answer to that question is positive, at least for longer-maturity contracts. For instance, French (1983) for copper and silver, Polakoff and Grier (1991) and Dezbachsh (1994) for the main FX markets, Meulbroek (1992) for eurodollar rates, all find statistically significant differences. Grinblatt and Jegadeesh (1996) find the same result for eurodollar yields but with the provision that the difference may stem from a mispricing of futures vis-à-vis forwards that has been slowly eliminated over time. In the same spirit, Benninga and Protopapadakis (1994) and Benninga et al. (2000) argue that differences between forward and futures prices should in most cases be theoretically small in a Lucas (1978) asset pricing model where default risk is absent. However, by modeling explicitly the risk of default present in forwards, Murawski (2003) shows that the theoretical spread between forward and futures prices could be large even for reasonable values of the parameters and empirically finds it is the case for crude oil contracts.

Modeling spot and futures prices. Since the cash-and-carry relationship does not hold for futures and no general formula exists, in particular when the convenience yield is stochastic, researchers have tried to explain the empirical behavior of futures prices or returns by factor models, either in isolation or together with the underlying spot prices. To take into account the influence of the behavior of the underlying asset on that of the futures, a factor model for the spot price itself [Schwartz (1997), Ross (1997), Schwartz and Smith (2000), and Korn (2004)] and/or a factor model for the convenience yield (commodity futures) is used [Schwartz (1997), Hilliard and Reis (1998), Casassus and Collin-Dufresne (2003), and Ribeiro and Hodges (2004)]. Siddique (2003), using the restrictions on expected returns and volatilities implied by Ross's APT (arbitrage pricing theory), shows that tests grounded on a latent variables methodology do not reject a single factor model with a common time-varying factor loading for the means and volatilities of returns on eight contracts (four interest rates, two stock indices, gold and crude oil). More generally, it is found that between one and three factors explain well the predictable variations in prices or returns. Casassus and Collin-Dufresne (2003) use a three-factor Gaussian model for spot prices, convenience yields and interest rates and find that the observed mean reversion in various commodity *spot* prices (copper, silver, crude oil and gold) are explained by time-varying risk premiums and/or level (of spot prices)-dependent convenience yields. Korn (2004) finds that an affine two-factor model is appropriate for crude oil contracts when the two factors are mean-reverting, thus compatible with stationary futures prices. Similarly, Ribeiro and Hodges (2004), using a mean-reverting CIR (Cox, Ingersoll and Ross (1985b)) process for the convenience yield, and a time-varying volatility for the spot price process, propose a two-factor model for commodity spot prices which they test from weekly data on crude oil futures.

Margin calls. A recurrent issue is whether the margin requirements imposed on participants by official futures markets are set at adequate levels, i.e. neither too high, so that trading is not discouraged, nor too low, so that default risk associated with a potentially extreme leverage remains negligible. This concern had been exacerbated during the periods following the October 1987 and October 1989 stock crashes and the pricking of the "internet bubble" in 2001 [see for instance Chatrath et al. (2001) for a discussion of margin setting in relation to the risk management system in futures markets; Dutt and Wein (2003) compares the merits of several margin systems on single stock futures contracts]. In general margins are deemed to be set at rather adequate or slightly too conservative levels. For instance, Day and Lewis (2004) find that margins on crude oil contracts traded on the NYME could safely be somewhat lowered. Cotter (2001) uses extreme value theory to show that margins on major European stock index futures are adequate.

Introduction of new contracts. Another concern is the creation of useful contracts that help complete an essentially incomplete market in which all risks cannot be hedged away. One aspect, studied by Pennings and Leuthold (2001), is whether launching a new contract increases or decreases the volume of trading on existing contracts. Another is the impact of listing new contracts on the return characteristics of the underlying asset. For instance, Detemple and Serrat (2003) argue that completing the market decreases the participants' liquidity constraints and thus lowers the market Sharpe ratio (through a smaller expected excess return). Clerc and Gibson (2000) find that, in the thinly traded Swiss stock market, the introduction of derivatives on stocks and the stock index (including options) lowered significantly the risk premium (per unit of risk). Similarly, McKenzie et al. (2001) document that the introduction of futures written on an individual stock (ISF) decreased the value of its beta and of its unconditional volatility while the effect was mixed on its conditional volatility. In a related area, Ang and Cheng (2004) report that the introduction of ISF has increased the market price efficiency on the relevant stocks. Also, Cuny (2002) documents that the spread contract on long term US Treasury bonds futures launched in January 2001 by the CBOT has increased the aggregate welfare of hedgers. This result is surprising on theoretical grounds since the spread contract is obviously redundant, as it can be trivially mimicked by a long and a short position on two futures contracts of different maturities. In an imperfect market, however, the spread contract seems to be valuable as market makers are able to lower their bid-ask spreads on this contract relatively to the original ones, as they incur smaller inventory costs and face less asymmetric information risk.

Practical uses of contracts. There exist various motivations for using forward or futures contracts, as well as different ways to proceed. The extant literature on *hedging* is enormous and will be discussed thoroughly in part II, with emphasis on theory. Among the topics that will not be covered, an important one is the incentives that firms have to hedge. In the Modigliani-Miller paradigm where markets are perfect and complete, hedging by firms is irrelevant since their market value is independent of such an activity. Indeed, ultimately, it is left to the individuals to decide what kind and amount of risk they bear, their decisions then being reflected in the equilibrium market prices. In the real world, many imperfections, such as liquidity constraints, the presence of transaction, information and bankruptcy costs, or fiscal reasons, may lead them to partially hedge some risks. Smith (1995) provides a survey of these incentives. For instance, the *optimal* amount of debt issued by a corporation in an imperfect market increases with hedging if such an activity reduces its probability of default. Graham and Smith (1998) also show that, if a firm faces a convex tax function (because of a progressive tax scheme), hedges that decrease the volatility of its taxable income will lower its expected tax liability, providing a tax incentive to hedge. Bartram et al. (2003) provide an impressive study on the use of financial derivatives (including options) by 7292 non-financial firms from 48 countries. They report that 60% of those firms use derivatives in general (44% of the contracts are foreign exchange, 33% interest rates and 10% commodities). Using derivatives may increase the firm's market value, in particular for a firm using interest rate derivatives (which decreases its weighted average cost of capital).

Since liquid futures contracts have relatively short maturities (less than one year), long term hedging requires *rolling* shorter term futures as time evolves. Neuberger (1999) examines this issue, performs tests on the crude oil futures market and concludes that the roll-over strategy is efficient.

Finally, another aspect that will not be considered in this book is *market making* activity. The presence of market makers generally improves the liquidity of the contracts, in exchange for a bid-ask spread. Tse and Zabotina (2004) for instance report that it is the case for the open outcry 10-year interest rate swap futures contract of the CBOT. The introduction in February 2002 of market makers seems to have significantly improved the liquidity on this market, as well as the speed and efficiency of the price discovery mechanism.

Endnotes

[1] See, for instance, Kolb (2002), Rendleman (2002) or Hull (2003).
[2] In the case of forwards, the P&L is exactly S(T) - G(t,T). In the case of futures, due to the daily margin requirements explained below, the P&L is approximately S(T) - H(t,T).

CHAPTER 2: STANDARD PRICING RESULTS UNDER DETERMINISTIC AND STOCHASTIC INTEREST RATES

Along with providing the way uncertainty is formalized in the considered economy, we establish in this chapter the assumptions that will be adopted throughout Part I of this book and the general principles governing asset pricing (§1), then the relationship between the spot and the forward prices of a risky asset (§2), and lastly that between the spot and the futures prices (§3). Any dividend (or coupon, or convenience yield) will always be assumed both continuous and deterministic.

2.1. GENERAL SETTING AND MAIN ASSUMPTIONS

In this framework, individuals can trade continuously on a frictionless and arbitrage free financial market until time τ_E, the horizon of the economy. A locally riskless asset and a number n of pure default-free discount bonds sufficient to complete the market are traded. The latter pay one dollar each at their respective maturities, respectively T_j, $j = 1,..., n$, with $T_{j-1} < T_j < \tau_E$. The following sets of assumptions provide the necessary details.

Assumption 1: Dynamics of the primitive assets.

- At each date t, the price $P(t,T_j)$ of a discount bond whose maturity is T_j, $j = 1,..., n$, is given by :

$$P(t,T_j)=\exp\left[-\int_t^{T_j} f(t,s)ds\right] \qquad (1)$$

where f(t,s) is the instantaneous forward rate (thereafter the forward rate) prevailing at time t for date s, with $t < s \leq \tau_E$.

- The instantaneous spot rate (thereafter the spot rate) is $r(t) = f(t,t)$. Agents are allowed to trade on a money market account yielding this continuous bounded spot rate. Let B(t) denote its value at time t, with B(0)=1. Then:

$$B(t) = \exp\left[\int_0^t r(u)du\right] \tag{2}$$

- To give our model some additional structure, we assume, following Heath, Jarrow and Morton (1992), that the forward rate is the solution to the following stochastic differential equation:

$$df(t,s) = \mu(t,s)dt + \Sigma(t,s)'dZ(t) \tag{3}$$

where $\mu(.)$, the drift term, and $\Sigma(t,s)$, the K-dimensional vector of diffusion parameters (volatilities), are assumed to satisfy the usual conditions[1] such that (3) has a unique solution, and "'" denotes a transpose. $Z(t)$ is a K-dimensional Brownian motion defined on the complete filtered space $(\Omega, F, \{F_t\}_{t\in[0,\tau_E]}, P)$, where Ω is the state space, F is the σ-algebra representing measurable events, and P is the actual (historical) probability. The forward rate is adapted to the augmented filtration generated by this Brownian motion. This filtration is denoted by $F \equiv \{F_t\}_{t\in[0,\tau_E]}$ and is assumed to satisfy the usual conditions [2]. The initial value of the forward rate, f(0,s), is observable and given by the initial yield curve prevailing on the market.

- Since the latter is arbitrage free, the drift term $\mu(t, s)$ in equation (3) is a specific function of the forward rates volatility $\Sigma(t, s)$ that involves the market prices of risk associated with the K sources of uncertainty. This is the so-called « drift condition ». If markets are complete, Proposition 3, on p. 86, of HJM (1992) establishes that this relationship between the drift and the volatility is unique. More precisely, it states that there exists a unique vector of *market prices of risk* $\phi(t)$ such that:

$$\mu(t,s) = -\sum_{j=1}^{K} \sigma_j(t,s)\left[\phi_j(t) - \int_t^s \sigma_j(t,u)du\right]$$

for all $s \in [0, \tau_E]$ and $t \in [0, s]$, where $\sigma_j(t,s)$ is the jth element of $\Sigma(t,s)$ and $\phi_j(t)$ is the jth element of $\phi(t)$.

Assumption 2: Absence of frictions and of arbitrage opportunities.

- The assumption of absence of arbitrage opportunities in a frictionless financial market leads to the First Theorem of asset pricing theory. Since Harrison and Kreps (1979), this assumption is in effect known to be tantamount to assuming the existence of a probability measure, defined with respect to a given numeraire and equivalent to P, such that the prices of all risky assets, deflated by this numeraire, are martingales[3].

- Now, applying Itô's lemma to (1) given (3) yields the stochastic differential equation satisfied by the discount bonds:

$$\frac{dP(t,T_j)}{P(t,T_j)} = \mu_P(t,T_j)dt + \Sigma_P(t,T_j)' dZ(t) \qquad j=1,...,n. \tag{4}$$

where $\Sigma_P(t,T_j)$ is the K-dimensional vector of the volatilities associated with the relative price changes of the discount bond maturing at T_j, $P(t,T_j)$. This vector is functionally related to the vector $\Sigma(.)$ of the forward rates volatilities. The drift $\mu_P(t,T_j)$ plays no particular role here, but could easily be computed as the sum of the riskless rate plus a risk premium that depends on the bond maturity date T_j. Note that, since the market is complete, we have $n \geq K$.

- The absence of arbitrage implies the existence of a martingale measure Q, associated with the locally riskless asset (more precisely the money market account B(t)) as the numeraire, and such that its Radon-Nikodym derivative with respect to the historical probability is equal to:

$$\left.\frac{dQ}{dP}\right|_{F_t} \equiv \eta(t) = \exp\left\{-\int_0^t \phi(s)' dZ(s) - \frac{1}{2}\int_0^t \phi(s)' \phi(s) ds\right\}$$

where $\phi(s)$ is the vector of market prices of risk. The latter is a predictable, F_t-adapted, process satisfying Novikov's condition $E^P\left[\exp\left(\frac{1}{2}\int_0^T \|\phi(s)\|^2 ds\right)\right] < \infty$, where the expectation E^P is taken under the true measure P. The probability Q is generally, but somewhat misleadingly, called the "*risk-neutral*" measure.

Now, the Second Theorem of asset pricing theory relates the uniqueness of the martingale measure Q to the completeness of the financial market. A market is complete if any risky asset can be replicated by a portfolio of existing (traded) assets, so that its price is unique. This requires that there exist, in addition to the riskless asset, as many risky assets traded on the market as there are fundamental sources of risk in the economy (the dimension of the Brownian motion, for instance, as here). A portfolio of existing assets, whose composition changes (in general) continuously over time, can then replicate any contingent claim. Therefore, the latter can be fairly priced. It also means that any risk can be perfectly hedged by the appropriate combination of existing assets.

When markets are complete, there exists only one martingale measure associated with a given numeraire. Thus, in our setting, Q is unique. When markets are incomplete, however, such a result breaks down and for each numeraire there exists more than one martingale measure. Consequently, there is possibly an infinite number of prices for each contingent claim. We will indicate in the sequel which results require completeness and which do not.

- Under Q, the price of a pure discount bond follows the dynamic process:

$$\frac{dP(t,T_j)}{P(t,T_j)} = r(t)dt + \Sigma_P(t,T_j)' d\hat{Z}(t) \qquad j=1,...,n. \tag{5}$$

where $\hat{Z}(t)$ is a K-dimensional Brownian motion under Q. Using Girsanov's theorem, it is related to the Brownian motion Z by:

$$d\hat{Z}(t) = dZ(t) + \phi(t)dt$$

Integrating (5) then yields:

$$P(t,T_j) = P(0,T_j)\exp\left[\int_0^t \left(r(s) - \frac{1}{2}\Sigma_P(s,T_j)'\Sigma_P(s,T_j)\right)ds + \int_0^t \Sigma_P(s,T_j)' d\hat{Z}(s)\right]$$

j= 1,…, n. (6)

- Consider any traded asset with payoff S(T) at time T and no intermediate cash flow. Its price today is S(t). T is assumed to be smaller than T_1 so that all the discount bonds are "long-lived" assets. By construction, we have:

$$\frac{S(t)}{B(t)} = E^Q\left[\frac{S(T)}{B(T)}\middle| F_t\right] \tag{7}$$

where $E^Q[.|F_t]$ denotes the conditional expectation under Q based upon all information available at time t.

- While the locally riskless money market account B(t) is by far the most extensively used numeraire, another one is frequently used when interest rates are stochastic. Recall that the sole objective of choosing a particular numeraire is to ease the mathematical burden of computing conditional expectations. Instead of choosing Q and its associated numeraire B(t), it is convenient to adopt the measure Q^T and its associated numeraire P(t,T), the value of the zero-coupon bond of maturity T. This measure, first used formally by Jamshidian (1987, 1989), is known as the "*T-forward-neutral*" probability. Under Q^T, the price of any non-dividend-paying asset deflated by P(t,T) is a martingale:

$$\frac{S(t)}{P(t,T)} = E^{Q^T}\left[\frac{S(T)}{P(T,T)}\middle| F_t\right] \tag{8}$$

which can be rewritten:

$$\frac{S(t)}{P(t,T)} = E^{Q^T}\left[S(T)\middle| F_t\right] \tag{9}$$

Formally, Q^T is defined as:

$$\left.\frac{dQ^T}{dQ}\right|_{F_t} = \frac{P(t,T)B(0)}{P(0,T)B(t)} = \frac{P(t,T)}{P(0,T)B(t)} \equiv \varepsilon_t^T, \forall t \leq T \tag{10}$$

where $B(t) = \exp\left[\int_0^t r(s)ds\right]$ is a stochastic process, as is P(t,T). Obviously, if interest rates are deterministic, the Radon-Nikodym derivative dQ^T/dQ is always equal to one in absence of arbitrage opportunities and the "T-forward-neutral" and "risk-neutral" measures are identical.

Assumption 3: Admissible strategies.

Our final set of assumptions concerns the economic agents' behavior. Each individual who can freely trade on the continuously open financial market adopts a portfolio strategy that consists in choosing the appropriate number of units of the locally riskless asset (the value of the money market account) and of each and every discount bond. Such strategies are assumed to be admissible[4], and in particular self-financing.

2.2. FORWARD PRICES

- Let G(t,T) be the price of the maturity-T forward contract written on one particular asset, say S(t). For the moment, this asset does not pay out dividends. When negotiated at t, the value of the forward contract is zero, so that:

$$0 = E^{Q}\left[\frac{G(t,T) - S(T)}{B(T)}\middle| F_t\right] \tag{11}$$

Rearranging terms yields:

$$G(t,T)E^{Q}\left[\frac{1}{B(T)}\middle| F_t\right] = E^{Q}\left[\frac{S(T)}{B(T)}\middle| F_t\right] \tag{12}$$

From the definition of Q, we have:

$$E^{Q}\left[\frac{1}{B(T)}\middle| F_t\right] = E^{Q}\left[\frac{P(T,T)}{B(T)}\middle| F_t\right] = \frac{P(t,T)}{B(t)} \text{ and } E^{Q}\left[\frac{S(T)}{B(T)}\middle| F_t\right] = \frac{S(t)}{B(t)}$$

Substituting into (12) yields the *cash-and-carry relationship without dividends:*

$$G(t,T) = \frac{S(t)}{P(t,T)} \tag{13}$$

This result can be derived alternatively, and even more rapidly, using the zero-coupon bond price P(t,T) as the numeraire. Under the Q^T-forward neutral probability, we have:

$$0 = E^{Q^T}\left[\frac{G(t,T) - S(T)}{P(T,T)}\middle| F_t\right] \tag{14}$$

and thus:

$$G(t,T) = E^{Q^T}\left[\frac{S(T)}{P(T,T)}\middle| F_t\right] = \frac{S(t)}{P(t,T)} \tag{15}$$

Remark that it is easy to go from (11) to (14), given the relationship between the two measures. Indeed, Bayes formula states that:

$$E^{Q^T}\left[X(T)\middle| F_t\right] = \frac{E^{Q}\left[X(T)Y(T)\middle| F_t\right]}{E^{Q}\left[Y(T)\middle| F_t\right]} \text{ where } \left.\frac{dQ^T}{dQ}\right|_{F_t} = Y(t)$$

It follows that:

$$E^{Q^T}\left[\frac{G(t,T) - S(T)}{P(T,T)}\middle| F_t\right] = \frac{E^{Q}\left[\frac{G(t,T) - S(T)}{P(T,T)} \frac{P(T,T)}{B(T)P(0,T)}\middle| F_t\right]}{E^{Q}\left[\frac{P(T,T)}{B(T)P(0,T)}\middle| F_t\right]}$$

Simplifying some terms yields:

$$E^{Q^T}\left[\frac{G(t,T)-S(T)}{P(T,T)}\middle|F_t\right]=\frac{E^Q\left[\frac{G(t,T)-S(T)}{B(T)}\middle|F_t\right]}{E^Q\left[\frac{P(T,T)}{B(T)}\middle|F_t\right]}$$

Since

$$E^Q\left[\frac{P(T,T)}{B(T)}\middle|F_t\right]=\frac{P(t,T)}{B(t)}$$

we have:

$$E^{Q^T}\left[\frac{G(t,T)-S(T)}{P(T,T)}\middle|F_t\right]=\frac{B(t)}{P(t,T)}E^Q\left[\frac{G(t,T)-S(T)}{B(T)}\middle|F_t\right]$$

Given that (14) holds, (11) must hold too.

We stress here that the cash-and-carry formula (13) or (15) is valid irrespective of whether the market is complete or not. Absence of frictions and arbitrage opportunities is enough. What is only required for (13) to hold is that agents are allowed to trade the asset underlying the forward contract and a discount bond maturing at time T.

- The preceding findings must be amended when the underlying asset pays out dividends. Assume a continuous dividend rate process $d_s(t)$. S(t) is the ex-dividend asset price. This price being the current value of the claim to the asset at date T plus all dividends up to T, it follows that, under the risk-neutral measure Q, we must have:

$$\frac{S(t)}{B(t)}=E^Q\left[\frac{S(T)e^{\int_t^T d_s(s)ds}}{B(T)}\middle|F_t\right] \tag{16}$$

Now, it is still true that:

$$0 = E^Q\left[\frac{G(t,T)-S(T)}{B(T)}\middle|F_t\right] = E^Q\left[\frac{G(t,T)}{B(T)}\middle|F_t\right] - E^Q\left[\frac{S(T)}{B(T)}\middle|F_t\right]$$
$$= G(t,T)E^Q\left[\frac{1}{B(T)}\middle|F_t\right] - E^Q\left[\frac{S(T)}{B(T)}\middle|F_t\right]$$
$$= G(t,T)E^Q\left[\frac{P(T,T)}{B(T)}\middle|F_t\right] - E^Q\left[\frac{S(T)}{B(T)}\middle|F_t\right]$$
$$= G(t,T)\frac{P(t,T)}{B(t)} - E^Q\left[\frac{S(T)}{B(T)}\middle|F_t\right]$$

Therefore:

$$G(t,T) = \frac{B(t)}{P(t,T)}E^Q\left[\frac{S(T)}{B(T)}\middle|F_t\right]$$

The last term is no longer a martingale under Q in general, unless the dividend process is deterministic. Assuming it is, we then have:

$$G(t,T) = \frac{B(t)}{P(t,T)}e^{-\int_t^T d_s(s)ds}E^Q\left[\frac{S(T)e^{\int_t^T d_s(s)ds}}{B(T)}\middle|F_t\right]$$

and thus, using (16), we obtain the *general cash-and-carry relationship:*

$$G(t,T) = \frac{S(t)e^{-\int_t^T d_s(s)ds}}{P(t,T)} \tag{17}$$

- Equation (17) takes on a particular form when the underlying asset of the forward contract is a *spot exchange rate*. In this case, it is *immaterial* whether domestic and foreign interest rates are deterministic or stochastic, as we will prove. Denoting by S(t) the exchange rate from the domestic viewpoint, i.e. the number of domestic monetary units per foreign monetary unit (say 1,21 US dollars exchanged for 1 Euro), and by $P^f(t,T)$ the foreign zero-coupon bond, the (T-t)-forward exchange rate is equal to:

$$G(t,T) = \frac{S(t)P^f(t,T)}{P(t,T)} \tag{17'}$$

To prove this, we make use of the *principle of international valuation*. According to the latter, in absence of arbitrage opportunity, the present value in domestic currency terms, $V_t^d[.]$, of a future payoff denominated in foreign exchange rate S(T) must be equal to the present value in foreign currency terms of that future payoff, $V_t^f\left[X^f(T)\right]$, times the current spot exchange rate S(t):

$$V_t^d\left[S(T)X^f(T)\right] = S(t)V_t^f\left[X^f(T)\right]$$

Now, consider a future certain payoff of 1 foreign currency unit ($X^f(T)$ =1). We have:

$$G(t,T) = \frac{V_t^d\left[S(T)1\right]}{P(t,T)} = S(t)\frac{V_t^f\left[1\right]}{P(t,T)} = S(t)\frac{P^f(t,T)}{P(t,T)}$$

which is the desired result, since the present value of 1 foreign currency unit received at T is obviously $P^f(t,T)$.

Equation (17') implies that if the level of domestic interest rates is lower (higher) than that of foreign rates, the forward exchange rate is smaller (larger) than the spot rate, since then P(t,T) is larger (smaller) than $P^f(t,T)$.

2.3. FUTURES PRICES

- Let H(t, T) be price of the futures contract of maturity T written on the spot asset S(t). Assume that the contract is marked to market on a continuous (rather than daily) time basis. We know that in absence of frictions and arbitrage opportunities H(T, T) = S(T). For a moment, assume also that there are no dividends paid out by the underlying asset.

To derive its current price H(t, T), consider the following general strategy: invest initially an amount X(0) = H(0,T) in the riskless asset (in lieu of investing S(0) in the underlying asset); trade at each date t ($0 \le t \le T$) $\Delta_H(t)$ units of the (infinitely divisible) contract and re-invest (algebraically) all the margins continuously generated by the futures contracts at the riskless rate. Then the margin account value at each time t, until maturity T, is equal to:

$$X(t) = X(0)\exp\left[\int_0^t r(s)ds\right] + \int_0^t \exp\left[\int_s^t r(s)ds\right]\Delta_H(s)dH(s,T)$$

Applying Ito's lemma to X(t) yields:

$$dX(t) = r(t)X(t)dt + \Delta_H(t)dH(t,T)$$

Now consider a particular strategy on the futures contracts such that:

$$\Delta_H(t) = \exp\left[\int_0^t r(s)ds\right]$$

The margin account dynamics will then be:

$$dX(t) = r(t)X(t)dt + \exp\left[\int_0^t r(s)ds\right]dH(t,T)$$

Applying Ito's lemma yields:

$$X(t) = H(t,T)\exp\left[\int_0^t r(s)ds\right]$$

Consequently,

$$X(T) = S(T)\exp\left[\int_0^T r(s)ds\right]$$

and X(0) is the price at time 0 of this payoff. Since X(0) = H(0,T), we have:

$$H(0,T) = E^Q\left[\frac{S(T)\exp\left[\int_0^T r(s)ds\right]}{\exp\left[\int_0^T r(s)ds\right]}\middle|F_0\right] = E^Q\left[S(T)\middle|F_0\right]$$

and for any date t (< T):

$$H(t,T) = E^Q\left[S(T)\middle|F_t\right] \tag{18}$$

Because of the continuous marking-to-market mechanism, the value of the futures contract is always zero. Therefore, it may seem rather intuitive that its price is a Q-martingale.

- When interest rates are deterministic, we have:

$$H(t,T) = E^Q\left[S(T)\middle|F_t\right] = B(T)E^Q\left[\frac{S(T)}{B(T)}\middle|F_t\right]$$

and, since then P(t,T) = B(t)/B(T) in absence of arbitrage, we get:

$$H(t,T) = B(T)\frac{S(t)}{B(t)} = \frac{S(t)}{P(t,T)} = G(t,T) \tag{19}$$

Under such interest rates, the forward and futures prices are *equal* and given by the *cash-and-carry relationship*. Without dividends, the latter is given by formula (13). With deterministic dividends, the relevant expression is (17).

- Under stochastic interest rates, comparing equations (15) and (18) makes it clear why current forward and futures prices differ: both are the expected value of the underlying asset at date T, S(T), but computed under two different measures: Q^T for the forward and Q for the futures.

To establish the relationship between the two prices, let us compute the drift of the forward price process, μ_G, under the risk-neutral probability Q. Applying Ito's lemma to the cash-and-carry relation (13), we obtain the drift:

$$\begin{aligned}\mu_G &= \mu_S - \mu_P(t,T) + \Sigma_P(t,T)(\Sigma_P(t,T) - \Sigma_S)' \\ &= \Sigma_P(t,T)(\Sigma_P(t,T) - \Sigma_S)' \\ &= -\Sigma_P(t,T)\Sigma_G(t,T)'\end{aligned}$$

where the second equality comes from the fact that, under Q, the drifts of the stock price and the bond price processes are equal to the riskless rate r(t), and the third equality uses again Ito's lemma applied to (13) for the diffusion parameters.

Therefore, under Q, the drift of G(t,T) is nothing but the covariance between the forward price relative changes and its underlying bond price relative changes.

We then can use the following well-known theorem. Consider a positive Itô process X(t), satisfying Novikov's condition $E^Q\left[\exp \frac{1}{2}\int_t^T \sigma_X(s)^2 ds \middle| F_t\right] < \infty$ such that, under the measure Q:

$$dX(t) = \mu_X(.)X(t)dt + \sigma_X(.)X(t)d\hat{Z}(t)$$

Then

$$X(t) = E_Q\left[X(T)\exp\left(-\int_t^T \mu_X(s)ds\right) \middle| F_t\right]$$

[<u>Proof</u>: Let $Y(t) = X(T)\exp\left(-\int_t^T \mu_X(s)ds\right)$. By Itô's lemma,

$$\frac{dY(t)}{Y(t)} = \frac{dX(t)}{X(t)} - \mu_X(t)dt = \sigma_X(.)d\hat{Z}(t)$$

Therefore, since Novikov's condition is satisfied, Y(t) is a Q-martingale, and we have:

$$Y(t) = E^Q[Y(T)|F_t]$$

Hence:

$$X(t)\exp\left(-\int_0^t \mu_X(s)ds\right) = E^Q\left[X(T)\exp\left(-\int_0^T \mu_X(s)ds\right)\middle|F_t\right]$$

which yields the result.]

Consequently, since G(T,T) = S(T), we can write:

$$G(t,T) = E^Q\left[S(T)\exp\left[\int_t^T \mathrm{cov}\left(\frac{dG(u,T)}{G(u,T)}, \frac{dP(u,T)}{P(u,T)}\right)du\right]\middle|F_t\right] \tag{20}$$

In the particular case where all variances and covariances are *deterministic*, we then have, using result (18):

$$G(t,T) = H(t,T)\exp\left[\int_t^T \mathrm{cov}\left(\frac{dG(u,T)}{G(u,T)}, \frac{dP(u,T)}{P(u,T)}\right)du\right] \tag{21}$$

The forward price thus is larger or smaller than its futures counterpart depending on the sign of the covariance between the forward price changes and the relevant zero-coupon price changes. Obviously, if interest rates are deterministic, this covariance vanishes and we recover G(t,T) = H(t,T). Note for completeness, however, that this assumption is not necessary for the latter equality to hold: it is in fact sufficient that the forward price of the underlying asset and the bond price are statistically independent under Q.

Endnotes

[1] See Heath et al. (1992).

[2] The filtration contains all the events whose probability with respect to P is null. See for instance Karatzas and Shreve (1991).

[3] This equivalence result holds only for simple strategies, i.e. strategies that need a portfolio reallocation only a finite number of times. See Harrison and Kreps (1979) and Harrison and Pliska (1981) for details.

[4] To save space, we do not specify the properties of admissible strategies. See Harrison and Kreps (1979), Harrison and Pliska (1981), Cox and Huang (1989) and Heath et al. (1992).

PART II

INVESTMENT AND HEDGING

Part II examines the optimal decisions made by individuals, financial institutions, or corporations in various contexts of different generality. In each chapter, optimal strategies using futures will be compared to strategies using the forward counterparts, as it is a recurrent theme of this book that these strategies differ significantly most of the time.

As hedging is empirically a main motivation for market participants, we start in Chapter 3 with a pure hedging problem, where the investor's objective is to reduce as much as possible, and in some cases cancel, the risk embedded in a given position on the underlying asset.

The scope of Chapter 4 is broader as it analyzes and solves the optimal portfolio problem of an investor endowed with a non-traded cash position. Therefore, unlike the previous chapter, hedges are part of a more general portfolio and the individual's utility function plays a major role.

Financial markets in the real world are in fact incomplete as all risks cannot be hedged away, even though one would be willing to pay the appropriate "insurance" price. The previous two chapters were set in a complete market framework. Chapter 5 is more general as it deals with an incomplete market where the price of a given asset may not be unique. It is however less general than Chapter 4 in the sense that it examines the investment, or speculation, problem only, without the hedging motivation.

Chapter 6 is specific to exchange risk. The latter is overwhelming in modern economies where a large share of trades is made across (currency) borders. Using a different approach, we solve the optimization problem of foreign investors who face a currency risk in addition to the risks associated with their investment abroad and with domestic and foreign stochastic interest rates.

A spread is a long position in one contract and a short position in an other contract of different maturity. It provides a simple way to speculate on the rise or fall of the underlying spot price without incurring too much risk. Chapter 7 thus examines the issue of using optimally such spreads and provides the characteristics of optimal spreads.

In many real world situations, in particular in commodities markets, the underlying spot asset generates a dividend or a convenience yield that is stochastic. Although we retain in Chapter 8 a complete market setting, this feature alone will be shown to invalidate most of the results regarding equilibrium prices and optimal strategies which obtain when this yield is deterministic.

CHAPTER 3: PURE HEDGING[1]

3.1. INTRODUCTION

Hedgers are investors who hold fixed portfolios of primitive assets that they do not or cannot trade, at least temporarily, either because of regulatory constraints, constraints imposed by their hierarchy or their clients, or because of the presence of prohibitive transaction and/or information costs. They thus enter the futures or forward market to hedge the risks associated with their portfolios. In fact, two types of hedging behavior are worth investigating, "pure" (or maximal) hedging on the one hand, and optimal hedging, on the other. "Pure" hedgers are investors whose objective is simply to minimize the (instantaneous) variance of their overall positions. This is the issue examined in this chapter, for reasons explained shortly below. The more general problem of optimal hedging is the one in which investors optimize, and thus only partially hedge, their portfolios, to achieve the optimal tradeoff between risk and expected return, given their non-traded position. Thus, investors will in this chapter express *maximal* hedging demands as opposed to *optimal* hedging ones, which will be analyzed in the following two chapters.

The literature on dynamic hedging is voluminous[2], but many papers have ignored the marking-to-market mechanism that characterizes futures contracts and treated the latter as though they were forward contracts. For some situations, this is not a major issue, either because interest rates can be assumed to be deterministic or because interest rate risk is of second order as compared to the main risk borne by the portfolio, as is the case for instance for stocks or stock indices, commodities, and insurance contracts[3]. In such cases, the marking-to-market mechanism brings about no difference in pricing and only a minor one in hedging. Indeed, as we will see later on, only the size of the futures position will differ from that of the otherwise equivalent forward position by what is called a "tailing factor" equal to the price of a pure discount bond whose maturity coincides with that of the futures contract[4].

When the underlying asset is a fixed income security and interest rates are stochastic, however, futures and forward contracts are no longer equivalent instruments. In particular, as explained in the previous chapter, the forward and futures prices are different[5]. More to the point here, the size of the hedging position using futures will differ from that of the forward position by more than a simple "tailing factor". In order to focus on the marking-to-market mechanism and assess its influence on hedging independently of the investors' preference parameters, we retain in this chapter the assumption of a "pure" hedger who minimizes the instantaneous variance of his/her overall position. The implications of this assumption will be discussed at the beginning of Section II.

Before, Section I presents the economic setting in which is framed our hedger's problem and the main assumptions necessary to derive the results. We use the Heath, Jarrow and Morton (1992) framework, hereafter HJM, to model the stochastic behavior of interest rates. In the HJM model, the evolution of the instantaneous forward rate is governed by an arbitrary number of factors. This allows the yield curve to take on a variety of different shapes and provides a convenient setting for deriving the respective hedging strategies using forwards or futures written on pure discount bonds. Section II discusses the pure hedger's optimal strategy first using forward contracts and then using futures. In Section III we illustrate the model by restricting the general HJM model to a simpler two-factor model and provide some numerical estimates of the two hedge ratios to assess the order of magnitude by which they differ. Section IV offers some concluding remarks.

3.2. THE ECONOMIC SETTING

In this economic framework, investors can trade continuously in the financial market until time τ_E, the horizon of the economy. We use continuous time for mathematical convenience but nothing essential at the economic level would be changed if discrete time were adopted. The market is assumed to be free of frictions and arbitrage opportunities. A word of caution is required here. Forward contracts, and also futures when interest rates are deterministic, are redundant instruments in perfect markets, because they can be exactly replicated by a combination of existing cash (primitive) assets. Therefore, the only meaningful way to introduce them without *explicitly* modeling imperfections is to assume that *implicit* differential transaction or information costs provide some investors (the hedgers defined below we are interested in) an incentive to trade on derivative markets rather than on primitive ones. Indeed, many investors do face higher trading and liquidity costs for cash instruments than for futures or forwards, information costs to find default-free cash assets, possible problems of differential taxation, and various regulatory constraints imposed on their balance sheets.

The reason we want to avoid modeling explicitly such imperfections is of course to obtain tractable results, and closed form solutions if possible.

Investors are allowed to trade on a locally riskless asset (a money market account) and on any number n of default-free zero-coupon bonds of various maturities. Note that we do not impose the condition that the market is complete. The bonds pay one dollar at their respective maturity dates T_j, j = 1, ...n, with $T_1 < T_2 < \ldots < T_n \leq \tau_E$.

At each time t, the price $P(t,T_j)$ of a discount bond of maturity T_j, j = 1, ...n, is given by:

$$P(t,T_j) = \exp\left[-\int_t^{T_j} f(t,s)ds\right] \tag{1}$$

where f(t,s) is the instantaneous forward rate (thereafter the forward rate) for maturity s at date t, with $s \leq \tau_E$.

Following HJM (1992), the forward rate is assumed to be the solution to the following stochastic differential equation:

$$df(t,s) = \mu(t,s)dt + \Sigma(t,s)' dZ(t) \tag{2}$$

where $\mu(.)$, the drift term, and $\Sigma(.)$, the K-dimensional vector of volatilities (diffusion parameters), are assumed to satisfy the usual conditions[6] such that (2) has a unique solution, and " ' " denotes a transpose. Z(.) is a K-dimensional Brownian motion defined on the complete filtered space $(\Omega, F, \{F_t\}_{t\in[0,\tau_E]}, P)$, where Ω is the state space, *F* is the σ-algebra representing measurable events, P is the actual (historical) probability and the filtration $\{F_t\}_{t\in[0,\tau_E]}$ is the augmented filtration generated by the Brownian Motion assumed to satisfy the usual conditions[7]. The forward rate is adapted to this filtration. The initial value of the forward rate, f(0,s), is observable and given by the initial yield curve prevailing in the market.

Since the latter is arbitrage free, the drift term $\mu(t, s)$ in equation (2) is a specific function of the forward rates volatility $\Sigma(t, s)$ that involves the market prices of risk associated with the K sources of uncertainty. This is the so-called « drift condition ». If markets are complete, Proposition 3, on p. 86, of HJM (1992) establishes that this relationship between the drift and the volatility is unique. More precisely, it states that there exists a unique vector of market prices of risk $\phi(t)$ such that:

$$\mu(t,s) = -\sum_{j=1}^{K} \sigma_j(t,s)\left[\phi_j(t) - \int_t^s \sigma_j(t,u)du\right]$$

for all $s \in [0, \tau_E]$ and $t \in [0, s]$, where $\sigma_j(t,s)$ is the jth element of $\Sigma(t,s)$ and $\phi_j(t)$ is the jth element of $\phi(t)$.

Now, substituting (2) in (1) and applying Itô's lemma yields the stochastic differential equation satisfied by the pure discount bonds:

$$\frac{dP(t,T_j)}{P(t,T_j)} = \mu_P(t,T_j)dt + \Sigma_P(t,T_j)' dZ(t) \qquad j = 1,\ldots,n \tag{3}$$

where $\Sigma_P(t,T_j)$ is the K-dimensional vector of the volatilities associated with the relative price changes of the discount bond maturing at T_j. This vector is functionally related to the vector $\Sigma(.)$ of the forward rates volatilities. The drift $\mu_P(t,T_j)$ plays no particular role here, but could easily be computed as the sum of the riskless rate plus a risk premium that depends on the bond maturity date T_j[8].

The instantaneous riskless rate of interest is r(t) = f(t,t), and so follows a stochastic process. The price at date t of the locally riskless asset (or money market account), the value of which is $1 at time t=0, thus is equal to:

$$B(t) = \exp\left[\int_0^t r(u)du\right] \tag{4}$$

Finally, there exists either a forward contract G(.) or a futures contract H(.) written on a discount bond of a given, arbitrary, maturity less than or equal to τ_E, say T_2. For simplicity and without any loss of generality, its maturity T_F ($= T_G = T_H$) is set at date T_1.

Consider first the case where investors can hedge their positions using *forward* contracts. The forward price at date $t \leq T_F$ is denoted by $G(t,T_F,T_2) \equiv G(t)$ for simplicity. Given that the market is free of frictions and arbitrage opportunities, it is equal to:

$$G(t) = \frac{P(t,T_2)}{P(t,T_F)} \tag{5}$$

Equation (5) gives the no-arbitrage forward *price* of the forward contract, which is nothing but the cash-and-carry relationship. Note that the current price of the forward contract is not its current *value*. The latter is zero at the inception of the contract since there is no cash payment involved between the buyer and the seller. As time goes by, however, and interest rates evolve, the contract's value becomes either positive or negative according to the favorable or unfavorable evolution of the bond price $P(t,T_j)$. For instance, if bond prices (interest rates) have increased (decreased) between $t=t$ and $t=T_F$, the buyer of the forward contract has a winning position at time T_F since then $G(t,T_F,T_2) < P(T_F,T_2)$, i.e. the (contractual) price he or she pays for delivery of the underlying bond is smaller than the current price of the latter.

Consider now the case where *futures*, not forward, contracts are available for trade. The futures *price* at date $t \leq T_F$ is denoted by $H(t,T_F,T_2) \equiv H(t)$ [9]. Again, the futures price should not be confused with its current *value*. As the futures contract is marked-to-market on a daily basis, the investor's daily gain (loss) is added to (subtracted from) his or her cash account. Here we assume continuous, rather than daily, marking-to-market, for mathematical tractability. Consequently, the current value of the futures contract is continuously zero, in contrast with the forward contract whose current value is generally not zero. Also note that the futures price is not given by the simple cash-and-carry relationship (5) due to the stochastic behavior of interest rates.

3.3. HEDGING WITH FORWARDS OR FUTURES

We present and discuss first the pure hedger's problem (§1), then derive its general solution (§2) and lastly offer comments, in particular as to the difference between using forward or futures contracts (§3).

3.3.1. Pure hedging.

Consider an economic agent who holds a fixed, non traded, portfolio of Π units of the discount bond maturing, say, at date T_2. This may seem restrictive but is actually innocuous and allows us to focus on the main issue at hand. If additional bonds of different maturities were introduced in the portfolio, the same results would apply to each one of them, with the suitable and obvious redefinition of asset proportions in the investor's wealth. Since he is constrained to hold the bonds, the financial market is actually incomplete for him. He will hedge his position by trading the derivative contracts of maturity $T_F < T_2$. Since we are not interested in pricing problems here, we implicitly assume that the market remains perfect and complete for unconstrained investors, so that both forward and futures contracts are fairly priced by arbitrageurs. Incipient arbitrage activity thus is implicit in this framework. The other market participants, including our hedger, are assumed to be price takers at these no-arbitrage prices. In addition, all of them adopt portfolio strategies that are assumed to be admissible, and in particular self-financing[10].

Our choice of a pure hedger is dictated by the fact that, in this chapter, we want to abstract entirely from any speculative component in the investor's forward or futures position and obtain a solution that is totally preference-free, i.e. independent of her utility function. In this way, the influence of the marking-to-market mechanism that discriminates between forward and futures contracts can be assessed as simply as possible. As is well known, the more general problem of maximizing the investor's expected utility of terminal wealth over some finite horizon would involve, even under the particular assumptions leading to the mean-variance paradigm, an additional (speculative) component that depends on both the hedger's risk aversion and her expectation as to the future average return on the derivative asset. This task is left to chapter 4 below. Note that, in actual economies, the overwhelming majority of agents that trade on derivative markets are firms and financial institutions. Modeling these entities as expected utility maximizers or pure hedgers, as opposed to market value maximizers, is subject to debate.

Pure hedgers' objective is supposedly to minimize, at each date t, the instantaneous variance of their overall position. This choice is inspired by the now abundant literature on hedging contingent claims in incomplete markets[11]. When the market is complete, any contingent claim, by definition, can be perfectly replicated by a dynamic and self-financing portfolio strategy that combines the underlying security, the riskless asset, and possibly other existing assets. However, in incomplete markets where the claim's pay-off is not perfectly replicable, the claim's buyer or seller who hedges the position must nonetheless bear some residual risk. However, in continuous time there exists a unique martingale measure, which belongs to the class of all martingale measures equivalent to the true (historical) probability, such that this residual risk is minimal[12]. The optimal (imperfectly) replicating strategy then is uniquely determined, can be computed in terms of this particular measure, and minimizes risk locally. The instantaneous variance reduction adopted here closely corresponds to this local risk minimization. In the same exact way an investor who follows the optimal replicating strategy will bear minimal residual risk irrespective of the date at which he chooses to close all his positions, a pure hedger following our optimal strategy will bear minimal risk independently of his actual investment horizon. It is very important to note the dynamic aspect of the optimal hedging strategy. It has been largely demonstrated in the empirical literature that, in actual practice, dynamic hedges yield far better results in terms of minimizing risk exposure than static hedges do[13].

3.3.2. Solutions.

We derive first the hedger's strategy that makes use of *forward* contracts, and then contrast it with the strategy using futures. When hedging takes place through forwards, the constrained investor's wealth at each time t is equal to:

$$W_G(t) = \Pi P(t,T_2) + P(t,T_F)\int_0^t \Delta_G(u)dG(u) \tag{6}$$

where the subscript G indicates the use of forward contracts, and $\Delta_G(u)$ is the number of forward contracts *held* (not traded) at date u, i.e. the number of forwards the hedger chooses to hold at any time[14]. The second term on the right hand side of equation (6) is the current (at t) value of the gains and losses incurred from the forward position. Since these cumulative forward gains/losses are realized at date T_F only, they must be discounted by the factor $P(t,T_F)$.

Note that the hedger does not use the money market account at all in this problem. This is because the contribution of this asset, which is locally riskfree, to the instantaneous variance of the hedged portfolio is zero. In other words, the investor's position in this account is here indeterminate and irrelevant. That will not be the case later with futures contracts, because of the margins called on the hedger's position.

Applying Itô's lemma to the wealth (6) yields the following dynamics:

$$\begin{aligned} dW_G(t) &= \Pi dP(t,T_2) + P(t,T_F)\Delta_G(t)dG(t) + \left[\int_0^t \Delta_G(u)dG(u)\right]dP(t,T_F) \\ &\quad + \Delta_G(t)dG(t)dP(t,T_F) \\ &= \Pi P(t,T_2)\frac{dP(t,T_2)}{P(t,T_2)} + \Delta_G(t)P(t,T_F)G(t)\frac{dG(t)}{G(t)} \\ &\quad + \left[\int_0^t \Delta_G(u)dG(u)\right]P(t,T_F)\frac{dP(t,T_F)}{P(t,T_F)} + \Delta_G(t)dG(t)dP(t,T_F) \end{aligned} \tag{7}$$

Similarly, applying Itô's lemma to G(t) yields:

$$dG(t) = G(t)\mu_G(t)dt + G(t)\Sigma_G(t)'d\hat{Z}(t) \tag{8}$$

where the instantaneous expected rate of price change $\mu_G(t)$ could be written out explicitly using equation (5) and $\Sigma_G(t)$ is the (K-dimensional) volatility of the forward contract relative price changes.

Thus, using the bond price dynamics (3) with j = 1 (recalling that $T_F = T_1$) and j = 2, and using result (8), the wealth dynamics (7) rewrites:

$$\begin{aligned} dW_G(t) = &\left\{ \begin{array}{l} \Pi P(t,T_2)\mu_P(t,T_2) + \Delta_G(t)P(t,T_F)G(t)\left(\mu_G(t) + \Sigma_G(t)'\Sigma_P(t,T_F)\right) \\ + \left[\int_0^t \Delta_G(u)dG(u)\right]P(t,T_F)\mu_P(t,T_F) \end{array} \right\} dt \\ &+ \left\{ \begin{array}{l} \Pi P(t,T_2)\Sigma_P(t,T_2) + \Delta_G(t)P(t,T_F)G(t)\Sigma_G(t) \\ + \left[\int_0^t \Delta_G(u)dG(u)\right]P(t,T_F)\Sigma_P(t,T_F) \end{array} \right\}' dZ(t) \end{aligned} \tag{9}$$

Now, if *futures* contracts are used as hedging vehicles instead of forwards, the constrained investor's wealth at time t is different from (6) and equal to:

$$W_H(t) = \Pi P(t,T_2) + X(t) \tag{10}$$

where the subscript H denotes the use of futures, and X(t) is the margin account associated with the investor's futures position. Since the investor can lend or borrow funds at the locally riskless rate of interest, X(t) is equal to :

$$X(t) = \int_0^t \exp\left[\int_u^t r(u)du\right]\Delta_H(u)dH(u)$$

where $\Delta_H(u)$ is the number of futures contracts *held* (not traded) at date u.

An implicit assumption underlying equation (10) is that the hedger can borrow against her wealth any amount X(t) at the prevailing locally riskless rate, should X(t) be negative. In other words, there is no cash constraint imposed on the hedger's position.

Applying Itô's lemma to the wealth (10) and to the price H(t) yields, respectively:

$$\begin{aligned} dW_H(t) &= \Pi dP(t,T_2) + dX(t) \\ &= \Pi dP(t,T_2) + r(t)X(t)dt + \Delta_H(t)dH(t) \end{aligned} \tag{11}$$

and

$$dH(t) = H(t)\mu_H(t)dt + H(t)\Sigma_H(t)' dZ(t) \tag{12}$$

where $\mu_H(t)$ is the instantaneous expected rate of price change of the futures contract and $\Sigma_H(t)$ is the (K-dimensional) volatility of the futures relative price changes.

Then, using equation (3) with j = 2 and equations (11) and (12) leads to:

$$dW_H(t) = (.)dt + \left\{ \Pi P(t,T_2)\Sigma_P(t,T_2) + \Delta_H(t)H(t)\Sigma_H(t) \right\}' dZ(t) \tag{13}$$

where the drift term (.)dt need not be made explicit since it will play no role in the derivation of the solution.

Indeed, to obtain the maximal hedging strategy, we minimize the instantaneous variance of the investor's wealth. This leads to the following propositions:

Proposition 1:

Under the assumptions of Section I and further assuming that the hedger minimizes the instantaneous variance of his or her overall position, the number of *forward* contracts he or she holds at any date t is equal to:

$$\Delta_G(t) = -\Pi \frac{\Sigma_G(t)' \Sigma_P(t,T_2)}{\Sigma_G(t)' \Sigma_G(t)} - \left(\frac{W_G(t)}{P(t,T_2)} - \Pi \right) \frac{\Sigma_G(t)' \Sigma_P(t,T_F)}{\Sigma_G(t)' \Sigma_G(t)} \tag{14}$$

and the number of *futures* contracts he or she holds at any time t is given by:

$$\Delta_H(t) = -\Pi \frac{P(t,T_2)}{H(t)} \frac{\Sigma_H(t)' \Sigma_P(t,T_2)}{\Sigma_H(t)' \Sigma_H(t)} \tag{15}$$

Proposition 2:

Under the assumptions of Proposition 1, the minimum variance hedge *ratio* using *forwards* is equal to:

$$\delta_G(t) = -\pi_G(t)\frac{\Sigma_G(t)'\Sigma_P(t,T_2)}{\Sigma_G(t)'\Sigma_G(t)} - (1-\pi_G(t))\frac{\Sigma_G(t)'\Sigma_P(t,T_F)}{\Sigma_G(t)'\Sigma_G(t)} \tag{16}$$

where $\delta_G(t) \equiv \Delta_G(t)G(t)P(t,T_F)/W_G(t)$ and $\pi_G(t) \equiv \Pi P(t,T_2)/W_G(t)$ is the proportion of the investor's wealth held in the non-traded bond,

and the minimum variance hedge *ratio* using *futures* is equal to:

$$\delta_H(t) = -\pi_H(t)\frac{\Sigma_H(t)'\Sigma_P(t,T_2)}{\Sigma_H(t)'\Sigma_H(t)} \tag{17}$$

where $\delta_H(t) \equiv \Delta_H(t)H(t)/W_H(t)$ and $\pi_H(t) \equiv \Pi P(t,T_2)/W_H(t)$ is the proportion of the investor's wealth held in the non-traded bond.

Proofs

a) *Forwards.* The variance of the random term present in the right hand side of equation (9) writes:

$$\begin{aligned}
\frac{Var(dW_G(t))}{dt} &= \Pi^2 P(t,T_2)^2\Sigma_P(t,T_2)'\Sigma_P(t,T_2) \\
&+ \Delta_G^2(t)P(t,T_F)^2G(t)^2\Sigma_G(t)'\Sigma_G(t) \\
&+ \left\{\left[\int_0^t \Delta_G(u)dG(u)\right]P(t,T_F)\right\}^2\Sigma_P(t,T_F)'\Sigma_P(t,T_F) + 2\Big\{\Pi P(t,T_2)\Delta_G(t)P(t,T_F) \\
&G(t)\Sigma_P(t,T_2)'\Sigma_G(t) + \Pi P(t,T_2)\left[\int_0^t \Delta_G(u)dG(u)\right]P(t,T_F)\Sigma_P(t,T_2)'\Sigma_P(t,T_F) \\
&+ \Delta_G(t)P(t,T_F)G(t)\left[\int_0^t \Delta_G(u)dG(u)\right]P(t,T_F)\Sigma_G(t)'\Sigma_P(t,T_F)\Big\}
\end{aligned}$$

Differentiating this expression with respect to $\Delta_G(t)$, setting the result equal to zero and dividing through by $2P(t,T_F)G(t)$ yields:

$$\begin{aligned}
0 &= \Delta_G(t)P(t,T_F)G(t)\Sigma_G(t)'\Sigma_G(t) \\
&+ \Pi P(t,T_2)\Sigma_P(t,T_2)'\Sigma_G(t) + \left[\int_0^t \Delta_G(u)dG(u)]\right]P(t,T_F)\Sigma_G(t)'\Sigma_P(t,T_F)
\end{aligned}$$

Knowing from equation (6) that:

$$\left[\int_0^t \Delta_G(u)dG(u)\right]P(t,T_F) = W_G(t) - \Pi P(t,T_2)$$

and using equation (5) to eliminate G(t) yields equation (14). Using the definitions of $\delta_G(t)$ and $\pi_G(t)$ and using equation (5) to eliminate G(t) yields equation (16).

b) *Futures.* Using the same procedure as above applied to (the simpler) equation (13) yields equations (15) and (17). □

3.3.3. Discussion.

Comparing solutions (14) and (15), or equivalently (16) and (17), elicits the following comments.

a) In both instances, the minimum variance hedging component, familiar in *static hedging*, that depends on the usual covariance (futures or forward price changes, underlying bond price changes) / variance (futures or forward price changes) ratio is present[15]. This ratio is not equal to one in general and can never be under stochastic rates if the underlying instrument to be hedged is a fixed income security, as here[16]. Not only there are several sources of uncertainty so that the covariance between the return on either contract and the return on the underlying asset is not equal to the variance of the return on either contract, but even in the case of only one source of uncertainty, this would also be the case.

To see this, assume momentarily for the sake of the discussion that Z(t) is one-dimensional. Then equations (14) and (15) become respectively:

$$\Delta_G(t) = -\Pi\frac{\sigma_{G(t),P(t,T_2)}}{\sigma^2_{G(t)}} - \left(\frac{W_G(t)}{P(t,T_2)} - \Pi\right)\frac{\sigma_{G(t),P(t,T_F)}}{\sigma^2_{G(t)}} \qquad (14')$$

where $\sigma_x(.)$ is a one-dimensional volatility (standard deviation) and $\sigma_{x,y}(.)$ a one-dimensional covariance, and:

$$\Delta_H(t) = -\Pi\frac{P(t,T_2)}{H(t)}\frac{\sigma_{H(t),P(t,T_2)}}{\sigma^2_{H(t)}} \qquad (15')$$

Even though the correlation coefficient between the underlying bond price changes and the forward (or futures) price changes is equal to one, a standard property of one-factor yield curve models, it does not follow that the hedge ratio is equal to one. The only exception would occur if the volatility of the underlying asset price changes were equal to that of the forward price changes. Yet this is impossible, when the underlying asset is a zero-coupon bond, as this equality would require that the maturities of the forward and its underlying bond coincide. This is obviously absurd since then the forward price would always be equal to one and its volatility consequently zero.

Here, the problem is compounded by the presence of multiple sources of risk that makes the hedge *imperfect* and the volatility of the hedged position strictly positive. This situation is referred to as "*cross-hedging*" in the literature and among practitioners.

b) Comparing the first term in the right hand side of (14) and the only term in the right hand side of (15) brings forward two differences. One is due to the presence of the term $P(t,T_2)/H(t)$ in (15) and the other to the disparity of the volatilities of forward and futures prices. First, the term $P(t,T_2)/H(t)$ is standard in the literature relative to hedging with futures and is commonly called the " tailing factor "[17]. It is due to the marking-to-market mechanism associated with futures. Note that it tends to increase through time towards one, because it is close to $P(t,T_2)/G(t)$ and the latter is equal to $P(t,T_F)$ from equation (5). Under stochastic interest rates following diffusion processes, $H(t)$ is equal to $G(t)$ times a multiplicative term that depends on the volatility characteristics of the relevant interest rates[18] (see the previous chapter and Section III below). For instance, if the underlying asset price and the forward price are positively correlated, as they are here, the forward price is larger than the futures price. However, because the forward and the futures price have different volatilities and covariances with their underlying bond price $P(t,T_2)$, one cannot infer which term is larger.

c) The essential, and striking, difference between the two solutions, however, is the presence in equations (14) or (16) of an extra term when the hedger uses forwards. Notice first that the latter term is positive or negative depending on whether $\pi_G(t)$, the proportion of the hedger's wealth held in the non-traded bond, is larger or smaller than one, i.e. on whether her forward position is losing or winning. Thus, when the latter is, say, currently winning, she logically increases the amount of forward contracts sold, all other things being equal. Second, this extra term has a straightforward financial interpretation: it is due to the presence of an interest rate risk on the cumulative profit or loss that has accrued so far to her forward position. Since in fact the cumulative gain or loss will be received or paid at the contract maturity date T_F only, this interest rate risk also depends on the covariance between the forward price $G(t) \equiv G(t,T_F,T_2)$ and the spot price $P(t,T_F)$ of the discount bond of maturity T_F. Third, this extra term can also be viewed as a minimum variance hedge against the relative price changes of the discount bond of maturity T_F that is implicit in the profit-and-loss account generated by the forward position. Obviously, this risk disappears when the position on the contract is marked-to-market, i.e. when futures are involved, since then gains (losses) are cashed in (out) immediately.

d) Because the forward and futures prices have different volatilities and also because the numbers of contracts sold short for hedging differ, the hedger's wealth, $W_G(t)$ or $W_H(t)$, will not exhibit the same volatility according to which kind of contract is actually used. This is, from both theoretical and empirical standpoints, an important result that concerns the core of the hedging issue. To show this, we substitute $\Delta_G(t)$ given by equation (14) in the stochastic part of equation (9) (using results (5) and (6)) and $\Delta_H(t)$ given by equation (15) in the stochastic part of equation (13). This yields, respectively:

$$\begin{aligned}&\Pi P(t,T_2)\left[\Sigma_P(t,T_2)-\frac{\Sigma_G(t)'\Sigma_P(t,T_2)}{\Sigma_G(t)'\Sigma_G(t)}\Sigma_G(t)\right]\\&\quad+(W_G(t)-\Pi P(t,T_2))\left[\Sigma_P(t,T_F)-\frac{\Sigma_G(t)'\Sigma_P(t,T_F)}{\Sigma_G(t)'\Sigma_G(t)}\Sigma_G(t)\right]\end{aligned} \tag{18}$$

and

$$\Pi P(t,T_2)\left[\Sigma_P(t,T_2)-\frac{\Sigma_H(t)'\Sigma_P(t,T_2)}{\Sigma_H(t)'\Sigma_H(t)}\Sigma_H(t)\right] \tag{19}$$

These diffusion coefficients, hence the volatility of the hedged portfolio, i.e. of the investor's wealth, are not equal. On those grounds, the hedger cannot be indifferent between using forward or futures contracts. While the volatility of the position hedged with futures involves one term only, it comprises two terms in the case of forwards. The first one, common to expressions (18) and (19), is the residual variance that remains due to the contract's inability to perfectly match the behavior of the non-traded bond (this is the "cross hedging" effect referred to earlier). It is proportional to the part of the investor's wealth that is held in the constrained bond position. The second component is the residual variance that is due to the imperfect correlation between the forward contract and the discount bond $P(t,T_F)$ implicit in the profit-and-loss position and whose maturity coincides with that of the forward.

It is instructive to compare this result with what would happen if the yield curve was driven by one source of uncertainty only, as in part of the discussion a) above. The terms inside all three brackets in expressions (18) and (19) would evidently cancel out, the hedge would be *perfect* and the hedger would consequently be *indifferent* between forward and futures contracts. This is because all interest rates and bond prices would be locally perfectly correlated. In our general setting, where the yield curve is driven by an arbitrary number of factors and volatilities themselves may be stochastic, the hedge is necessarily *imperfect*. Unfortunately, to assess whether the hedger would be better off using one type of derivatives or the other would require the exact knowledge of both the diffusion and the drift terms of the hedged portfolio value process.

Suppose for illustrative purposes that the volatilities $\Sigma(t,s)$ of the forward rates (see equation (3)) are either linear in maturity $[\Sigma(t,s)=(s-t)\sigma]$ or exponential $\left[\Sigma(t,s)=a^{-1}\left(1-e^{-a(s-t)}\right)\sigma\right]$. Then the futures and forward prices are known to differ by a deterministic term only and thus have the same instantaneous volatility[19] [see Section III below for a numerical example]. Therefore, we can substitute $\Sigma_G(t)$ for $\Sigma_H(t)$ in equation (19). However, expressions (18) and (19) are still different because of the second term present in (18). In particular, the residual risk achieved with futures is in these two cases smaller than the one obtained with forwards, a particularly interesting result.

e) In the same way, it is fruitful to assess the difference between the drift terms of the investor's wealth dynamics (its instantaneous expected absolute change). To do so, we sort out the exact expression for the drift term of the process $dW_G(t)$ present in equation (7) where forwards are used :

$$\Pi P(t,T_2)\mu_P(t,T_2)+\Delta_G(t)P(t,T_F)G(t)\mu_G(t)$$
$$+\left(\int_0^t \Delta_G(u)dG(u)\right)P(t,T_F)\mu_P(t,T_F)+\Delta_G(t)P(t,T_F)G(t)\Sigma_G(t)'\Sigma_P(t,T_F)$$

Substituting $\Delta_G(t)$ given by equation (14) in the above expression and rearranging terms yields:

$$\Pi P(t,T_2)\left[\mu_P(t,T_2)-\frac{\Sigma_G(t)'\Sigma_P(t,T_2)}{\Sigma_G(t)'\Sigma_G(t)}\left[\mu_G(t)+\Sigma_G(t)'\Sigma_P(t,T_F)\right]\right]$$
$$+(W_G(t)-\Pi P(t,T_2))\left[\mu_P(t,T_F)-\frac{\Sigma_G(t)'\Sigma_P(t,T_F)}{\Sigma_G(t)'\Sigma_G(t)}\left[\mu_G(t)+\Sigma_G(t)'\Sigma_P(t,T_F)\right]\right]$$

(20)

The first term in equation (20) is the expected return on the investor's hedged portfolio, i.e. the expected return on the non-traded bonds minus the expected *adjusted* return on the forwards. The adjustment is due to both the imperfect correlation between the forward and its underlying bond of maturity T_2 and the correlation between the forward and the discount bond of identical maturity T_F that is implicit in the forward position. The second term in expression (20) is the expected return on the profit-and-loss account, i.e. the expected return on the discount bond of maturity T_F, minus that (also twice adjusted) on the forwards held to hedge this account.

Another interesting feature is that the adjusted term $[\mu_G(t)+\Sigma_G(t)'\Sigma_P(t,T_F)]$ present in both terms of expression (20) is the expected return on the *futures* contract under *deterministic* volatilities (recall that, under these circumstances, $\Sigma_G(t) = \Sigma_H(t)$). Thus there is a link in this case between the drift terms of the hedged portfolio dynamics obtained through forwards and through futures. Nonetheless, the second term in (20) is different when futures are used. Indeed, using the same method as above for forwards, the drift term of $dW_H(t)$ is equal to:

$$r(t)W_H(t)+\Pi P(t,T_2)\left(\mu_P(t,T_2)-r(t)-\frac{\Sigma_H(t)'\Sigma_P(t,T_2)}{\Sigma_H(t)'\Sigma_H(t)}\mu_H(t)\right) \quad (21)$$

The second term in equation (20) is replaced by the term $r(t)X(t)$ that represents the instantaneous return on the cash position generated by the marking-to-market mechanism, an intuitive result.

3.4. A NUMERICAL ILLUSTRATION

To assess the order of magnitude of the difference in hedge ratios between the two strategies, this section provides numerical estimates in a specialized version of the HJM model where explicit closed form solutions for the futures price can be derived. As argued earlier, this is the case when the volatilities of the forward rates are either linear in maturity or exponential, which we assume here. The futures price and the forward price then differ by a deterministic term only and thus have the same instantaneous volatility. Since we want to preserve realism and avoid perfect correlations and perfect hedges, we first retain a two-factor model. Then, for the sake of comparison, we will briefly consider the one-factor model where perfect hedges can be performed.

3.4.1. A two-factor model

Formally, we specialize equation (3) as follows:

$$df(t,T)=\mu(t,T,f(t,T))dt+\sigma_1 dZ_1(t)+\sigma_2 dZ_2(t) \tag{22}$$

where σ_1 and σ_2 are constant. Assumption (22) is convenient as it allows for rather general forms of the yield curve while keeping the closed form solutions tractable.

Now, substituting (22) in (1) and applying Itô's lemma yields the stochastic differential equation satisfied by the pure discount bonds:

$$\frac{dP(t,\tau_i)}{P(t,\tau_i)}=[b(t,\tau_i)+r(t)]dt-\sigma_1(\tau_i-t)dZ_1(t)-\sigma_2(\tau_i-t)dZ_2(t)$$

The dynamics followed by the *forward* price $G(t)\equiv P(t,T_2)/P(t,T_F)$ thus is given by :

$$\begin{aligned}dG(t)=\mu_G(t)G(t)dt-\sigma_1(T_2-T_F)G(t)dZ_1(t)\\ -\sigma_2\left(e^{-(T_F-t)}-e^{-(T_2-t)}\right)G(t)dZ_2(t)\end{aligned}$$

The arbitrage relationship between forward and futures prices, given at the end of Chapter 2, reads:

$$H(t)=G(t)\exp\left\{\int_t^{T_F}\operatorname{cov}\left(\frac{dG(s)}{G(s)};\frac{dP(s,T_F)}{P(s,T_F)}\right)ds\right\}$$

An easy computation then shows that the *futures* price is equal to:

$$\begin{aligned}H(t)=\frac{P(t,T_D)}{P(t,T_F)}\exp\Big\{-\frac{\sigma^2}{2}(T_2-T_F)(T_F-t)^2\\ -\frac{\sigma_2^2}{2}\left[\left(e^{-(T_2-T_F)}-1\right)+\left(e^{-(T_F-t)}-e^{-(T_2-t)}\right)\left(2-e^{-(T_F-t)}\right)\right]\Big\}\end{aligned}$$

and its dynamics to:

$$dH(t)=\mu_H(t)dt-\sigma_1(T_2-T_F)H(t)dZ_1(t)-\sigma_2\left(e^{-(T_F-t)}-e^{-(T_2-t)}\right)H(t)dZ_2(t)$$

Equations (14) and (15), respectively, then become:

$$\Delta_G(t)=-\Pi-\left(\frac{W_G(t)}{P(t,T_2)}\right)\frac{\sigma_1^2(T_2-T_F)(T_F-t)+\sigma_2^2\left(e^{-(T_F-t)}-e^{-(T_2-t)}\right)\left(1-e^{-(T_F-t)}\right)}{\sigma_1^2(T_2-T_F)^2+\sigma_2^2\left(e^{-(T_F-t)}-e^{-(T_2-t)}\right)^2} \tag{23}$$

and

$$\Delta_H(t) = -\Pi\, P(t,T_F)\frac{\sigma_1^2(T_2 - T_F)(T_2 - t) + \sigma_2^2\left(e^{-(T_F - t)} - e^{-(T_2 - t)}\right)\left(1 - e^{-(T_2 - t)}\right)}{\sigma_1^2(T_2 - T_F)^2 + \sigma_2^2\left(e^{-(T_F - t)} - e^{-(T_2 - t)}\right)^2}$$
$$\exp\left\{\frac{\sigma_1^2}{2}(T_2 - T_F)(T_F - t)^2 + \frac{\sigma_2^2}{2}\left[\left(e^{-(T_2 - T_F)} - 1\right) + \left(e^{-(T_F - t)} - e^{-(T_2 - t)}\right)\left(2 - e^{-(T_F - t)}\right)\right]\right\} \tag{24}$$

Some numerical values for the number of forward and futures contracts the hedger will hold under various plausible conditions are provided in Table 3.1. Throughout the Table, the interest rate used to compute the bond price $P(t,T_F)$ appearing in equation (24) is equal to 5% compounded continuously. The current date t is set equal to zero, without loss of generality. The forward rate volatilities σ_1 and σ_2 are annualized. The duration T_F of the contracts and the duration T_2 of the bond to be covered are expressed in years. The non-traded position Π is set equal to one (unit) without loss of generality. The letters A, B and C appearing in the first cell of the last three columns of Table 3.1 refer to the following situations:

- A denotes the case where no gains or losses have so far accrued to the hedger's forward position, so that $[W_G(0)/P(0,T_2)]$ is in fact equal to Π (=1);
- B denotes the case where $[W_G(0)/P(0,T_2)]$ is set equal to 1.1Π because of accrued gains;
- and C is the case where $[W_G(0)/P(0,T_2)]$ is equal to 0.9Π because of accrued losses.

These assumptions are obviously arbitrary but cover realistic situations. The values in the columns labeled "Delta G" and "Delta H" are computed under assumption A, and are provided to give some insight as to the order of magnitude of the hedge ratios. Lastly, the differences "Diff (%)" appearing in the last three columns are computed as $100\,[\Delta_G/\Delta_H - 1]$.

The minimum variance hedge ratios are, as expected, always larger than one (in absolute value, since the position to be hedged can in fact be long or short). These ratios however tend towards one as the duration of the non-traded bond $P(t,T_2)$ lengthens, for a given value of the duration T_F of the derivative contract. This is because the "cross hedging" effect that reflects imperfect correlation tends to become small as the value of the forward or futures contract converges towards that of their underlying bond when the duration of the latter increases (in equation (5), G(t) tends to $P(t, T_2)$ for a given (short) T_F as T_2 lengthens).

Table 3.1. Number of forward and futures contracts held for hedging purposes

The interest rate used throughout is 5% compounded continuously. Sigma 1 and sigma 2 (columns two and three) are the (annualized) forward rate volatilities used in the two-factor HJM model [equation (21)]. The first four groups of assumptions (column one) illustrate cases for which $\sigma_1 = \sigma_2$, and the last two cases for which $\sigma_1 > \sigma_2$ or $\sigma_1 < \sigma_2$. T_F is the duration, expressed in years, of both the forward and the futures contracts. T_2 is the duration, also expressed in years, of the bonds to be hedged. The number of such bonds, Π, is normalized to 1. Delta G and Delta H are the numbers of forward contracts and futures contracts, respectively, held under Assumption A. According to the latter, no gains or losses have so far accrued to the hedger's forward position (i.e. current wealth is equal to 1). According to assumption B (respectively, C), current wealth is equal to 1.1 (respectively 0.9) due to accrued gains (respectively, losses). The differences Diff(%) appearing in the last three columns are equal to 100 $[\Delta_G/\Delta_H - 1]$.

Group	sigma1	sigma2	TF	T2	Delta G	Delta H	Diff(%) A	Diff(%) B	Diff(%) C
I	0.04	0.04	0.5	1	2.12	2.07	2.53	7.94	-2.89
	0.04	0.04	0.5	2	1.38	1.34	2.51	5.32	-0.30
	0.04	0.04	0.5	3	1.22	1.19	2.49	4.37	0.62
	0.04	0.04	0.5	5	1.12	1.09	2.45	3.55	1.35
	0.04	0.04	0.5	10	1.06	1.03	2.35	2.88	1.82
II	0.04	0.04	1	2	2.09	1.99	5.06	10.54	-0.41
	0.04	0.04	1	3	1.54	1.46	4.99	8.65	1.32
	0.04	0.04	1	5	1.26	1.20	4.82	7.00	2.65
	0.04	0.04	1	10	1.11	1.07	4.41	5.47	3.34
	0.04	0.04	1	20	1.05	1.02	3.57	4.10	3.05
III	0.06	0.06	1	2	2.09	1.99	4.99	10.46	-0.49
	0.06	0.06	1	3	1.54	1.47	4.81	8.48	1.15
	0.06	0.06	1	5	1.26	1.21	4.45	6.62	2.28
	0.06	0.06	1	10	1.11	1.08	3.51	4.57	2.45
	0.06	0.06	1	20	1.05	1.04	1.67	2.18	1.15
IV	0.04	0.04	2	5	1.68	1.53	9.52	13.95	5.10
	0.04	0.04	2	10	1.25	1.16	7.79	9.96	5.62
	0.04	0.04	2	15	1.15	1.09	6.08	7.50	4.66
	0.04	0.04	2	20	1.11	1.06	4.39	5.44	3.35
V	0.06	0.02	2	5	1.67	1.54	8.17	12.50	3.84
	0.06	0.02	2	10	1.25	1.20	4.35	6.44	2.26
	0.06	0.02	2	15	1.15	1.15	0.66	2.00	-0.69
	0.06	0.02	2	20	1.11	1.14	-2.90	-1.93	-3.87

Table 3.1. (Continued)

Group	sigma1	sigma2	TF	T2	Delta G	Delta H	Diff(%) A	Diff(%) B	Diff(%) C
VI	0.02	0.06	2	5	1.77	1.60	10.39	15.18	5.61
	0.02	0.06	2	10	1.27	1.15	9.96	12.27	7.65
	0.02	0.06	2	15	1.16	1.06	9.52	11.03	8.01
	0.02	0.06	2	20	1.11	1.02	9.08	10.20	7.96

Differences in the hedge ratios appear to be notable in general. When the impact on the agent's wealth of the forward position is negligible (column A), they range in absolute value between 0.7% and 10.4% with all values but one positive as expected. When the hedger's position presents cumulative gains (column B), the difference between the two hedge ratios as expected increases, and ranges from 2% to 15%. When losses instead have accumulated (column C), the difference decreases to the range 0.3% to 8 %.

When the duration of the forward or futures contracts (T_F) is less than or equal to one year, both the hedge ratios and their relative difference are quite insensitive to changes in the volatilities σ_1 and σ_2 [compare Groups II and III]. For longer contracts [see Groups IV to VI], variations in these volatilities, in particular in their relative magnitude, bring about somewhat significant changes either in the hedge ratios or in their relative difference. Overall, these simulations confirm that the minimum variance hedge ratios vary significantly according to which kind of contract is actually used and that the residual risks associated with a forward hedge and a futures hedge also differ materially, because both hedges are imperfect.

3.4.2. A one-factor model

By contrast, both hedges are perfect under the assumption of a one-factor model, because of perfect local correlation between interest rates. The distinction between the two contracts then becomes essentially irrelevant in this very special and rather unrealistic case, except that the expressions for the minimum variance hedge ratio still differ.

First notice that equation (14'), using the fact that, from the cash-and-carry relation (5) and Ito's lemma, $[\sigma_P(t, T_2) - \sigma_P(t, T_F)]$ is equal to $\sigma_G(t)$, can be rewritten:

$$\Delta_G(t) = -\Pi - \frac{W_G(t)}{P(t,T_2)} \frac{\sigma_{G(t),P(t,T_2)}}{\sigma^2_{G(t)}}$$

In the particular case of the previous model with σ_2 set equal to zero, this equation (or, equivalently, equation (23)) becomes:

$$\Delta_G(t) = -\Pi - \left(\frac{W_G(t)}{P(t,T_2)}\right) \frac{\sigma_1^2 (T_F - t)}{\sigma_1^2 (T_2 - T_F)} = -\Pi - \left(\frac{W_G(t)}{P(t,T_2)}\right) \frac{(T_F - t)}{(T_2 - T_F)} \quad (23')$$

where, interestingly, the hedge makes use of the duration ratio $(T_F\text{-}t)/(T_2\text{-}t)$ and not of the standard deviation σ_1 (which vanishes because of perfect correlation), as in standard static hedges of fixed-income securities.

Similarly, equation (15'), or equivalently equation (24), rewrites:

$$\begin{aligned}\Delta_H(t) &= -\Pi \frac{P(t,T_2)}{H(t)} \frac{\sigma_{H(t),P(t,T_2)}}{\sigma^2_{H(t)}} \\ &= -\Pi\, P(t,T_F) \frac{(T_2 - t)}{(T_2 - T_F)} \exp\left\{\frac{\sigma_1^2}{2} (T_2 - T_F)(T_F - t)^2\right\} \\ &= -\Pi \frac{P(t,T_2)}{H(t)} \frac{(T_2 - t)}{(T_2 - T_F)}\end{aligned}$$

The expression for the minimum variance hedge ratio is still simpler with futures than with its forward counterpart because the latter requires the computation of the position value $W_G(t)$ at all dates t. It is left as an exercise to the reader to show that in both cases, however, the hedge is perfect so that the residual variance of the covered position is zero.

3.5. CONCLUDING REMARKS

In contrast to conventional wisdom according to which the difference between hedging through forward contracts and futures is rather immaterial, it turns out that, in an economy where interest rates are stochastic, the minimum variance hedge ratio using forwards is significantly more involved than its futures counterpart. In particular, it comprises an extra term, due to the fact that profits or losses incurred are locked-in in the forward position up to the investor's horizon date, thereby inducing a need for additional interest rate risk hedging. For the same reason, the investor's total wealth (also) appears in the hedging formula using forwards while only the non-traded cash position appears in the formula involving futures. This sheds some additional light on the respective features of forward and futures contracts written on interest rate sensitive securities, although we have ignored a number of important features that characterize these derivatives in the real world. These include transaction costs, default risk and liquidity issues. Despite these simplifications, the impact on hedging of the marking-to-market mechanism seems to be significant when the stochastic feature of interest rates is taken into account.

Simple simulations performed under some plausible assumptions in the particular case of a two-factor yield curve with deterministic volatilities suggest that, in many instances, the magnitude of the difference between the maximal hedge ratios may be sizeable. However, since both the drift and the diffusion terms for the constrained investor's optimal wealth are different according to which derivative contract is used, nothing general can be said about which contract should overall be preferred.

Endnotes

[1] This chapter draws heavily from our article Lioui and Poncet (2000a) published in *Management Science.*
[2] See for instance Anderson and Danthine (1983), Breeden (1984), Ho (1984), Stulz (1984), Adler and Detemple (1988a, 1988b), Duffie and Jackson (1990), Poncet and Portait (1993), Svensson and Werner (1993) and Lioui and Poncet (1996a, 1996b, 2000a, 2002).
[3] Recall from the previous chapter that if the covariance of the futures or forward price changes with the relevant zero-coupon bond price changes is null or negligible, the futures and forward prices are equal.
[4] See for instance Figlewski, Landskroner and Silber (1991).
[5] See also Cox et al. (1981), Richard and Sundaresan (1981) or Duffie and Stanton (1992).
[6] See HJM (1992).
[7] The filtration contains all the events whose probability with respect to P is null. See for instance Karatzas and Shreve (1991).
[8] See equation (8) on page 82 of HJM (1992).
[9] Relevant references for the pricing of futures contracts include Jarrow and Oldfield (1981), (1988), Duffie and Stanton (1992) and Flesaker (1993).
[10] The properties of admissible strategies are specified, for instance, in Harrison and Kreps (1979), Harrison and Pliska (1981), Cox and Huang (1989), or HJM (1992).
[11] Pioneer references are Föllmer and Sondermann (1986) and Föllmer and Schweizer (1991).
[12] This unique measure is called, following Föllmer and Schweizer (1991), the *minimal* martingale measure. It is the equivalent measure that preserves the most the structure of the true measure subject to the constraint that all asset price processes are martingales under it.
[13] See for instance Brealey and Kaplanis (1995).
[14] The net number of contracts *traded* between dates u^- and u^+ is equal to $d\Delta_G(u)$. Since what is of interest to us is the investor's hedging position at any date t, our modeling, although equivalent, is more natural.
[15] In the typical situation where a static hedge of the position is performed, the usual simple

formula for this ratio is: $\delta = -\sigma_{FS}/\sigma^2_F$, where S stands for "spot" and F stands for either "futures" or "forward". This is easily derived from the following static problem: choose the number of contracts Δ so that the variance at date T of the fully covered position, Variance[Π.S(T) + Δ.F(T)], is minimized. That is: Min $[\Pi^2\sigma^2_S + \Delta^2\sigma^2_F + 2\Pi\Delta\,\sigma_{FS}]$. Setting the derivative of this expression with respect to Δ equal to zero and defining $\delta = \Delta/\Pi$ yields directly the result.

[16] Obviously here, if interest rates are deterministic, making bond prices deterministic as well, the hedging problem does not exist at all.

[17] See for example Figlewski et al. (1991).

[18] This term is stochastic when interest rate volatilities themselves are stochastic, so that futures prices and forward prices in this case will have different volatilities.

[19] See for instance El Karoui and Rochet (1989), or Benninga and Protopapadakis (1994).

CHAPTER 4: OPTIMAL DYNAMIC PORTFOLIO CHOICE IN COMPLETE MARKETS[1]

4.1. INTRODUCTION

The preceding chapter solved the hedging problem of an investor endowed with a non-traded bond position and seeking to minimize his interest rate risk exposure. This chapter examines the more general issue of an investor's optimal bond portfolio strategy when he maximizes the expected utility of his terminal wealth, is endowed with a non-traded position in one particular cash bond but can freely trade on the other bonds, the locally riskless asset and on forwards or futures written on the constrained bond. For instance, all financial institutions, most non-financial firms and many individual investors face this situation.

One route that can be followed, and will be in some chapters later on, to solve this problem is to use the stochastic dynamic programming technique, leading to the Hamilton-Jacobi-Bellman equation. We follow a different route here and use the martingale approach and the methodology developed by Cox and Huang (1989, 1991). We show that the optimal strategy involving futures includes, in addition to the pure hedge and speculative components, two extra hedging elements. The first one is associated with interest rate risk and the second one with the risk brought about by the co-movements of the spot interest rate and the market prices of risk. When the strategy involves forward contracts, yet another hedging term is present. Moreover, the investor's horizon will be shown explicitly to play a crucial role in the optimal strategy design.

Previous research, pioneered by Merton (1971) and Breeden (1979) in a multi-period context, has revealed that investors in general do not make myopic decisions. A portfolio strategy is said to be myopic when each period decision is made as if it were the last one, using no information regarding future investment opportunities. In a complete information economy where the (fully observable) state variables are stochastic and asset returns are correlated with them, myopia results only from logarithmic (Bernoulli) utility[2]. Barring such a utility function, optimal portfolios exhibit so called Merton-Breeden components that are preference-dependent and are used by non-myopic investors as hedges against the unfavorable changes in their investment opportunity set brought about by the economic state variables. For instance, Breeden (1984) showed in a continuous time model that if futures contracts existed that were written on the state variables and were of *instantaneous* maturity, investors would optimally use them as hedges against such unfavorable fluctuations.

We specialize the investor's utility function to the Constant Relative Risk Aversion (CRRA) class, contrasting the isoelastic case and the logarithmic case, in order to derive quasi-explicit solutions in the general framework, draw useful implications and assess the significance of non-myopic (as opposed to myopic) behavior.

The chapter is organized as follows. Section 2 presents the general economic framework, and focuses on the characteristics that make it different from that of the previous chapter. Section 3 is devoted to deriving the optimal strategy for both the isoelastic and the Bernoulli investors and to interpreting the results. To gain further insights as to the interpretation of the general results, Section 4 examines a particular case that leads to completely closed-form solutions. Section 5 concludes and discusses the prospects of some possible extensions.

4.2. THE ECONOMIC SETTING

The economic framework adopted here is essentially that of the previous chapter. In particular, equations (2.1) to (2.4) are assumed to hold. However, we impose here that the market is *complete*, i.e. that the number of traded risky assets (n) is at least as large as the dimension (K) of the Brownian motion.

The assumption of absence of arbitrage opportunities in a frictionless financial market is well known, since Harrison and Kreps (1979), to be tantamount to assuming the existence of a probability measure, defined with respect to a given numeraire and equivalent to the historical measure P, such that the asset relative prices with respect to the numeraire are martingales[3]. When the numeraire is the locally riskless asset yielding r(t), the new, so called "risk-neutral", measure Q is defined by the following Radon-Nikodym derivative:

$$\left.\frac{dQ}{dP}\right|_{\mathcal{F}_t} \equiv \eta(t) = \exp\left\{-\int_0^t \phi(s)'\,dZ(s) - \frac{1}{2}\int_0^t \phi(s)'\,\phi(s)ds\right\} \tag{1}$$

Note (i) that Q is unique since the market is complete (even without the futures or the forward contract defined below), and (ii) that the market price of risk $\phi(t)$ is in general a stochastic process.

There exists *either* a forward contract G(.) *or* a futures contract H(.), whose maturity is T_F (= T_G = T_H), written on a pure discount bond. The latter has a maturity less than or equal to τ_E, say, without loss of generality, T_1 (>T_F). It is essential to recall from the previous chapter that for *unconstrained* investors the market is complete, so that these derivative instruments are *redundant*, but that for the *constrained* investor whose optimal strategy we want to derive the market is completed by the presence of either one of these derivatives.

The price at date $t \leq T_F < T_1$ of the *forward* contract written on the pure discount bond $P(t,T_1)$ is denoted by $G(t,T_F,T_1) \equiv G(t)$ for simplicity, and in an arbitrage-free market is equal to:

$$G(t) = \frac{P(t,T_1)}{P(t,T_F)} \tag{2}$$

The price at date $t \leq T_F < T_1$ of the *futures* contract is denoted by $H(t,T_F,T_1) \equiv H(t)$ and is only assumed to follow a diffusion process.

4.3. THE OPTIMAL DYNAMIC STRATEGY

We present and discuss first the investor's problem (§1), then derive its general solution (§2) and lastly offer comments, in particular as to the differences that stem from adopting alternative utility functions and from using forward or futures contracts (§3).

4.3.1. The Investor's Program

The investor is endowed with Π units of default-free discount bonds of, say, maturity T_1 that he chooses not to trade until time $\tau < T_F$, where τ is his investment horizon[4]. He can trade on the following assets: (n-1) default-free discount bonds of maturities T_j, where j = 2,..., n, the riskless asset and a futures *or* a forward contract written on the bond of maturity T_1. He will use them as speculative investments and/or means of hedging his non-traded cash bond position. His problem is to choose an optimal (expected utility maximizing) portfolio strategy, i.e. the optimal number of units of the locally riskless asset, of the (n-1) bonds, and of futures or forward contracts.

The futures contract is assumed to be continuously (rather than daily) marked-to-market and the investor's margin account at each date t thus is:

$$X(t) = \int_0^t \exp\left[\int_s^t r(u)du\right]\Gamma_H(s)dH(s) \tag{3}$$

where $\Gamma_H(t)$ stands for the number of futures held at time t.

The investor's wealth at each date t then is:

$$V_H(t) = \Pi P(t,T_1) + \Gamma_B(t)B(t) + \sum_{j=2}^{n} \Gamma_{P(t,T_j)}(t)P(t,T_j) + X(t) \tag{4}$$

where $\Gamma_B(t)$ and $\Gamma_{P(t,T_j)}(t)$ stand for the number of units of the riskless asset and of the discount bonds of maturities T_j, respectively.

When the investor trades on the forward contract, his wealth at each time t is equal to:

$$V_G(t) = \Pi P(t,T_1) + \Delta_B(t)B(t) + \sum_{j=2}^{n} \Delta_{P(t,T_j)}(t)P(t,T_j) + P(t,T_F)\int_0^t \Delta_G(s)dG(s) \tag{5}$$

where $\Delta_B(t)$ and $\Delta_{P(t,T_j)}(t)$ stand for the number of units of the riskless asset and of the discount bonds of maturities T_j, respectively.

To derive explicit solutions, two types of specialized utility functions belonging to the well-known and convenient HARA (Hyperbolic Absolute Risk Aversion) class are investigated. Since the instantaneous forward rate is Markovian, however, the economic thrust of the results would be preserved under more general Von Neumann-Morgenstern utility functions. In this framework, no intuition is lost because of this assumption.

The first function is the Constant Relative Risk Aversion (CRRA, or iso-elastic) utility such that:

$$u(V(\tau,\omega)) = \frac{1}{\alpha} V(\tau,\omega)^{\alpha}, \omega \in \Omega, -\infty < \alpha < 1 \tag{6}$$

where $(1-\alpha)$ is the (positive) coefficient of relative risk aversion[5].

The second one is the logarithmic function that characterizes a Bernoulli investor. It has been shown by Rubinstein (1976) to be the relevant "benchmark" utility in finance in a multi-period context due to its unique myopic property: the individual optimises her investment decisions at each date t as if her horizon was t +1 (in discrete time) or t+dt (here). It writes:

$$u(V(\tau,\omega)) = Ln(aV(\tau,\omega)), \quad \omega \in \Omega \tag{7}$$

where a is a mere scale parameter. This case corresponds to the limit of the isoelastic utility function for $\alpha = 0$. The relative risk aversion coefficient thus is equal to 1. This is very convenient, as it suffices to derive results for the isoelastic case then set alpha equal to zero. Hence one need consider explicitly the latter case only. Although technically the log utility investor exhibits a constant relative risk aversion too, we will routinely refer to the "CRRA investor" when α is different from zero and to the "Bernoulli investor" otherwise.

4.3.2. Solutions

The martingale approach is used to solve the problem[6]. When markets are complete, the pricing function is the martingale measure (1).

The investor's portfolio problem writes:

$$\begin{cases} \text{Max } E^P\left[\dfrac{V(\tau)^\alpha}{\alpha}\right] \\ \text{s.t. } E^P\left[\dfrac{V(\tau)}{h(\tau)}\right] = V(0) = \Pi P(0,T_1) \end{cases} \tag{8}$$

where $\alpha < 1$ [$\alpha = 0$ for the log utility] and where $h(\tau)$ is the value at time t of the optimal growth portfolio.

To simplify the computation of the investor's optimal strategy, it is convenient to use h(t), the numeraire, or optimal growth, portfolio. The latter makes the h-denominated value process of any admissible portfolio a martingale under the historical probability measure P[7]. Formally, h(t) is defined as:

$$h(t) \equiv B(t)\frac{dP}{dQ}\bigg|_{F_t} = \exp\left\{\int_0^t \phi(s)' dZ(s) + \int_0^t \left(r(s) + \frac{1}{2}\phi(s)'\phi(s)ds\right)\right\} \tag{9}$$

This portfolio h(t) is the Bernoulli investor's optimal portfolio, another reason why it is useful to adopt it.

Using Cox and Huang (1991), the program (8) has a unique solution. The first-order condition for an optimum writes:

$$V(\tau) = \lambda^{\frac{1}{\alpha-1}} h(\tau)^{\frac{1}{1-\alpha}}$$

where the Lagrange multiplier λ is characterized by:

$$V(0)=\lambda^{\frac{1}{\alpha-1}}E^{P}\left[h(\tau)^{\frac{\alpha}{1-\alpha}}\right]$$

In the log utility case ($\alpha = 0$), $V(0) = \lambda^{-1}$ and $V(\tau) = h(\tau)V(0)$, which incidentally justifies the interpretation of $h(t)$ as the optimal growth portfolio.

It follows that:

$$\frac{V(t)}{h(t)}=E^{P}\left[\frac{V(\tau)}{h(\tau)}|F_t\right]=\lambda^{\frac{1}{\alpha-1}}E_t^{P}\left[h(\tau)^{\frac{\alpha}{1-\alpha}}\right]$$

where $E^P_t[.]$ denotes the expectation under the historical measure P conditional on the information F_t available at date t.

Thus optimal wealth at t is equal to:

$$V(t)=\lambda^{\frac{1}{\alpha-1}}h(t)E_t^{P}\left[h(\tau)^{\frac{\alpha}{1-\alpha}}\right]=\left\{\lambda^{\frac{1}{\alpha-1}}h(t)^{\frac{1}{1-\alpha}}\right\}E_t^{P}\left[\left(\frac{h(\tau)}{h(t)}\right)^{\frac{\alpha}{1-\alpha}}\right] \quad (10)$$

Expression (10) allows for the useful following definitions. First notice that, when $\alpha = 0$, only the first term in brackets $\{\lambda^{-1} h(t)\}$ remains. For this reason, only a *speculative* component and a *pure hedging* element (in the sense used in the previous chapter) will appear in the investor's optimal strategy. In the isoelastic case, however, there exists a second term $E_t^P[.]$ that will generate *dynamic hedging* components in the strategy. This term can be made more explicit as follows:

$$E_t^{P}\left[\left(\frac{h(\tau)}{h(t)}\right)^{\frac{\alpha}{1-\alpha}}\right]=E_t^{P}\left[\left(\frac{B(\tau)\eta(\tau)^{-1}}{B(t)\eta(t)^{-1}}\right)^{\frac{\alpha}{1-\alpha}}\right]$$

since, from definitions (1) and (9), $h(t) = B(t)\eta(t)^{-1}$. Then $V(t)$ reads:

$$V(t)=\left\{\lambda^{\frac{1}{\alpha-1}}h(t)^{\frac{1}{1-\alpha}}\right\}\left[E_t^P\left[\left(\frac{B(\tau)}{B(t)}\right)^{\frac{\alpha}{1-\alpha}}\right].E_t^P\left[\left(\frac{\eta(\tau)^{-1}}{\eta(t)^{-1}}\right)^{\frac{\alpha}{1-\alpha}}\right]\right.$$
$$\left.+\mathrm{Cov}_t\left[\left(\frac{B(\tau)}{B(t)}\right)^{\frac{\alpha}{1-\alpha}};\left(\frac{\eta(\tau)^{-1}}{\eta(t)^{-1}}\right)^{\frac{\alpha}{1-\alpha}}\right]\right] \tag{11}$$

The hedging component inside the biggest brackets is due to the existence of two particular sources of risk (plus the risk due to the generally non-zero correlation between them). The first is the interest rate risk related to the random evolution of the money market account value B(t) due to the process r(t) being stochastic. The second is the risk associated with the random fluctuations of the market prices of risk (hereafter MPR) $\phi(t)$ that are the constituents of the Radon-Nicodym derivative $\eta(t)$. It is important to note already that, since the spot interest rate r(t) also appears in the elements of $\phi(t)$, it will play a dual role in the investor's optimal strategy. Furthermore, if the frequently used but clearly heroic assumption that the MPR follows a deterministic process were adopted, the first source of risk would still be present.

Expression (10) for wealth at time t can be written in a way that eases the economic interpretation of the investor's optimal strategy:

$$\begin{aligned}V(t)&=\lambda^{\frac{1}{\alpha-1}}h(t)E_t^P\left[h(\tau)^{\frac{\alpha}{1-\alpha}}\right]\\&=\lambda^{\frac{1}{\alpha-1}}h(t)^{\frac{1}{1-\alpha}}P(t,\tau)^{\frac{\alpha}{\alpha-1}}E_t^P\left[\left(\frac{P(t,\tau)h(\tau)}{P(\tau,\tau)h(t)}\right)^{\frac{\alpha}{1-\alpha}}\right]\\&=\lambda^{\frac{1}{\alpha-1}}h(t)^{\frac{1}{1-\alpha}}P(t,\tau)^{\frac{\alpha}{\alpha-1}}E_t^P\left[\theta(t,\tau)^{\frac{\alpha}{\alpha-1}}\right]\end{aligned} \tag{12}$$

where we have introduced the price $P(t,\tau)$ of the discount bond whose maturity coincides with the investor's horizon. Since the market is complete, this bond either happens to exist and be traded or is redundant, therefore replicable by a portfolio of existing bonds. This choice is not arbitrary since this bond is the only one for which it is true that $P(\tau,\tau) = 1$.

Now, $\theta(t,\tau) \equiv \frac{P(\tau,\tau)\, h(t)}{P(t,\tau)\, h(\tau)}$ is the Radon-Nicodym derivative associated with the change of numeraire from the growth optimum portfolio h(t) to the discount bond price P(t, τ). In other words, θ(t, τ) is the density that makes the prices of all risky assets using this bond price as numeraire martingales under this new probability measure. It is also the Arrow-Debreu price for one unit of this discount bond in every possible state of the world.

According to equation (12), part of the CRRA investor's strategy can conveniently be analysed as including the discount bond P(t, τ) as a hedging device against interest rate risk. Thus the role of the investor's horizon τ emerges in a natural manner in the optimal portfolio dynamics.

Defining $E_t^P\left[\theta(t,\tau)^{\frac{\alpha}{\alpha-1}}\right] \equiv J(\alpha\,;\,t,\tau)$ and applying Itô's lemma to J(.) yields:

$$\frac{dJ(.)}{J(.)} = (.)dt + \sum_{i=1}^{n} \sigma_{Ji}(\alpha\,;\,t,\tau)dZ_i(t)$$

where $\sigma_J(\alpha\,;\,t,\tau)'$ is the (1 x n) diffusion vector of the process dJ(.)/J(.), and J(α ; t, τ) is the instantaneous conditional (α/(α-1)) "moment" of the Arrow-Debreu prices of the discount bond of maturity τ.

Applying Itô's lemma to equation (12) in turn yields the *optimal* wealth dynamics:

$$\frac{dV(t)}{V(t)} = (.)dt + \left[\frac{1}{1-\alpha}\phi(t)' - \frac{\alpha}{1-\alpha}\Sigma_P(t,\tau)' + \sigma_J(\alpha\,;\,t,\tau)'\right]dZ(t) \qquad (13)$$

We now calculate the dynamics of actual wealth (4) or (5) depending on which contract (futures or forward) is used. Applying Ito's lemma to (4) yields the dynamics:

$$\begin{aligned}\frac{dV_H(t)}{V_H(t)} &= (\;)dt \\ &+ \left\{\pi_H(t)\Sigma_P(t,T_1) + \sum_{j=2}^{n} \gamma_{P(t,T_j)}(t)\Sigma_P(t,T_j)' + \gamma_H(t)\Sigma_H(t,T_F)'\right\}dZ(t)\end{aligned} \qquad (14)$$

where:

$$\begin{aligned}\pi_H(t) &\equiv \frac{\Pi P(t,T_1)}{V_H(t)}\\ \gamma_{P(t,T_j)}(t) &\equiv \frac{\Gamma_{P(t,T_j)}(t)P(t,T_j)}{V_H(t)}\\ \gamma_H(t) &\equiv \frac{\Gamma_H(t)H(t)}{V_H(t)}\end{aligned} \tag{15}$$

and $\Sigma_H(t,T_F)$ stands for the volatility of the futures price.

Likewise, if the investor trades on the forward contract, her wealth dynamics writes:

$$\begin{aligned}\frac{dV_G(t)}{V_G(t)} = (\ )dt + \Big\{&\pi_G(t)\Sigma_P(t,T_1) + \sum_{j=2}^{n}\delta_{P(t,T_j)}(t)\Sigma_P(t,T_j)'\\ &+\delta_G(t)\Sigma_G(t,T_F)' + \varphi_G(t)\Sigma_P(t,T_F)'\Big\}dZ(t)\end{aligned} \tag{16}$$

where:

$$\begin{aligned}\pi_G(t) &\equiv \frac{\Pi P(t,T_1)}{V_G(t)}\\ \varphi_G(t) &\equiv \frac{P(t,T_F)\int_0^t \Delta_G(s)dG(s)}{V_G(t)}\\ \delta_G(t) &\equiv \frac{P(t,T_F)\Delta_G(t)G(t)}{V_G(t)}\end{aligned} \tag{17}$$

Now, identifying the diffusion terms of *admissible* wealth (14) or (16) and *optimal* wealth (13) leads to the following two propositions.

<u>Proposition 1:</u>

a) Given the assumptions adopted in this chapter, the optimal strategy the CRRA investor using futures follows is given by:

$$\begin{aligned}\begin{bmatrix}\gamma_{P(t,T_2)}\\ \cdot\\ \gamma_{P(t,T_n)}\\ \gamma_H(t)\end{bmatrix} &= -\Lambda_H(t)^{-1}\Sigma_P(t,T_1)\pi_H(t) + \frac{1}{1-\alpha}\Lambda_H(t)^{-1}\phi(t)\\ &\quad -\frac{\alpha}{1-\alpha}\Lambda_H(t)^{-1}\Sigma_P(t,\tau) + \Lambda_H(t)^{-1}\sigma_J(\alpha\,;t,\tau)\end{aligned} \tag{18}$$

where:

$$\Lambda_H(t)=[\Sigma_P(t,T_2) \;\; . \;\; \Sigma_P(t,T_n) \;\; \Sigma_H(t,T_F)]$$

b) and the optimal strategy the CRRA investor using forwards follows is given by:

$$\begin{bmatrix} \delta_{P(t,T_2)}(t) \\ . \\ \delta_{P(t,T_n)}(t) \\ \delta_G(t) \end{bmatrix} = -\Lambda_G(t)^{-1}\Sigma_P(t,T_1)\pi_G(t)+\frac{1}{1-\alpha}\Lambda_G(t)^{-1}\phi(t)$$

$$-\frac{\alpha}{1-\alpha}\Lambda_G(t)^{-1}\Sigma_P(t,\tau)+\Lambda_G(t)^{-1}\sigma_J(\alpha\,;t,\tau) \qquad (19)$$

$$-\Lambda_G(t)^{-1}\Sigma_P(t,T_F)\varphi_G(t)$$

where:

$$\Lambda_G(t)=[\Sigma_P(t,T_2) \;\; . \;\; \Sigma_P(t,T_n) \;\; \Sigma_G(t,T_F)]$$

Proposition 2:

a) Given the assumptions adopted in this chapter, the optimal strategy the Bernoulli investor using futures follows is given by:

$$\begin{bmatrix} \gamma_{P(t,T_2)} \\ . \\ \gamma_{P(t,T_n)} \\ \gamma_H(t) \end{bmatrix} = -\Lambda_H(t)^{-1}\Sigma_P(t,T_1)\pi_H(t)+\Lambda_H(t)^{-1}\phi(t) \qquad (20)$$

b) and the optimal strategy the Bernoulli investor using forwards follows is given by:

$$\begin{bmatrix} \delta_{P(t,T_2)}(t) \\ . \\ \delta_{P(t,T_n)}(t) \\ \delta_G(t) \end{bmatrix} = -\Lambda_G(t)^{-1}\Sigma_P(t,T_1)\pi_G(t)+\Lambda_G(t)^{-1}\phi(t)-\Lambda_G(t)^{-1}\Sigma_P(t,T_F)\varphi_G(t) \qquad (21)$$

Due to the generality of the adopted framework, it is not possible to disentangle the specific roles of the futures or forward contract and the bonds. The following discussion therefore does not attempt to discriminate between the two types of assets.

4.3.3. Discussion

a) We comment first the CRRA case involving *futures*. The first component of strategy (18) is the traditional, pure, preference-free, minimum-variance component that offsets the risk present in the non-traded cash position $\Pi P(t,T_1)$. It depends in particular on what is essentially the covariance between the cash bond price changes and all the assets price changes over the variance of all assets price changes. Simple examination of equation (18) indicates that the minimum-variance offsetting component of the futures strategy is not equal in size to the non-traded position and must be continuously rebalanced throughout the investment period. Moreover, this hedge ratio also depends on time through the time dimension inherent in the underlying bond price volatility. Continuous rebalancing of the offsetting component thus is called for[8].

The second component of the investor's strategy is the speculative element. Recalling from equation (1) the definition of the MPR $\phi(t)$ associated with the discount bonds, this speculative component is a usual mean-variance type term. It is of course a decreasing function of the investor's risk aversion $(1-\alpha)$. Also, since the investor has access to the locally riskfree asset yielding $r(t)$, it is the risk premiums present in the definition of the MPR vector $\phi(t)$ that show up in the numerator instead of the drifts of the price processes.

The third and fourth terms differ markedly from what was traditionally offered in the abundant literature on inter-temporal portfolio choices. For instance, Breeden (1984), Adler and Detemple (1988a,b), or Poncet and Portait (1993), using the stochastic dynamic programming approach pioneered in finance by Merton, write the investor's value function as a function of the state variables that are assumed to drive the investment opportunity set and derive the optimal demands. This produces (so called Merton-Breeden) hedging terms against the random fluctuations of each and every state variable. In contrast, our investor's strategy exhibits only two hedging terms against what will be interpreted below as (i) the interest rate risk measured up to the individual's investment horizon and (ii) a mixture of the bond price volatility and of the MPR volatility.

The third ingredient in (18) is in fact an informationally based component that hedges against unfavorable shifts in the investment opportunity set that are due to interest rate fluctuations. It is somewhat akin to (but different from) a Merton-Breeden hedge since the latter hedges against the random fluctuations of a particular state variable. Furthermore, this third component possesses a distinctive feature: the asset that the investor *implicitly* uses is neither the money market account nor the futures contract itself, assets which are common to all investors, but the discount bond whose maturity date coincides with her *own investment horizon*, $P(t, \tau)$. By "implicitly", we mean that the computation of this component of the optimal strategy (18) requires that one takes into account the risk associated with the discount bond $P(t, \tau)$. This result is intuitive in so far as she wishes to hedge against changes in her opportunity set for a time period that extends up to her horizon, but not beyond. It is important to note that (i) this bond $P(t, \tau)$ is in general a *synthetic* asset that the investor can easily manufacture (using the futures, the money market account and the existing bonds) since the market is complete, even for her, and (ii) this implicit synthetic asset is found *endogenously* as part of the solution to the investor's problem[9]. The investor's horizon has thus been shown explicitly to play a crucial role in the optimal strategy design, in sharp contrast with the traditional decomposition.

Although the last term in equation (18) is couched in more abstract terms, it nevertheless lends itself to a rather intuitive economic interpretation. As shown above, $J(\alpha; t, \tau)$ is related to the contingent Arrow-Debreu prices $\theta(t,\tau)$ for one unit of the discount bond $P(t,\tau)$ maturing at the investor's horizon in every state of the world, conditional on the information available at date t. Thus, $\sigma_J(\alpha; t, \tau)$, the diffusion vector of the stochastic process $dJ(\alpha; t, \tau)/ J(\alpha; t, \tau)$, is a measure of the risk associated with the random volatility of these contingent Arrow-Debreu prices and therefore represents essentially both the volatility of the discount bond price volatility and that of the MPR. Accordingly, the fourth component of strategy (18) also qualifies as a hedge. It is investor specific as it depends on both her risk aversion coefficient and her horizon. In a way, $\theta(t,\tau)$ plays the role of a state variable that encompasses the random fluctuations of both the yield curve and the MPR. Thus, in that sense, this component can be interpreted as a kind of Merton-Breeden hedging term. However, like the third term in (18), it is a hedge, not against the random fluctuations of a specific state variable, but against the random *volatility* of the contingent Arrow-Debreu prices $\theta(t,\tau)$ relevant to the investor's horizon.

It may be instructive to draw an analogy between these results and those obtained by Breeden (1979). In his economy, as in Merton's (1973), the investment opportunity set is driven by state variables, thus changes over time in a stochastic manner. Yet, in contrast with Merton, whose Capital Asset Pricing Model (CAPM) exhibits two (or more) betas, one vis-à-vis the market portfolio and one (or more) vis-à-vis the state variable(s), his consumption-based CAPM exhibits a single beta, which is defined vis-à-vis aggregate consumption. This is because the ultimate concern of all investors is real consumption, and that the latter is affected by all the sources of risk that plague the economy. His insight thus leads to a parsimonious model that is (at least in theory) more tractable than its multi-betas rivals. Our approach also leads to a strategy that is "parsimonious" vis-à-vis standard results and whose implementation is much easier. Indeed, it only involves the estimation of the characteristics of two sets of elements that are well identified and relatively easy to interpret and work out, namely the yield curve and the market prices of risk. The latter can for instance be deduced from the market prices of interest rate options. By contrast, the implementation of the more traditional approach is very problematic as the investor must identify first all the numerous and generally unknown relevant state variables and then estimate their distribution characteristics.

b) When the investor trades on *forward* contracts, his optimal strategy (19) includes an additional term, which is akin to the extra term encountered in the previous chapter when pure hedging was undertaken with forwards. This term is positive or negative depending on the sign of $\varphi_G(t)$, the proportion of the investor's wealth held in the forward contracts, i.e. on whether his forward position is winning or losing. Suppose that all correlations are positive, a realistic assumption for interest rate instruments. Then, when the position is, say, currently losing, he logically decreases his holdings in all assets, all other things being equal. In addition, as compared to the first term of (19) relative to the constrained bond holdings $\pi_G(t)$, it is readily seen that this extra term involves the covariance between all asset returns and that of the bond of the same maturity T_F as the forward contract, not that of the bond of maturity T_1. This finding has a straightforward financial interpretation. Since the cumulative profit or loss that has accrued so far to his forward position will be received or paid at the contract maturity date T_F only, the interest rate risk thus borne depends on the covariance between the forward price and the spot price of the discount bond of maturity T_F. Therefore, this extra term is a minimum variance hedge against the relative price changes $P(t, T_F)$ of the discount bond implicit in the profit-and-loss account generated by the forward position.

c) We turn now to the "benchmark" case of log utility. Scrutiny of equations (20) and (21) readily reveals the Bernoulli investor's myopic behavior: the two dynamic hedge components have vanished, the investor paying no attention to possible changes in her (next period) opportunity set. This is well known and was expected. Also, the pure hedge component is of course identical to the one encountered in the CRRA case, and the speculative component is essentially unaffected, except for the value of the relative risk aversion parameter. The difference between optimal strategies using futures and forwards still is materialized by the presence of an extra term in expression (21) vis-à-vis result (20).

d) A final remark concerns the overall risk borne by the investor's wealth. Since the investor is an expected utility maximizer, and his risk aversion is not infinite, his optimal hedged portfolio offers the best possible trade-off between risk and expected return, thus has a non-zero variance. Plugging either one of the solutions (18) and (20) into equation (14) and either one of the solutions (19) and (21) into equation (16) gives the admissible wealth's dynamics. This yields in all four cases a non-zero diffusion vector, although the diffusion term involving $\pi(t)$ vanishes, as expected.

4.4. AN EXAMPLE USING FUTURES

In order to provide further insights as to the hedging terms present in equation (18), in particular the one involving the Arrow-Debreu prices of the discount bond $P(t,\tau)$, we specialize the general case of the previous section in the following manner.

Note first that we restrict the analysis to the case of futures, as we already know that the forward case will involve an extra term due to the interest rate risk brought about by the forward strategy itself. Now suppose (without much loss of generality) that there exists only one tradable asset, so that $(n - 1) = 1$. Since we want our market to remain complete, assume that this asset is a stock (more generally a stock index), denoted by $S(t)$, rather than a bond (in the following special framework, any two bonds or futures written on a bond are perfectly correlated, so that the market cannot be completed by adding such bonds or futures). Assume further that the Brownian motion driving the stock index price, $Z_1(t)$, is one-dimensional and the Brownian motion driving the instantaneous forward rate, $Z_2(t)$, is also one-dimensional and independent of $Z_1(t)$. Finally assume that the drift and diffusion parameters of $S(t)$ and $f(t,T)$ are known constants[10]:

$$\frac{dS}{S} = \varepsilon dt + \sigma_S dZ_1(t) \tag{22}$$

$$df(t,T) = \mu dt + \nu dZ_2(t) \tag{23}$$

In this case, the dynamics of the discount bond price $P(t, T_1)$ and that of the futures price $H(t,T_F)$ write, respectively:

$$\frac{dP(t,T_1)}{P(t,T_1)} = [b(t,T_1)+r(t)]dt-(T_1-t)\nu dZ_2(t) \tag{24}$$

$$\frac{dH(t,T_F)}{H(t,T_F)} = \mu_H(t,T_F,T_1)dt-(T_1-T_F)\nu dZ_2(t) \tag{25}$$

where it should be emphasized that the $b(t, T_1)$ part of the first drift is now deterministic, as is the drift of the futures price. Also, the diffusion part of the second equation stems from the fact that the futures price $H(t,T_F, T_1)$ is equal to $G(t,T_F, T_1)\, g(t,T_F, T_1)$ where $G(t,T_F, T_1)$ is the forward price equal to $P(t, T_1)/P(t,T_F)$ and the g(.) function is deterministic since the diffusion parameter of $df(t,T)$ is itself deterministic[11].

The two-dimensional MPR vector $\phi(t)$ is now equal to:

$$\phi(t)=\begin{bmatrix}(\varepsilon-r(t))/\sigma_S \\ -b(t,T_1)/(T_1-t)\nu\end{bmatrix}\equiv\begin{bmatrix}\phi_1(t)\\ \phi_2(t)\end{bmatrix} \tag{26}$$

where the only stochastic component is $r(t)$. Hence all the risk associated with the random evolution of the MPR comes from the spot rate itself.

In this framework, we can compute explicitly the term $E_t^P\left[\left(\frac{h(\tau)}{h(t)}\right)^{\frac{\alpha}{1-\alpha}}\right]$ present in equation (10).

Proposition 3:

The investor's optimal wealth using futures is:

$$V_H(t)=\left\{\lambda^{\frac{1}{\alpha-1}}h(t)^{\frac{1}{1-\alpha}}\right\}A(t,\tau)P(t,\tau)^{-\frac{\alpha}{1-\alpha}\left(1-\frac{\varepsilon}{\sigma_S^2}\right)}\exp\left(\frac{\alpha}{1-\alpha}\frac{\nu(\tau-t)}{\sigma_S^2}Z_2(t)\right) \tag{27}$$

where $A(t,\tau)$ is the exponential of a deterministic function.

Proof:

We have:

$$\left(\frac{h(\tau)}{h(t)}\right)^{\frac{\alpha}{1-\alpha}} = \exp\left\{\frac{\alpha}{1-\alpha}\int_t^\tau r(s)ds + \frac{\alpha}{1-\alpha}\int_t^\tau \phi(s)' dZ(s) + \frac{\alpha}{2(1-\alpha)}\int_t^\tau \phi(s)'\phi(s)ds\right\} \tag{28}$$

Let us compute the first integral, using:

$$r(t) = f(t,t) = (.) + f(0,t) + \nu Z_2(t)$$

$$\int_t^\tau f(t,s)ds = (.) + \int_t^\tau f(0,s)ds + \nu(\tau - t)Z_2(t)$$

Hence:

$$\begin{aligned}\int_t^\tau r(s)ds &= (.) + \int_t^\tau f(0,s)ds + \int_t^\tau \nu Z_2(s)ds \\ &= (.) + \int_t^\tau f(t,s)ds - \nu(\tau - t)Z_2(t) + \int_t^\tau \nu Z_2(s)ds\end{aligned}$$

But (integrating by parts):

$$\int_t^\tau \nu Z_2(s)ds = \nu(\tau - t)Z_2(t) + \nu\int_t^\tau (\tau - s)dZ_2(s)$$

Hence:

$$\int_t^\tau r(s)ds = (.) + \int_t^\tau f(t,s)ds + \nu\int_t^\tau (\tau - s)dZ_2(s) \tag{29}$$

Let us compute the second integral in (28):

$$\begin{aligned}\int_t^\tau \phi(s)' dZ(s) &= \int_t^\tau \phi_1(s)dZ_1(s) + \int_t^\tau \phi_2(s)dZ_2(s) \\ &= \int_t^\tau \frac{\varepsilon}{\sigma_S}dZ_1(s) - \frac{1}{\sigma_S}\int_t^\tau r(s)dZ_1(s) - \int_t^\tau \frac{b(s,T_1)}{(T_1 - s)\nu}dZ_2(s) \\ &= \int_t^\tau \frac{\varepsilon}{\sigma_S}dZ_1(s) - \frac{1}{\sigma_S}\left[\int_t^\tau (.)dZ_1(s) + \nu\int_t^\tau Z_2(s)dZ_1(s)\right] - \int_t^\tau \frac{b(s,T_1)}{(T_1 - s)\nu}dZ_2(s)\end{aligned}$$

and thus

$$\begin{aligned}\int_t^\tau \phi(s)' dZ(s) = &\int_t^\tau \frac{\varepsilon}{\sigma_S}dZ_1(s) \\ &-\frac{1}{\sigma_S}\left[\int_t^\tau (.)dZ_1(s) + \nu\int_t^\tau [Z_2(s) - Z_2(t)]dZ_1(s) + \nu Z_2(t)\int_t^\tau dZ_1(s)\right] \\ &-\int_t^\tau \frac{b(s,T_1)}{(T_1 - s)\nu}dZ_2(s)\end{aligned} \tag{30}$$

Finally, the last integral in (28) is equal to:

$$\int_t^\tau \phi(s)'\phi(s)ds = \int_t^\tau \left(\frac{b(s,T_1)}{(T_1-s)\nu}\right)^2 ds + \int_t^\tau \left(\frac{\varepsilon - r(s)}{\sigma_S}\right)^2 ds$$
$$= \int_t^\tau (.)ds + \frac{1}{\sigma_S^2}\int_t^\tau r^2(s)ds - \frac{2\varepsilon}{\sigma_S^2}\int_t^\tau r(s)ds \tag{31}$$

which yields after tedious computations involving the second integral:

$$\int_t^\tau \phi(s)'\phi(s)ds = \int_t^\tau (.)ds + \frac{1}{\sigma_S^2}\int_t^\tau (.)dZ_2(s) + \frac{2(\tau-t)\nu}{\sigma_S^2}Z_2(t) - \frac{2\varepsilon}{\sigma_S^2}\int_t^\tau r(s)ds \tag{32}$$

Taking the conditional expectation of (28) using (29), (30) and (32) yields (recalling that b(t, T_1) is here deterministic):

$$E_t^P\left[\left(\frac{h(\tau)}{h(t)}\right)^{\frac{\alpha}{1-\alpha}}\right] = A(t,\tau)$$
$$\exp\left\{\frac{\alpha}{1-\alpha}\int_t^\tau f(t,s)ds + \frac{\alpha}{1-\alpha}\frac{\nu(\tau-t)}{\sigma_S^2}Z_2(t) - \frac{\alpha}{1-\alpha}\frac{\varepsilon}{\sigma_S^2}\int_t^\tau f(t,s)ds\right\}$$

where A(t,τ) is an exponential of a deterministic function.

Now, since $P(t,\tau) = \exp\left\{-\int_t^\tau f(t,s)ds\right\}$, we have:

$$E_t^P[.] = A(t,\tau)P(t,\tau)^{-\frac{\alpha}{1-\alpha}\left(1-\frac{\varepsilon}{\sigma_S^2}\right)}\exp\left\{\frac{\alpha}{1-\alpha}\frac{\nu(\tau-t)}{\sigma_S^2}Z_2(t)\right\}$$

so that result (27) obtains■.

Now, applying Itô's lemma to $V_H(t)$ given by (27) yields:

$$\frac{dV_H(t)}{V_H(t)} = (.)dt + \frac{1}{1-\alpha}\phi_1(t)dZ_1(t)$$
$$+\left[\frac{1}{1-\alpha}\phi_2(t) + \frac{\alpha}{1-\alpha}\left(1-\frac{\varepsilon}{\sigma_S^2}\right)(\tau-t)\nu + \frac{\alpha}{1-\alpha}\frac{(\tau-t)\nu}{\sigma_S^2}\right]dZ_2(t) \tag{33}$$

Admissible wealth given by equation (5) becomes:

$$\frac{dV_H(t)}{V_H(t)} = (.)dt + \gamma_S(t)\sigma_S dZ_1(t) + [-\pi(t)(T_1 - t)\nu - \gamma_H(t)(T_1 - T_F)\nu]dZ_2(t) \quad (34)$$

Identifying the diffusion terms of (33) and (34), using the definitions of $\phi_1(t)$ and $\phi_2(t)$ and rearranging terms yields the following proposition:

Proposition 4:

a) Under the simplifying assumptions of this section, the iso-elastic investor's optimal strategy using futures is given by:

$$\begin{aligned} \gamma_S(t) &= \frac{1}{1-\alpha}\frac{\varepsilon - r(t)}{\sigma_S^2} \\ \gamma_H(t) &= -\pi(t)\frac{(T_1 - t)\nu}{(T_1 - T_F)\nu} + \frac{1}{1-\alpha}\frac{b(t,T_1)}{(T_1 - t)\nu(T_1 - T_F)\nu} \\ &\quad - \frac{\alpha}{1-\alpha}\frac{(\tau - t)\nu}{(T_1 - T_F)\nu} - \frac{\alpha}{1-\alpha}\frac{(\tau - t)\nu}{(T_1 - T_F)\nu}\left(\frac{1-\varepsilon}{\sigma_S^2}\right) \end{aligned} \quad (35)$$

and b) the Bernoulli investor's optimal strategy by:

$$\begin{aligned} \gamma_S(t) &= \frac{\varepsilon - r(t)}{\sigma_S^2} \\ \gamma_H(t) &= -\pi(t)\frac{(T_1 - t)\nu}{(T_1 - T_F)\nu} + \frac{b(t,T_1)}{(T_1 - t)\nu(T_1 - T_F)\nu} \end{aligned} \quad (36)$$

Note that we have *not* simplified some terms in these equations by cancelling ν out where it was possible, in order to keep track of the volatility meaning of those terms.

It is clear why all the hedging terms, the "pure" one involving $\pi(t)$ as well as the Merton-Breeden ones, appear only in the futures part of the strategy. The structure of investment in stocks is left unaffected by the yield curve being stochastic, because of our independence assumption regarding $Z_1(t)$ and $Z_2(t)$. Hence we will focus the discussion on the $\gamma_H(t)$ part of the strategy only. The $\gamma_S(t)$ part is straightforward as it involves only the usual risk-return trade-off in addition to the investor's relative risk aversion coefficient.

In both equations (35) and (36) we recover the preference-free minimum variance component that offsets the risk brought about by the non-traded bond position and depends on the usual ratio of the covariance between futures price changes and cash price changes over the variance of futures price changes. Here, due to the perfect correlation between the instantaneous changes in futures prices and in bond prices, this covariance/variance ratio collapses to a volatility (standard deviation) ratio, which itself collapses, since ν is a constant, to a duration ratio. Since $t \leq \tau$ and $\tau < T_F$, the ratio $(T_1 - t) / (T_1 - T_F)$ is always larger than one. Thus the difference in absolute size between the cash position and the pure hedge component is due to the interest rate risk difference in volatility between the futures and its underlying asset. Hence, in absolute terms, this part of the investor's strategy over-hedges his cash position.

However, this ratio decreases continuously to the value $(T_1 - \tau) / (T_1 - T_F) > 1$, as time elapses. Thus the pure hedge component must be continuously rebalanced over the investment period due to the time dimension of the non-traded bond volatility. Furthermore, since we use futures, not forward, contracts, we recover a term $P(t, T_F)$ that is standard in the literature devoted to hedging with futures[12]. This term is commonly called the "tailing factor" and is due to the marking-to-market mechanism associated with the investor's position[13]. This tailing factor is also responsible for the need to continuously rebalance that component of the strategy.

The second component of (35) and (36) is the speculative component discussed in Section 3. Due to our independence assumption, only the covariance between the futures price and the cash bond price (in addition to the risk premium b(.)) comes into play.

The third and fourth terms in (35), which are absent from (36) due to the Bernoulli investor's myopia, clearly involve both the investor's preferences and his investment horizon τ. The third term is, like the first one, a minimum variance component that offsets the interest rate risk brought about by shifts in the investment opportunity set. It too depends on the ratio of the covariance between futures price changes and cash price changes over the variance of futures price changes, which also degenerates into a duration ratio. However, as explained in the previous section, the cash bond involved is not the non-traded one but the bond whose maturity coincides with the investor's horizon. Consequently, this hedge term tends to zero as the investor's horizon shrinks. The fourth term is of course the most interesting in this section and constitutes in fact the motivation for it. Recall from Section 3 our interpretation of this term as akin to a Merton-Breeden hedge against the random fluctuations of the MPR related to interest rates and the MPRs related to stocks. The influence of these shocks is here explicit and materialized by the term involving ν (as well as τ, T_1 and T_F) and the term involving ε and σ^2_S, respectively. Therefore, in spite of the assumed independence between $Z_1(t)$ and $Z_2(t)$, the randomness of interest rates that affects the MPR of financial instruments not directly related to interest rates such as stocks impinges on the optimal futures strategy. Something is then lost when this strategy is considered in isolation, for instance when the investor's portfolio is assumed to consist of bonds or bills only.

4.5. CONCLUDING REMARKS

Using the martingale approach, we have investigated the influence of stochastic interest rates on investors' behavior. The optimal strategy of an investor endowed with an interest rate sensitive non-traded cash position and whose utility function exhibits a constant relative risk aversion has been explicitly derived. When futures are used, this strategy is composed of two or four elements, according to whether the investor's behavior is myopic or not. The speculative and pure hedge components are always present. The latter is shown not to be equal in size to the non-traded position and to be time dependent. In contrast with previous studies in which the number of Merton-Breeden hedging terms is equal to that of the state variables, we have shown that the optimal strategy can be simplified to include only two such elements, whatever the number of state variables is. The first one is associated with interest rate risk and the second one with the risk brought about by the co-variations of the spot interest rate and the various market prices of risk. This greatly facilitates the practical implementation of the optimal portfolio strategy. The two Merton-Breeden components, which vanish in the case of a myopic investor, involve a synthetic asset that is found endogenously to be a bond the maturity of which coincides with the investor's horizon.

When forwards are used, the investor's optimal strategy involves an extra term vis-à-vis the strategy using futures, namely a hedge term that offsets the interest rate risk borne by the forward position.

One possible extension of this framework would be to consider other preferences. An obvious candidate would be a general HARA function, of which the isoelastic and logarithmic functions are special cases. This would make the results more intricate but still tractable under the complete market assumption. Another, important, extension would be to examine the effects of incomplete markets. This would occur if the number of sources of risk (Brownian motions) exceeded N in the framework adopted here. This generalization is rather difficult because, although the methodology pioneered by He and Pearson (1991) and Karatzas et al. (1991) is well suited for pure investment decisions, it must be significantly modified when an hedging problem is added.

Endnotes

[1] This Chapter is grounded on Lioui and Poncet (2001b).
[2] See for instance Hakansson (1971), Merton (1971), Rubinstein (1976), Breeden (1979), Cox, Ingersoll, and Ross (1985a) and recently Kim and Omberg (1996). Merton (1973), Kraus and Litzenberger (1975), Breeden (1984), Cox, Ingersoll, and Ross (1985b), Adler and Detemple (1988a) and Lioui and Poncet (2000b, 2001b) have underlined the particular relevance of log utility to optimal hedging theory.
[3] The definition of admissible strategies adopted here is the one given by Cox and Huang (1989). The equivalence result holds only for simple strategies, i.e. strategies that need a portfolio reallocation only a finite number of times (see Harrison and Kreps (1979) and Harrison and Pliska (1981)).
[4] See the previous chapter for a detailed justification and a discussion of this assumption.
[5] Kim and Omberg (1996) pointed out to the possibility of "Nirvana" solutions when this parameter is between 0 and 1. Such solutions arise when following a given portfolio stragegy the investor is able to achieve infinit expected utility. Korn and Kraft (2004) give some examples of such strategies.
[6] See Duffie (2001) and the seminal papers of Karatzas, Lehoczky and Shreve (1987) and Cox and Huang (1989, 1991).
[7] See for instance Long (1990) or Bajeux-Besnainou and Portait (1997).
[8] This is in sharp contrast with some traditional results, such as in Poncet and Portait (1993).
[9] By contrast, Poncet and Portait (1993) for instance solve the hedging problem by manufacturing, in an *exogenous* manner, synthetic assets that are perfectly correlated with their state variables.
[10] This specification does not preclude negative values for the forward rate. However, these events are relatively rare for realistic values of the process parameters. In addition, Amin and Morton (1994) have shown that the Gaussian models of the yield curve perform empirically better than log-normal ones. For a lucid discussion of this issue, see Subrahmanyam (1996). Using for instance the so-called affine term structure model (see Duffie (2001) or Dai and Singleton (2000) for discussions) would prevent this drawback, but would also prevent closed-form solutions, the main objective of this illustrative special case.
[11] Relevant references include Duffie and Stanton (1992), for continuous resettlement, and Flesaker (1993) for a discrete day-by-day marking-to-market. It is easy to show that here

$$g(t,\tau_F,\tau_D)=\exp\left[-\frac{v^2}{2}(\tau_D-\tau_F)(\tau_F-t)^2\right].$$

[12] To see why a term $P(t,T_F)$ is implicitly involved, recall that $\gamma_H(t) = \Gamma_H(t)H(t)/V_H(t)$, that $\pi(t) = \Pi\, P(t,T_1)/V_H(t)$ and that $H(t) = [P(t,T_1)/P(t,T_F)]g(t,T_F,T_1)$. Consequently, the number of futures contracts $\Gamma_H(t)$ depends on $-\Pi\, P(t,T_F)$, the "adjusted" number of non-traded bonds.
[13] See Figlewski et al. (1991). The "tailing factor" is equal to $P(t,T_F)$ when the short rate of interest is deterministic. When the latter is stochastic, as here, $P(t,T_F)$ is multiplied by an extra term.

CHAPTER 5: OPTIMAL DYNAMIC PORTFOLIO CHOICE IN INCOMPLETE MARKETS[1]

5.1. INTRODUCTION

The purpose of this chapter is to investigate whether the general results of the previous chapter extend to the case of an incomplete market. We consider a hedger-speculator who is still endowed with a non-traded position in one particular cash bond [2] and chooses to intervene (speculate) *only* in the bond forward or futures market. This individual decides to participate in the latter market only typically because he faces *implicit* differential information and/or transaction costs that provide *him* (not necessarily other types of investors) an incentive to trade on derivative rather than on primitive markets. Hence, although we retain the assumption that markets are frictionless and free of arbitrage opportunities and market participants are price takers at these no-arbitrage prices, the market open for trade to our hedger-speculator is in effect incomplete. Because of this incompleteness, the technical derivation of this investor's optimal strategy is somewhat more involved than in the previous chapters. Consequently, to eliminate the influence of random changes in the state variable(s), focus on the stochastic nature of interest rates and still obtain tractable results, we will examine only the case of a myopic, Bernoulli, investor whose coefficient of relative risk aversion is one.

The distinction between forward and futures contracts remains a crucial ingredient to the analysis. Since interest rates are stochastic, the opportunity sets spanned by the forward and the futures contracts, respectively, are different. In other words, the risk-return relationship offered to speculators in the derivative market differs according to whether they can trade futures or forwards. It turns out that the results continue to be strikingly different according to which derivative is used. While the strategy using futures presents the usual structure with one hedge component and one speculative element, the strategy involving forwards exhibits an extra term. The latter will be interpreted as a special hedge.

The main Section (I) derives the Bernoulli investor's optimal strategy using futures or forward contracts. In particular, it explains in details the methodology developed by He and Pearson (1991) and Karatzas, Lehoczky, Shreve and Xu (1991) that we have adopted. Section II provides a discussion of the results and their implication. A brief Section III offers some concluding remarks.

5.2. OPTIMAL INVESTMENT AND HEDGING

The relevant economy is that of the previous chapter. Consider a speculator endowed with an arbitrary initial wealth W(0) invested in (at least temporarily) Π non-traded bonds of initial value $P(0, T_1)$. His investment horizon is $\tau < T_F < T_1$. She chooses to trade on the forward, or futures, market, but not on the bond market, so as to maximize the expected log-utility of her terminal wealth $W(\tau)$. That is, she adopts the portfolio strategy that solves:

$$\begin{cases} \text{Max}_{\Delta_i,\Gamma_i} E_Q\left[\text{Ln}W_i(\tau)\right] \\ \text{s.t. the portfolio strategy is admissible and satisfies} \\ \text{the budget constraint} \end{cases} \tag{1}$$

where i = H, G, and the budget constraint writes either:

$$W_H(t) = \Pi P(t,T_1) + \int_0^t \exp\left[\int_u^t r(u)du\right]\Delta_H(u)dH(u) + \Gamma_H(t)B(t) \tag{2}$$

or:

$$W_G(t) = \Pi P(t,T_1) + P(t,T_F)\int_0^t \Delta_G(u)dG(u) + \Gamma_G(t)B(t) \tag{3}$$

where the subscript H (resp. G) indicates the use of futures (resp. forward) contracts, $\Delta_i(t)$ is the number of contracts held (not traded) at date t and $\Gamma_i(t)$ is the number of units of the money market account held at instant t. The first term on the RHS of (2) is the margin account associated with the investor's position in futures. The first term on the RHS of (3) is the current (at date t) value of the profits and losses incurred from the forward position, but cashed-in or -out at date T_F only, therefore discounted by the factor $P(t, T_F)$.

The presence of the locally riskless asset is required. Since the logarithmic individual invests in the optimum growth portfolio, she must use the riskless asset to replicate this portfolio by trading derivatives instead of bonds. Note that this is analogous to replicating the option with its underlying asset and the riskfree asset in the Black-Scholes world. The reason is that, except for margin calls, trading on forwards (or futures) involves no investment up to her horizon τ. Wealth thus is essentially invested in the riskless asset, except for the value of the non-traded bond holdings.

We face here a technical problem when trying to solve program (1) since the financial market is incomplete for the speculator-hedger. We need first to characterize the no-arbitrage assumption on the market she has access to. When markets are incomplete, the martingale measure associated with a given numeraire is not unique. The set of martingale measures can, however, be characterized by using the diffusion matrix of the futures, or forward, price[3]. We then use the approach developed by Karatzas et al. (1991) and He and Pearson (1991). We state the results then establish the proof.

Proposition:

a) The Bernoulli investor's optimal dynamic strategy using futures is given by:

$$\hat{\delta}_H(t)=\phi_H(t)'\Sigma_H(t)\left(\Sigma_H(t)'\Sigma_H(t)\right)^{-1}-\pi_H(t)\Sigma_P(t,T_1)'\Sigma_H(t)\left(\Sigma_H(t)'\Sigma_H(t)\right)^{-1} \quad (4)$$

where the hat " ^ " denotes an optimal solution, and

$\hat{\delta}_H(t)\equiv\hat{\Delta}_H(t)H(t)/\hat{W}_H(t)$ is the « value » of the futures position relative to that of total wealth,

$\phi_H(t)$ is the (stochastic) market price of the risk associated with the futures,

$\Sigma_P(t,T_1)$ is the K-dimensional volatility of the cash bond of maturity T_1,

$\Sigma_H(t)$ is the K-dimensional volatility of the futures price, and

$\pi_H(t)\equiv\dfrac{\Pi P(t,T_1)}{V_H(t)}$ is the proportion of total wealth held in the non-traded bond position.

b) The Bernoulli investor's optimal dynamic strategy using forward contracts is given by:

$$\begin{aligned}\hat{\delta}_G(t)\Sigma_G(t)=\;&\phi_G(t)'\Sigma_G(t)\left(\Sigma_G(t)'\Sigma_G(t)\right)^{-1}\\&-(1-\hat{\gamma}_G(t)-\pi_G(t))\Sigma_P(t,T_F)'\Sigma_G(t)\left(\Sigma_G(t)'\Sigma_G(t)\right)^{-1} \quad (5)\\&-\pi_G(t)\Sigma_P(t,T_1)'\Sigma_G(t)\left(\Sigma_G(t)'\Sigma_G(t)\right)^{-1}\end{aligned}$$

where

$\hat{\delta}_G(t) \equiv \hat{\Delta}_G(t)P(t,T_1)/\hat{W}_G(t)$ is the « value » of the forward position relative to that of total wealth,

$\phi_G(t)$ is the (stochastic) market price of the risk associated with the forward contract,

$\Sigma_P(t,T_F)$ is the K-dimensional volatility of the cash bond of maturity T_F,

$\Sigma_G(t)$ is the K-dimensional volatility of the forward price, and

$\hat{\gamma}_G(t) \equiv \hat{\Gamma}_G(t)B(t)/\hat{W}_G(t)$ and $\pi_G(t) \equiv \dfrac{\Pi P(t,T_1)}{V_G(t)}$ are the proportions of wealth invested in the riskless asset and the non-traded bonds, respectively.

Proof

Since the technique used in the case of futures is the same as that of forwards, we focus on the latter, which is slightly more complicated, and then solve the former more rapidly. We use the martingale approach to portfolio choice in incomplete markets, as developed by Karatzas et al. (1991) and He and Pearson (1991).

First apply Itô's lemma to G(t) given by the cash-and-carry formula to obtain :

$$dG(t) = G(t)\mu_G(t)dt + G(t)\Sigma_G(t)'dZ(t)$$

Since markets are arbitrage free, there exists a stochastic process $\phi_G(t)$ followed by the market price of risk associated with the forward contract that is assumed to satisfy the Novikov's condition :

$$E^Q\left[\exp\left\{\frac{1}{2}\int_0^t \phi_G(u)'\phi_G(u)du\right\}\right] < \infty, \qquad t \le T_F,$$

so that the process $\eta^G(T_F)$ defined below is a Q-martingale[4]. A martingale measure associated with the locally riskless asset as the numeraire can be constructed such that:

$$\left.\frac{dQ^G}{dQ}\right|_{F_{T_F}} \equiv \eta^G(T_F) = \exp\left\{-\int_0^{T_F}\phi_G(t)'dZ(t) - \frac{1}{2}\int_0^{T_F}\phi_G(t)'\phi_G(t)dt\right\} \qquad (6)$$

Since the market is not complete (for our investor), the measure Q^G is not unique. Let

$$\mathrm{Ker}\left(\Sigma_G(t)^{'}\right) \equiv \left[\theta(t) \in R^K \middle| \Sigma_G(t)^{'}\theta(t) = 0\right]$$

be the kernel of vector $\Sigma_G(t)^{'}$. We can construct other martingale measures such that:

$$\begin{aligned} \frac{dQ_\theta^G}{dQ}\bigg|_{F_{T_F}} &\equiv \eta_\theta^G(T_F) \\ &= \exp\left\{-\int_0^{T_F}(\phi_G(t)+\theta(t))^{'}dZ(t) - \frac{1}{2}\int_0^{T_F}\left(\phi_G(t)^{'}\phi_G(t)+\theta(t)^{'}\theta(t)\right)dt\right\} \end{aligned} \quad (7)$$

The choice of the martingale measure that will be the pricing rule for the Bernoulli investor is part of the solution to his problem.

We solve the problem in three steps. First, we choose an arbitrary vector $\theta(t)$ from $\mathrm{Ker}\left(\Sigma_G(t)^{'}\right)$ and fix a martingale measure Q_θ^G. We find the optimal wealth the investor will reach using this measure, given his budget constraint. This optimal wealth obviously depends upon the selected vector $\theta(t)$. If markets were complete for the investor, we could be sure that there exists a forward strategy that enables him to reach this wealth. However, in an incomplete market, the wealth obtained in the first step may not be reachable. The second step then consists of choosing the particular vector of $\mathrm{Ker}\left(\Sigma_G(t)^{'}\right)$ that ensures that this wealth is indeed reachable. This vector is chosen such as to yield the minimum of the investor's expected utility to reflect the fact that he is constrained by the market being incomplete. This also characterizes a particular martingale measure. In the third and last step, this martingale measure is used to construct the portfolio strategy that allows the replication of optimal wealth.

First step. The speculator 's program writes:

$$\begin{cases} \max\limits_{W_G(\tau)} E^Q[\mathrm{Ln} W_G(\tau)] \\ \text{s.t. } E^{Q_\theta^G}\left[\dfrac{W_G(\tau)}{B(\tau)}\right] = W(0) \end{cases}$$

the solution to which is :

$$\hat{W}_G(\tau) = W(0)B(\tau)\left(\eta_\theta^G(\tau)\right)^{-1} \quad (8)$$

The value function of the program is $J_G(\theta) \equiv E^Q\left[\mathrm{Ln}\hat{W}_G(\tau)\right]$. Using (7) and (8), we obtain:

$$J_G(\theta) = \mathrm{Ln}W(0) + E^Q\left[\int_0^\tau r(s)ds\right] + \frac{1}{2}E^Q\left[\int_0^\tau \phi_G(t)'\phi_G(t)dt\right] + \frac{1}{2}E^Q\left[\int_0^\tau \theta(t)'\theta(t)dt\right]$$

Second step. We have to find θ such that:

$$\begin{cases} \min_\theta J_G(\theta) \\ \text{s.t. } \Sigma_G(t)'\theta(t) = 0 \text{ for } t \in [0,\tau] \end{cases}$$

Solving this program is equivalent to solving:

$$\begin{cases} \min_\theta \frac{1}{2}\theta(t)'\theta(t) \\ \text{s.t } \Sigma_G(t)'\theta(t) = 0. \end{cases}$$

whose solution is obviously the null vector: $\theta(t) = 0$. This surprising result is uniquely valid for the logarithmic utility. Thus, the martingale measure is given by (6) and optimal wealth (8) is equal to:

$$\hat{W}_G(\tau) = W(0)B(\tau)\left(\eta^G(\tau)\right)^{-1}$$

Its value at each time t is equal to:

$$\frac{\hat{W}_G(t)}{B(t)} = E^{Q^G}\left[\frac{\hat{W}_G(\tau)}{B(\tau)}\middle|F_t\right] = W(0)E^{Q^G}\left[\left(\eta^G(t)\right)^{-1}\middle|F_t\right] = W(0)\left(\eta^G(t)\right)^{-1} \quad (9)$$

where we have used lemma 2.5 on page 43 of Cox and Huang (1989) (Bayes formula). Applying Itô's lemma to (9), we get the dynamics of optimal wealth:

$$d\hat{W}_G(t) = (.)dt + \hat{W}_G(t)\phi_G(t)'dZ(t) \quad (10)$$

From equation (3), the dynamics of the speculator's wealth is also given by:

$$\begin{aligned} d\hat{W}_G(t) = (.)dt + \hat{\Delta}_G(t)P(t,T_F)G(t)\Sigma_G(t)'dZ(t) \\ +\left(\int_0^t \hat{\Delta}_G(u)dG(u)\right)P(t,T_F)\Sigma_P(t,T_F)'dZ(t) \\ +\Pi P(t,T_1)\Sigma_P(t,T_1)'dZ(t) \end{aligned}$$

Now using the definitions

$\hat{\gamma}_G(t) \equiv \hat{\Gamma}_G(t)B(t)/\hat{W}_G(t)$

$\pi_G(t) \equiv \Pi P(t,T_1)/\hat{W}_G(t)$ and

$\hat{\delta}_G(t) \equiv \hat{\Delta}_G(t)P(t,T_1)/\hat{W}_G(t) = \hat{\Delta}_G(t)P(t,T_F)G(t)/\hat{W}_G(t)$ (using the cash-and-carry formula) and recalling, from (3), that:

$$P(t,T_F)\int_0^t \hat{\Delta}_G(u)dG(u) = \hat{W}_G(t) - \hat{\Gamma}_G(t)B(t) - \Pi P(t,T_1)$$

and $d\hat{W}_G(t)$ rewrites:

$$\begin{aligned} d\hat{W}_G(t) = (.)dt &+ \hat{\delta}_G(t)\hat{W}_G(t)\Sigma_G(t)'dZ(t) \\ &+(1-\hat{\gamma}_G(t)-\pi_G(t))\hat{W}_G(t)\Sigma_P(t,T_F)'dZ(t) \\ &+\pi_G(t)\hat{W}_G(t)\Sigma_P(t,T_1)'dZ(t) \end{aligned} \tag{11}$$

Identifying the diffusion coefficients in (10) and (11) yields the result.

Let us apply the same methodology to derive the investor's *futures* strategy. First apply Itô's lemma to H(t) to obtain :

$$dH(t) = H(t)\mu_H(t)dt + H(t)\Sigma_H(t)'dZ(t)$$

The process $\phi_H(t)$ followed by the market price of risk associated with the futures contract is assumed to satisfy the Novikov's condition. Following the same steps as above, we derive:

$$d\hat{W}_H(t) = (.)dt + \hat{W}_H(t)\phi_H(t)'dZ(t) \tag{12}$$

From equation (2), the speculator's wealth dynamics is also given by:

$$d\hat{W}_H(t) = (.)dt + \hat{\Delta}_H(t)H(t)\Sigma_H(t)'dZ(t) + \Pi P(t,T_1)\Sigma_P(t,T_1)'dZ(t) \tag{13}$$

Using the definition $\hat{\delta}_H(t) \equiv \hat{\Delta}_H(t)H(t)/\hat{W}_H(t)$ and identifying the diffusion coefficients in (12) and (13) yields the desired result. □

5.3. DISCUSSION

- We examine first the case of futures, for which result (4) conforms to standard portfolio theory when only primitive (cash) assets are involved. The logarithmic investor's position in futures has two elements only, the first one being speculative and the second one a hedge, exactly as in equation (4.20) of the previous chapter. We thus recover the Bernoulli individual's myopic behavior. The speculative component yields a long position in futures provided the market price of risk $\phi_H(t)$ associated with this derivative asset is positive. The optimal number of contracts the speculator holds, ignoring the hedge component, is proportional to (i) the value of his optimal wealth, and (ii) the market price of risk $\phi_H(t)$. The hedge component yields the usual short position in futures, provided the covariance of relative price changes in the non-traded bond with those in the futures is, as expected, positive.

- Strategy (4) presents two important differences with strategy (4.20). First, obviously, only the volatility of the futures price influences the speculative part, and only the volatility of the futures and its covariation with the non-traded bond matter in the hedging part. Second, and more importantly, the market price of risk that is relevant here is that associated with the futures price only because the market is for this investor in effect incomplete. Also, it is noteworthy that, due to the myopia that characterizes the logarithmic utility, the fictitious risky assets that complete the market are (shown in the proof to be) ones that offer no risk premia at all. This is the reason why equation (4) has its familiar aspect, although the market is incomplete.

- The result obtained with forward contracts strikingly differs from that achieved with futures. First and foremost, as its counterpart (4.21) in the preceding chapter, there is an extra term in (5) that involves the fraction of wealth not invested in the non-traded bond and in the money market account, $(1-\hat{\gamma}_G(t)-\pi_G(t))$, times a usual covariance/variance ratio. It stems from the fact that since the forward position is not marked-to-market, it faces an additional interest rate risk (vis-à-vis the case of futures) on the cumulative paper profits or losses that have accrued so far.

- In the framework adopted here, two sources of randomness can be distinguished. The first one, which is classical, comes from the random fluctuations of the very *market price of risk* associated with the forward price, $\phi_G(t)$. All investors but the Bernoulli investor hedge against this risk (and the hedge is preference dependent, since the opportunity set is affected). The second source is the *interest rate risk induced by the forward trading strategy itself.* Because she anticipates that one period ahead the current value of her cumulative forward position (also) will have changed, even the Bernoulli speculator will optimally hedge against unfavorable interest rate moves brought about by her investment strategy. This hedge is preference-free, since the opportunity set is not affected by the strategy per se, but, as intuition suggests, depends on the fraction of wealth $(1 - \hat{\gamma}_G(t) - \pi_G(t))$ that is generated by the forward strategy. As it is elicited by the trading strategy itself, one could refer to it as an « endogenous risk » hedge.

- Furthermore, as is the case with futures, and ignoring the hedging term involving $-\pi(t)$, the logarithmic speculator will always start with a long position in the forward market, along with a positive investment in the money market account, provided the market price of risk $\phi_G(t)$ is positive. However, since $\hat{\gamma}_G(t)$, the proportion of wealth invested in the riskless asset, is smaller than one in the case of a winning forward position, and since the covariance between the forward price changes and the $P(t,T_F)$ bond price changes is presumably positive, the extra risk involved leads the speculator to reduce, other things being equal, her holdings in the forward contracts, which could even become theoretically negative. The converse is true if she is currently losing on her forward position. Thus, ignoring again the hedge term in $-\pi(t)$, this strategy loses the proportionality in wealth and in the market price of risk that characterized the strategy involving futures.

- Lastly, as in the futures case, it remains true that the fictitious assets that complete the market offer no risk premia, because of the unique shape of the logarithmic utility function.

5.4. CONCLUDING REMARKS

In a complete information economy where all state variables are stochastic but fully observable, logarithmic utility is sufficient to produce myopia of portfolio decisions involving primitive (cash) financial assets. Portfolio strategies thus involve one speculative term and one hedging term only. This remains true when Bernoulli investors trade on interest rate futures. However, when they trade on interest rate forwards, they follow a more complex strategy, which does not qualify any more as myopic.

The debate relative to the respective benefits and drawbacks of over-the-counter forwards and officially organized futures generally focused on transaction costs, safety considerations, counterparty risk and liquidity-related issues. None of these practically very important features is relevant in this somewhat abstract setting. Even so, precise account of the marking to market mechanism allows one to substantiate the claim that using futures on interest rate instruments differs significantly from using forwards under stochastic interest rates. Indeed, even for a Bernoulli investor, optimal wealth levels and trading strategies differ materially. The strategy involving forwards exhibits an extra hedge term vis-à-vis the one using futures (or cash assets) that retains the traditional, simpler, structure. This term, different from a Merton-Breeden component, can be interpreted as a hedge against an « endogenous risk », namely the interest rate risk brought about by the optimal trading strategy itself.

Our findings thus have some bearing on the issue of optimal design of financial contracts. Given that interest rates are indeed stochastic in the real world, we already know from financial theory that forward and futures prices should be different. Whether this difference is in practice economically significant or not depends partly on the instruments underlying the derivatives and partly on subjective assessments. Empirically, as intuition suggests, the difference is more pronounced for instruments directly related to interest rates than for stocks, for instance, or commodities. The issue examined here is different. It consists in assessing whether an optimal speculative strategy using futures should differ from the one using forwards. It has been shown in chapter 3[5] that optimal hedging of a non-traded cash bond position using futures also involves a simpler formula than hedging with forwards. It thus appears that the optimal strategies followed by most market participants are in theory easier to compute, implement and control when futures contracts are used. At the practical level, it is clear that an additional source of risk must be recognized and properly managed when forward contracts are traded. If markets were complete, the necessary correction would be easy to compute, while still time-consuming. Since real financial markets are incomplete, however, the additional risk cannot be perfectly hedged. As using futures eliminates the implied residual risk, risk averse agents will find them attractive relative to forward contracts, other things being equal. Although nothing precise can be said on economic welfare at the aggregate level since the net supply of derivatives is zero, these results thus are rather heartening from the perspective of officially organized markets. Not only marking to market is an efficient mechanism to prevent default or counterparty risk, it also prevents the necessity to perform extra hedging.

Endnotes

[1] This chapter extends the results of Lioui and Poncet (2000b) to the case where the investor holds a non-traded cash bond position in addition to speculating on the futures or forward market.

[2] The generalization to a non-traded portfolio of bonds of different maturities is technically

trivial (some vectors would replace some scalars) and offers no additional economic intuition.
[3] See He and Pearson (1991) for a technical discussion and relevant references.
[4] See Karatzas and Shreve (1991) page 198.
[5] Recall that optimal hedge ratios typically differ from 1 to 15% in absolute value for reasonable parameters.

CHAPTER 6: OPTIMAL CURRENCY RISK HEDGING[1]

6.1. INTRODUCTION

This chapter examines the issue of optimal currency risk hedging strategies, using forward or futures contracts, followed by investors who invest in at least momentarily non-traded foreign financial or real assets and thus face exchange rate risks in addition to investment risks. The decision not to trade until a given horizon may be dictated by considerations pertaining to (foreign and/or domestic) regulatory constraints, long term investment strategy or policy, or the presence of prohibitive transaction and/or information costs. More generally, theory as well as empirical evidence suggest that (i) currency hedging improves the risk-return trade-off of international portfolios (see Solnik (1991) or Glen and Jorion (1993)) and (ii) continuously rebalanced strategies enhance hedging effectiveness, as documented for example in Brealey and Kaplanis (1995), in particular when the fact that domestic and foreign interest rates are stochastic is taken into account.

Since exchange rates and international interest rates are intertwined, it is inconsistent to assume the former stochastic and the latter deterministic, or the other way around. To characterize the random behavior of both foreign and domestic interest rates, we adopt the general version of Heath, Jarrow and Morton's (1992) model, where instantaneous forward rates are influenced by an arbitrary number of sources of risk. Similarly, we assume that the spot exchange rate between the two relevant currencies also follows a general diffusion process driven by the same fundamental sources of risk.

Hedgers enter the futures or forward market to hedge the risks associated with their non-traded portfolios. Preliminary work on dynamic currency risk hedging in a context of stochastic interest rates has been produced by Briys and Solnik (1992) and Tong (1996). Our approach here will be more general with respect to the diffusion processes considered, the proper inclusion in the investor's wealth dynamics of the actual changes in the hedge value, and the adequate comparison between forwards and futures.

The next Section presents the economic framework and the main assumptions underlying the model. For modelling the yield curve, we use a general version of Heath, Jarrow and Morton (1992), HJM hereafter, in which all drifts and diffusion parameters depend on an arbitrary number of state variables, in the spirit of de Jong and Santa Clara (1999). Section 2 derives and interprets the hedger's optimal strategy using futures, using again the stochastic dynamic programming approach leading to the Hamilton-Jacobi-Bellman equation. Section 3 examines the case of forwards and compares the two strategies. Finally, Section 4 offers some simulations that intend to measure the practical differences between the two strategies.

6.2. ECONOMIC SETTING

The international financial market is frictionless and trading takes place continuously over the time interval $[0,\tau]$, τ denoting the horizon of both the foreign and domestic economies. There are N (arbitrary) sources of risk across the two economies, represented by N independent Brownian motions $\{Z_k(t);\ t \in [0,\tau];\ k = 1, \ldots, N\}$ defined on the complete, filtered, probability space $(\Omega,\ F,\ \{F_t\}_{t\in[0,\tau]},\ P)$. The domestic and foreign yield curves, the exchange rate between the two currencies and the value of the non-traded foreign asset are diversely affected by these sources of risk. All the processes defined below are adapted to the augmented filtration generated by the N Brownian motions.

There are K state variables affecting the international investment opportunity set, and their dynamics solves the following SDE:

$$dY(t) = \mu_Y(t,T,Y(t))dt + \Sigma_Y(t,T,Y(t))dZ(t) \tag{1}$$

where $Z(t)$ is the N-dimensional Brownian motion defined on (Ω, F, P), $\Sigma_Y(t,T,Y(t))$ is the $(K\times N)$-dimensional matrix of diffusion coefficients and $\mu_Y(t,T,Y(t))$ is the $(K\times 1)$- dimensional vector of drifts. The drift vector and the diffusion matrix satisfy the usual conditions such that the preceding SDE has a unique solution[2]. These state variables diversely affect the dynamics of all international asset returns.

The domestic instantaneous forward interest rate solves the following SDE:

$$df_d(t,T) = \mu_d(t,T,Y(t))dt + \sigma_d(t,T,Y(t))' dZ(t) \tag{2}$$

where $\sigma_d(.)$ is the N-dimensional vector of diffusion coefficients and " ' " denotes a transpose.

Assuming that state variables affect the dynamics of interest rates is compatible with HJM model since state variables determine only the future evolution of interest rates, not their current level, which is given. Also, the convenient Markovian feature of all stochastic processes used here is preserved.

The dynamics of the domestic instantaneous spot rate, $r_d(t) \equiv f_d(t,t)$, then writes:

$$dr_d(t) = \mu_d^r(t, Y(t))dt + \sigma_d(t, Y(t))' dZ(t) \tag{3}$$

Denote by $P_d(t, \tau_i)$ the price of a domestic default-free pure discount bond maturing at time $\tau_i < \tau$. It is equal to:

$$P_d(t, \tau_i) = \exp\left[-\int_t^{\tau_i} f_d(t, T)dT\right] \tag{4}$$

Applying Itô's lemma yields:

$$\frac{dP_d(t, \tau_i)}{P_d(t, \tau_i)} = [b_d(t, \tau_i, Y(t)) + r_d(t)]dt + v_d(t, \tau_i, Y(t))' dZ(t) \tag{5}$$

where $b_d(.)$ is the instantaneous risk premium, and the diffusion vector $v_d(.)$ is related to the diffusion vector $\sigma_d(.)$ since the volatility of bond prices depends on that of interest rates[3].

In addition to domestic bonds, investors have access to an instantaneously riskless money market account that yields $r_d(t)$. With $B_d(0) = 1$, its value at date t thus is:

$$B_d(t) = \exp\left[\int_0^t r_d(s)ds\right] \tag{6}$$

The foreign economy has a similar structure. First, the foreign instantaneous forward interest rate obeys the following SDE:

$$df_f(t, T) = \mu_f(t, T, Y(t))dt + \sigma_f(t, T, Y(t))' dZ(t) \tag{7}$$

From equations (2) and (7), it is clear that the domestic and foreign yield curves are correlated, but that correlation is not perfect in general.

The foreign instantaneous spot rate, $r_f(t) \equiv f_f(t,t)$, then follows:

$$dr_f(t) = \mu_f^r(t, Y(t))dt + \sigma_f(t, Y(t))' dZ(t) \tag{8}$$

The price at date t of the foreign default-free pure discount bond maturing at time τ_i is equal to $P_f(t, \tau_i) = \exp\left[-\int_t^{\tau_i} f_f(t, T)dT\right]$ and its dynamics reads:

$$\frac{dP_f(t,\tau_i)}{P_f(t,\tau_i)} = [b_f(t,\tau_i,Y(t)) + r_f(t)]dt + \mathrm{v}_f(t,\tau_i,Y(t))' dZ(t) \qquad (9)$$

Now, the spot exchange rate between the two relevant currencies, expressed in units of the domestic currency, solves the SDE:

$$\frac{dS(t)}{S(t)} = \mu_s(t,Y(t))dt + \mathrm{v}_S(t,Y(t))' dZ(t) \qquad (10)$$

This specification allows the exchange rate to be possibly influenced by sources of risk that does not affect either one or the two yield curves, if some elements of the vectors $\sigma_d(.)$ and/or $\sigma_f(.)$ are equal to zero. These sources of risk could be exogenous shocks that affect the exchange rate such as real shocks in either economy and/or shocks brought about by interactions between the two economies under scrutiny and other economies.

Consider a FOREX (FX) contract to buy or sell one unit of the foreign currency at a given maturity, say τ_1. Absence of arbitrage opportunities directly implies that the *forward* exchange rate, denoted by $G(t, \tau_1)$, is equal to:

$$G(t,\tau_1) = \frac{P_f(t,\tau_1)}{P_d(t,\tau_1)} S(t) \qquad (11)$$

and its dynamics is given by:

$$\frac{dG(t,\tau_1)}{G(t,\tau_1)} = \mu_G(t,\tau_1,Y(t))dt + \mathrm{v}_G(t,\tau_1,Y(t))' dZ(t) \qquad (12)$$

where, using Itô's lemma and equations (5) and (9) for $\tau_i = \tau_1$, we could make the drift $\mu_G(.)$ and diffusion vector $\mathrm{v}_G(.)$ explicit.

Denote by $H(t,\tau_1)$ the price of the *futures* contract of maturity τ_1 written on the exchange rate S. Then, the dynamics of $H(t,\tau_1)$ is given by:

$$\frac{dH(t,\tau_1)}{H(t,\tau_1)} = \mu_H(t,\tau_1,Y(t))dt + \mathrm{v}_H(t,\tau_1,Y(t))' dZ(t) \qquad (13)$$

where the drift $\mu_H(.)$ differs, as always, from $\mu_G(.)$, and the diffusion vector $\mathrm{v}_H(.)$ differs from $\mathrm{v}_G(.)$ because interest rates are stochastic.

Finally, the value of the foreign investment in which the domestic agent invests, expressed in units of the foreign currency, is denoted by V(t). Its dynamics obeys the following SDE:

$$\frac{dV(t)}{V(t)} = \mu_V(t, Y(t))dt + \nu_V(t, Y(t))' dZ(t) \tag{14}$$

Note that the value of this investment could be influenced by more than the N sources of risk $\mathbf{Z}_k$, k = 1, ...N. Any number of additional sources could easily have been introduced into the analysis to account for the influence on V(t) of various kinds of uncertainty, different from the ones affecting the yield curves and the exchange rate. In particular, V(t) could be the value of a real asset, such as a plant or a mall. However, this introduction would have no effect whatsoever on the results.

Assuming the domestic investor consumes in his own country, the value of the foreign asset must be converted in terms of his own currency. Expressed in units of the domestic currency, this value is denoted by $\overline{V}(t)$, with the obvious relationship: $\overline{V}(t) = V(t)S(t)$. Given equations (10) and (14), the dynamics of $\overline{V}(t)$ reads:

$$\frac{d\overline{V}(t)}{\overline{V}(t)} = [\mu_S(t) + \mu_V(t) + \nu_V(t)' \nu_S(t)]dt + [\nu_V(t) + \nu_S(t)]' dZ(t) \tag{15}$$

where, for simplicity, we have omitted the influence of the state variables Y(t) on the drift and diffusion terms.

6.3. OPTIMAL STRATEGY USING FUTURES

Consider now the problem faced by a domestic investor endowed with a position in the foreign investment that he chooses not to trade until time T_I ($< \tau$), his investment horizon, for reasons invoked in the introduction to this chapter. He will trade on a currency futures contract of maturity τ_1, such that $T_I < \tau_1 < \tau$, to hedge the currency risk brought about by this non-traded position.

His portfolio strategy is characterized by the number $\psi(t)$ of futures contracts and the number $\Gamma(t)$ of units of the locally riskless domestic asset held at each date t. Without loss of generality, we can set $\Gamma(0)$ equal to zero. Note that while the optimal value of $\Gamma(t)$ presents no particular interest per se, it must be introduced into the problem because the investor's strategy must be self-financing so that trading on the riskless asset then is compulsory.

Futures positions being continuously (rather than daily) marked to market, the investor's margin account at date t is equal to:

$$X(t) = \int_0^t \exp\left[\int_s^t r_d(s)ds\right]\psi(s)dH(s,\tau_1)$$

The investor's wealth at each time t, $\hat{W}(t)$, thus is:

$$\hat{W}(t) = \overline{V}(t) + X(t) + \Gamma(t)B_d(t) \tag{16}$$

where the hat ^ indicates that futures (not forwards) are used.

Substituting for $\overline{V}(t)$ given by (15) and applying Itô's lemma yields the wealth dynamics:

$$\begin{aligned} d\hat{W}(t) = & \left[\left\{\mu_S(t) + \mu_V(t) + \nu_V(t)^\nabla \nu_S(t)\right\}\overline{V}(t) + r_d(t)\left\{X(t) + \Gamma(t)B_d(t)\right\}\right. \\ & \left. + \mu_H(t,\tau_1)\psi(t)H(t,\tau_1)\right]dt \\ & + \left[\left\{\nu_V(t) + \nu_S(t)\right\}\overline{V}(t) + \psi(t)H(t,\tau_1)\nu_H(t,\tau_1)\right]' dZ(t) \end{aligned} \tag{17}$$

To obtain an optimal hedge *ratio*, we define the following proportions: $\hat{\pi}(t) \equiv \dfrac{\overline{V}(t)}{\hat{W}(t)}$ is the fraction of the investor's total wealth invested in the foreign asset, and $\hat{\delta}(t) \equiv \dfrac{\psi(t)H(t,\tau_1)}{\hat{W}(t)}$ is the nominal value of the futures position in the foreign currency per unit of total wealth, namely the *hedge ratio*.

Using the definitions and equation (16) to eliminate the term $\{X(t) + \Gamma(t) B_d(t)\}$ yields:

$$\begin{aligned} d\hat{W}(t) = & \begin{bmatrix} \left\{\mu_S(t) + \mu_V(t) + \nu_V(t)^\nabla \nu_S(t)\right\}\hat{\pi}(t) \\ + r_d(t)(1-\hat{\pi}(t)) + \hat{\delta}(t)\mu_H(t,\tau_1) \end{bmatrix}\hat{W}(t)dt \\ & + \hat{W}(t)\left[\left(\nu_V(t) + \nu_S(t)\right)\hat{\pi}(t) + \hat{\delta}(t)\nu_H(t,\tau_1)\right]' dZ(t) \end{aligned} \tag{18}$$

Notice that the position in the riskless asset vanishes from the budget constraint.

The investor maximizes the expected utility of terminal wealth at the horizon date T_I:

$$\begin{cases} \underset{(\hat{\delta})}{\text{Max}} \; E[U(\hat{W}(T_I))] \\ \qquad \text{s.t. } \hat{W}(t), \; 0 < t \le T_I, \text{ obeys (18)} \end{cases} \tag{19}$$

where U(.) is as usual a Von Neumann-Morgenstern utility function that is state independent and exhibits risk aversion (U' > 0, U'(0) = + ∞, U'' < 0).

Since the financial market is here incomplete, the martingale approach is cumbersome. We thus take advantage of the property that all processes are Markovian in this setting to apply the classical results of stochastic dynamic programming. Define the investor's value (indirect utility) function $\hat{J}(t, \hat{W}(t), Y(t))$:

$$\hat{J}(t, \hat{W}(t), Y(t)) \equiv E[U(\hat{W}(T_I)) \mid F_t].$$

The optimal futures strategy solves the following Hamilton-Jacobi-Bellman (HJB) equation:

$$0 = \underset{(\hat{\delta})}{\text{Max}} \begin{cases} -\hat{J}_t + \hat{J}_W \hat{W}\left[(\mu_V + \mu_S + \nu_V{}' \nu_S)\hat{\pi} + (1-\hat{\pi})r_d + \hat{\delta}\mu_H\right] + \hat{J}_Y{}' \mu_Y \\ + \frac{1}{2}\hat{J}_{WW}\hat{W}^2\left[(\nu_V + \nu_S)\hat{\pi} + \hat{\delta}\nu_H\right]'\left[(\nu_V + \nu_S)\hat{\pi} + \hat{\delta}\nu_H\right] \\ + J_{WY}\hat{W}\Sigma_Y\left[(\nu_V + \nu_S)\hat{\pi} + \hat{\delta}\nu_H\right] + \frac{1}{2}\hat{J}_{YY}\left\|\Sigma_Y \Sigma_Y{}'\right\|^2 \end{cases}$$

where the subscripts on $\hat{J}$ denote partial derivatives and, for brevity, the time dependence of the variables has been deleted. Differentiating the HJB equation with respect to $\hat{\delta}(t)$ to obtain the first-order condition for an optimum yields the optimal hedging strategy:

$$\hat{\delta} = -\hat{\pi}\frac{(\nu_V + \nu_S)' \nu_H}{\nu_H{}' \nu_H} - \frac{\hat{J}_W}{\hat{J}_{WW}\hat{W}}\left[\frac{\mu_H}{\nu_H{}' \nu_H}\right] - \sum_{j=1}^{K}\frac{\hat{J}_{Wy_j}}{\hat{J}_{WW}\hat{W}}\frac{\nu_H{}' \sigma_{y_j}}{\nu_H{}' \nu_H} \tag{20}$$

The first component of this optimal strategy, $\hat{\delta}_1 \equiv -\hat{\pi}(\nu_V + \nu_S)' \nu_H / (\nu_H{}' \nu_H)$, is the traditional minimum variance hedge ratio that aims at offsetting the risk brought about by the foreign investment. It results from the minimization of the variance of instantaneous changes in wealth and thus is preference-free. It depends on the usual ratio of the covariance between the futures price and the foreign asset value over the variance of the futures price. The covariance is itself the sum of two components. The first one is associated with the volatility ν_S of the spot exchange rate and thus is macroeconomic by nature. The second one is associated with the volatility ν_V of the foreign investment held, and thus has a microeconomic, or asset specific, dimension. The covariance/variance ratio is multiplied by $\hat{\pi}(t) \equiv \overline{V}(t)/\hat{W}(t)$, so that, as expected, the minimum variance hedge ratio depends proportionally on the amount of wealth invested abroad. Both the covariance/variance ratio and $\hat{\pi}(t)$ may be smaller or larger than one, the result on $\hat{\pi}(t)$ depending on whether the futures position is currently winning [$\hat{\pi}(t)<1$] or losing [$\hat{\pi}(t)$ possibly >1]. Hence, the first term $\hat{\delta}_1(t)$ may, in absolute terms, over-hedge or under-hedge the investor's position in the foreign asset.

The second term, $\hat{\delta}_2(t) \equiv -\frac{\hat{J}_W}{\hat{J}_{WW}\hat{W}}\left[\frac{\mu_H}{\nu_H{}'\nu_H}\right]$, is the speculative, mean-variance, term. Recall that $(-\hat{J}_W/\hat{J}_{WW}\hat{W})$ is akin to a relative risk tolerance coefficient and thus is positive. If the drift μ_H of the futures price process is negative, a situation referred to by practitioners as "contango", then $\hat{\delta}_2(t)$ is negative. It is therefore optimal to sell more futures contracts than is implied by the first term $\hat{\delta}_1(t)$, to benefit (on average) from this negative trend. On the contrary, if the drift μ_H is positive, a so-called "normal backwardation" situation, the optimal strategy consists in selling a smaller number of futures than is implied by $\hat{\delta}_1(t)$ to take advantage (on average) of this positive trend. Since this strategy is in fact risky, $\hat{\delta}_2(t)$ naturally depends positively on the investor's relative risk tolerance coefficient.

The last K terms are the Merton-Breeden dynamic hedges against the unfavorable changes of the state variables. The investor adjusts his futures position so as to protect his wealth against situations in which it is smaller because of shifts in the investment opportunity set brought about by changes in state variables. This is of course possible only if the correlation between the changes in the state variables and those in the futures price H is different from zero. In addition, these hedging components are preference dependent. The terms $-\hat{J}_{Wx_j}/\hat{J}_{WW}\hat{W}$ reflect that dependence and each one of them can be interpreted as a coefficient of relative risk tolerance vis-à-vis the relevant state variable along the wealth's optimal path. A multi-period investor behaves in a non-myopic manner (unless his utility function turns out to be logarithmic) because he knows that he will have to rebalance his portfolio in the next period when his opportunity set will have been randomly affected.

Therefore, he builds Merton-Breeden hedges against these contingencies.

6.4. THE CASE OF FORWARD CONTRACTS

We consider now the case where investors have access to forward, not futures. Due to the marking-to-market mechanism, the preceding results will be shown to be affected in much the same way they were in the preceding chapters.

It must be noted at the outset that we need not assume that the investor trades on the domestic instantaneously riskless asset for his strategy to be self-financing. This is because, in this case, no cash payments are involved up to the investor's horizon T_I. However, we still maintain the assumption, to make the comparison between the futures and the forward strategies more precise· Evidently, it cannot hurt the investor to be allowed to trade on the money market account.

Let $\phi(t)$ the number of forward contracts held at time t. The current value of this forward position is equal to $P_d(t,\tau_1)\int_0^t \phi(s)dG(s,\tau_1)$, the discount factor $P_d(t, \tau_1)$ being required as the cumulative profit or loss is cashed-in or cashed-out at date τ_1 only. Consequently, the investor's wealth is equal to:

$$W(t) = \overline{V}(t) + P_d(t,\tau_1)\int_0^t \phi(s)dG(s,\tau_1) + \Gamma(t)B_d(t) \qquad (21)$$

where the hat ^ on W(t) has disappeared to indicate that forwards (not futures) are used. Substituting for $\overline{V}(t)$ given by (15) and applying Itô's lemma yields the wealth dynamics:

$$dW(t)=\Bigg[\Big\{\mu_S(t)+\mu_V(t)+\nu_V(t)^\nabla\nu_S(t)\Big\}\,\overline{V}(t)$$
$$+\Big\{P_d(t,\tau_1)\int_0^t\phi(s)dG(s,\tau_1)\Big\}\Big\{b_d(t,\tau_1)+r_d(t)\Big\}$$
$$+\phi(t)P_d(t,\tau_1)G(t,\tau_1)\Big\{\mu_G(t,\tau_1)-\nu_G(t,\tau_1)^\nabla\nu_d(t,\tau_1)\Big\}+\Gamma(t)r_d(t)B_d(t)\Bigg]dt$$
$$+\Bigg[\Big\{\nu_V(t)+\nu_S(t)\Big\}\,\overline{V}(t)-\Big\{P_d(t,\tau_1)\int_0^t\phi(s)dG(s,\tau_1)\Big\}\,\nu_d(t,\tau_1)$$
$$+\phi(t)P_d(t,\tau_1)G(t,\tau_1)\nu_G(t,\tau_1)\Bigg]'\,dZ(t) \tag{22}$$

Let us define the following proportions:

$\pi(t)\equiv\dfrac{\overline{V}(t)}{W(t)}$ is the fraction of the investor's total wealth invested in the foreign asset, $\gamma(t)\equiv\dfrac{\Gamma(t)B_d(t)}{W(t)}$ is the fraction of wealth invested in the domestic riskless asset, and $\delta(t)\equiv\dfrac{\phi(t)P_d(t,\tau_1)G(t,\tau_1)}{W(t)}$ is the discounted nominal value of the forward position in the foreign currency per unit of total wealth, namely the *hedge ratio*.

Using these definitions and equation (21) to get rid of the cumbersome term $P_d(t,\tau_1)\int_0^t\phi(s)dG(s,\tau_1)$, equation (22) rewrites:

$$dW(t)=\Bigg[\Big\{\mu_S(t)+\mu_V(t)+\nu_V(t)'\,\nu_S(t)\Big\}\pi(t)$$
$$+(1-\pi(t))(b_d(t,\tau_1)+r_d(t))-\gamma(t)b_d(t,\tau_1)$$
$$+\delta(t)\Big(\mu_G(t,\tau_1)-\nu_G(t,\tau_1)'\,\nu_d(t,\tau_1)\Big)\Bigg]W(t)dt$$
$$+W(t)\big[(\nu_V(t)+\nu_S(t))\pi(t)-(1-\pi(t)-\gamma(t))\nu_d(t,\tau_1)+\delta(t)\nu_G(t,\tau_1)\big]'\,dZ(t) \tag{23}$$

The investor's program thus reads:

$$\begin{cases}\underset{(\delta,\gamma)}{\text{Max}}\;\; E[U(W(T_I))] \\ \qquad \text{s.t. } W(t),\ 0<t\le T_I,\ \text{obeys (23)}\end{cases} \tag{24}$$

Denoting by J(.) the investor's value function $J(t,W,Y) \equiv E[U(W(T_I)) \mid F_t]$, the optimal forward strategy solves the HJB equation:

$$0 = \underset{(\delta,\gamma)}{\mathrm{Max}} \left\{ \begin{array}{l} -J_t + J_W W \begin{bmatrix} (\mu_V + \mu_S + \nu_V{}' \nu_S)\pi + (1-\pi)(b_d + r_d) \\ + \delta(\mu_G - \nu_G{}' \nu_d) - \gamma b_d \end{bmatrix} \\ + J_Y{}' \mu_Y + \frac{1}{2} J_{YY} \left\| \Sigma_Y \Sigma_Y{}' \right\|^2 \\ + J_{WY} W \Sigma_Y \left[(\nu_V + \nu_S)\pi - (1-\pi-\gamma)\nu_d + \delta \nu_G \right] \\ + \frac{1}{2} J_{WW} W^2 \left[(\nu_V + \nu_S)\pi - (1-\pi-\gamma)\nu_d + \delta \nu_G \right]' \\ \qquad \left[(\nu_V + \nu_S)\pi - (1-\pi-\gamma)\nu_d + \delta \nu_G \right] \end{array} \right\}$$

Differentiating the HJB equation with respect to $\delta(t)$ and $\gamma(t)$, then eliminating $\gamma(t)$ across the two resulting equations, yields the optimal hedging strategy with forwards:

$$\begin{aligned} \delta = & -\frac{\pi}{\kappa} \left[(\nu_V + \nu_S)' \left(\nu_G - \nu_d \frac{\nu_d{}' \nu_G}{\nu_d{}' \nu_d} \right) \right] \\ & -\frac{1}{\kappa} \frac{J_W}{J_{WW} W} \left[\mu_G - \nu_d{}' \nu_G + b_d \left(\frac{\nu_d{}' \nu_G}{\nu_d{}' \nu_d} \right) \right] \\ & -\frac{1}{\kappa} \sum_{j=1}^{K} \frac{J_{Wx_j}}{J_{WW} W} \left[\nu_G{}' \sigma_{x_j} - \frac{\nu_d{}' \nu_G}{\nu_d{}' \nu_d} \nu_d{}' \sigma_{x_j} \right] \end{aligned} \qquad (25)$$

where $\kappa \equiv \nu_G{}' \nu_G - \dfrac{(\nu_d{}' \nu_G)^2}{\nu_d{}' \nu_d}$.

As the reader is now aware, the optimal hedging strategy using forwards is significantly more involved than its counterpart using futures (equation (20)). Indeed, in all components, there exist additional terms that make the economic interpretation less easy but richer.

All these extra terms contain the ratio $\rho \equiv \left(\dfrac{\nu_d{}' \nu_G}{\nu_d{}' \nu_d} \right)$, i.e. the covariance between the forward exchange rate and the domestic bond price over the variance of the latter. It appears both in the κ term present in the denominators and in the last terms of the numerators. Note that its sign is probably *negative*: when, consequently to a fall in domestic rates, the domestic bond price $P(t, \tau_1)$ increases, the spot exchange rate, given foreign interest rates, presumably decreases[4] and thus the forward exchange rate $G(t, \tau_1)$ falls for two reasons (see equation (11)). This makes the covariance between the domestic bond price and the forward exchange rate negative. Now, the presence of the additional terms in expression (25) is easily interpreted as it is due to the additional interest rate risk borne on the "paper" (not yet realized) profit or loss that has accumulated so far in the forward position. Since in fact this (algebraic) gain will be paid off only at date τ_1, the induced interest rate risk depends on the covariance between the forward exchange rate $G(t, \tau_1)$ and the price $P(t, \tau_1)$ of the domestic discount bond of maturity τ_1. This risk, which obviously affects all the components of the hedge, is the interest rate risk induced by the forward trading strategy itself, exactly like in the case of a purely domestic setting. Because the investor anticipates that the current value of his cumulative forward position will have changed on the next period, he will optimally hedge against unfavorable interest rate moves that his very strategy brings about. This risk vanishes when the position is marked-to-market, which greatly simplifies solution (20).

Consider the preference-free, minimum variance, component (denoted by $\delta_1(t)$ below). The term involving ρ is $(\nu_V + \nu_S)' \nu_d$, the covariance between the value of the foreign asset expressed in domestic currency and the value of the domestic bond. This covariance is probably positive, unless the foreign asset value depends positively on interest rates. Since $\kappa \equiv \nu_G' \nu_G - \dfrac{(\nu_d' \nu_G)^2}{\nu_d' \nu_d}$ is most likely smaller than $\nu_H' \nu_H$ (the variance of the forward and that of the futures are very similar, if not identical), the absolute value of $\delta_1(t)$ is larger than its futures counterpart $\hat{\delta}_1(t)$, provided ρ is negative as argued in the preceding paragraph. Thus, under these plausible assumptions, the investor will sell, all other things being equal, more forward contracts than he would futures to minimize the variance of his overall position. In financial terms, if the forward exchange rate $G(t, \tau_1)$ falls, the hedger's short position is winning (in present value terms), and all the more so because the discount factor $P_d(t, \tau_1)$, which is negatively correlated with G(t, τ_1), increases. If the forward exchange rate rises, the short position is losing in present value terms, but all the less so because the discount factor decreases. Thus, as far as the minimum variance component is concerned, the investor will over-hedge when using forwards. In chapter 3, we have already shown that optimal hedge ratios typically differ from 1 to 15% in absolute value for reasonable sets of parameters. Although the present investor is not a pure hedger and the framework is more general, the order of magnitude will remain significant in practical implementations, and may be larger when interest rates become volatile, as will be seen below.

The comparison between futures and forwards is not as conclusive regarding the speculative and the Merton-Breeden hedging terms, whose absolute magnitudes, incidentally, are much smaller than the first one. This is due to conflicting influences. For instance, provided the risk premium b_d is positive, one extra term in the bracketed numerator of the second, mean-variance component, has a sign opposite to that of the other extra term. In addition, the drift μ_G may be larger or smaller than its futures counterpart μ_H. The same indeterminacy affects the last K dynamic hedging components.

Rewriting (25) as:

$$\delta = -\pi \frac{(\nu_V + \nu_S)' \nu_G}{\nu_G' \nu_G} + \left(-\frac{J_W}{J_{WW} W}\right)\left[\frac{\mu_G}{\nu_G' \nu_G} - \frac{\nu_d' \nu_G}{\nu_G' \nu_G}\right] + (1 - \pi - \gamma)\frac{\nu_d' \nu_G}{\nu_G' \nu_G} - \sum_{j=1}^{K} \frac{J_{Wy_j}}{J_{WW} W} \frac{\nu_G' \sigma_{y_j}}{\nu_G' \nu_G} \tag{26}$$

sheds more light on the differences between the optimal strategy using futures and that using forwards. From (26), the latter strategy contains (3+K) terms. The last K information-based hedging terms are similar to those that appear in (20). The first term in (26), i.e. the pure hedge that offsets the risk involved by the foreign position, is now similar to the first term of the futures strategy (20). The main difference between forwards and futures as hedging vehicles thus lies in the second and third terms of (26). The latter is a pure, preference-free, component that hedges the interest rate risk embedded in the profit or loss accruing from the forward position. This term is the ratio of the covariance between the domestic bond price and the forward exchange rate over the variance of the latter. It vanishes when futures are used. The second, speculative, component in (26) differs from its futures counterpart (the second term in (20)) in that it is adjusted for the interest rate risk brought about by the forward strategy. The adjustment factor is nothing but the hedge ratio of this interest rate risk, i.e. the covariance/variance ratio that appears in the third component. Therefore, the presence of the interest rate risk borne by the forward position induces, as intuition suggests, a switch from speculation to hedging.

6.5. SIMULATION RESULTS

To assess whether the differences between strategies using futures or forwards are sizeable, we now resort to simulation and provide numerical estimates. To focus on the main characteristics of the model of Section 1, namely (i) exchange rate risk and (ii) domestic interest rate risk, while avoiding a multiplicity of parameters that would blur the overall picture, we analyze a particular case that nevertheless preserves the essential spirit of the framework. We assume that foreign interest rates are equal to zero and the value V(t) of the foreign investment, expressed in units of the *foreign* (local) currency, is deterministic [$V_V(t, Y(t)) = 0$]. Consequently, $\overline{V}(t) = V(t)S(t)$ is random because of the spot exchange rate only. Also, the domestic interest rate will play here the role of a (single) state variable.

The evolution of the domestic instantaneous forward rate is specialized as:

$$df_d(t,T) = \mu_d dt + \sigma_{d1} dZ_1(t) \tag{2'}$$

Then the price of a domestic discount bond of maturity τ_i obeys:

$$\frac{dP_d(t,\tau_i)}{P_d(t,\tau_i)} = [b_d(t,\tau_i) + r_d(t)]dt - \sigma_{d1}(\tau_i - t)dZ_1(t) \tag{5'}$$

where $b_d(t,\tau_i)$, the instantaneous risk premium, is equal to:

$$b_d(t,\tau_i) = -\mu_d(\tau_i - t) + \frac{1}{2}\sigma_{d1}{}^2(\tau_i - t)^2 \tag{27}$$

Assume the exchange rate dynamics is given by:

$$\frac{dS(t)}{S(t)} = \mu_S dt + \sigma_{S1} dZ_1(t) + \sigma_{S2} dZ_2(t) \tag{10'}$$

Note that the possibility of a non-zero correlation between the exchange rate and the domestic interest rate is preserved.

Since foreign rates are equal to zero, equation (11) for the forward exchange rate simplifies to $G(t,\tau_1) = S(t)/P_d(t, \tau_1)$. Applying Ito's formula gives:

$$\frac{dG(t,\tau_1)}{G(t,\tau_1)} = \mu_G(t,\tau_1)dt + (\sigma_{S1} + \sigma_{d1}(\tau_1 - t))dZ_1(t) + \sigma_{S2}dZ_2(t) \quad (12')$$

As to the currency futures contract, we make use of a result found in Amin and Jarrow (1991):

$$H(t,\tau_1) = G(t,\tau_1)\exp\left\{\int_t^{\tau_1} \rho(s,\tau_1)ds\right\} \quad (13')$$

with

$$\rho(t,\tau_1) \equiv \sigma_{d1}(\tau_1 - t)(\sigma_{S1} + \sigma_{d1}(\tau_1 - t)) \quad (28)$$

In this special case, the futures and the forward exchange rates differ by a deterministic term only and thus have the same instantaneous volatility. Accordingly, we will use the simpler notation $\nu_G = \nu_H \equiv \nu$. In addition, it is easy to show that:

$$\mu_H(t,\tau_1) = \mu_G(t,\tau_1) - \rho(t,\tau_1) \quad (29)$$

Then, the strategies (20) using futures and (25) using forwards simplify, respectively, to:

$$\hat{\delta}\hat{W} = -\hat{\pi}\hat{W}\frac{\nu_S{}'\nu}{\nu'\nu} - \frac{\hat{J}_W}{\hat{J}_{WW}}\left[\frac{\mu_H}{\nu'\nu}\right] - \frac{\hat{J}_{Wr_d}}{\hat{J}_{WW}}\frac{\nu'\sigma_{r_d}}{\nu'\nu} \quad (20')$$

and

$$\begin{aligned}\delta W = &-\frac{\pi W}{\kappa}\left[\nu_S{}'\left(\nu - \nu_d\frac{\nu_d{}'\nu}{\nu_d{}'\nu_d}\right)\right]\\ &-\frac{1}{\kappa}\frac{J_W}{J_{WW}}\left[\mu_G - \nu_d{}'\nu + b_d\left(\frac{\nu_d{}'\nu}{\nu_d{}'\nu_d}\right)\right]\\ &-\frac{1}{\kappa}\frac{J_{Wr_d}}{J_{WW}}\left[\nu{}'\sigma_{r_d} - \frac{\nu_d{}'\nu}{\nu_d{}'\nu_d}\nu_d{}'\sigma_{r_d}\right]\end{aligned} \quad (25')$$

where we have multiplied through by $\hat{W}$ and W, respectively. Using (29) to eliminate μ_H from (20'), these strategies, re-formulated in terms of *numbers* of contracts held, become:

$$\psi(t) = -\frac{\overline{V}(t)}{H(t,\tau_1)}\frac{\nu_S{}'\nu}{\nu'\nu} - \frac{\hat{J}_W}{H(t,\tau_1)\hat{J}_{WW}}\left[\frac{\mu_G - \rho}{\nu'\nu}\right] - \frac{\hat{J}_{Wr_d}}{H(t,\tau_1)\hat{J}_{WW}}\frac{\nu'\sigma_{r_d}}{\nu'\nu} \quad (20'')$$

and

$$\phi(t) = -\frac{\overline{V}(t)}{P_d(t,\tau_1)G(t,\tau_1)\kappa}\left[\nu_S{}'\left(\nu - \nu_d \frac{\nu_d{}'\nu}{\nu_d{}'\nu_d}\right)\right]$$
$$-\frac{1}{P_d(t,\tau_1)G(t,\tau_1)\kappa}\frac{J_W}{J_{WW}}\left[\mu_G - \nu_d{}'\nu + b_d\left(\frac{\nu_d{}'\nu}{\nu_d{}'\nu_d}\right)\right] \quad (25'')$$
$$-\frac{1}{P_d(t,\tau_1)G(t,\tau_1)\kappa}\frac{J_{Wr_d}}{J_{WW}}\left[\nu'\sigma_{r_d} - \frac{\nu_d{}'\nu}{\nu_d{}'\nu_d}\nu_d{}'\sigma_{r_d}\right]$$

The various volatility matrices reduce to:

$$\nu = \begin{pmatrix}\sigma_{S1} + \sigma_{d1}(\tau_1 - t)\\ \sigma_{S2}\end{pmatrix} \nu_S = \begin{pmatrix}\sigma_{S1}\\ \sigma_{S2}\end{pmatrix} \nu_d = \begin{pmatrix}-\sigma_{d1}(\tau_1 - t)\\ 0\end{pmatrix} \sigma_{r_d} = \begin{pmatrix}\sigma_{d1}\\ 0\end{pmatrix} \quad (30)$$

Furthermore, applying Itô's lemma to $G(t,\tau_1)$ gives:

$$\mu_G = \mu_S + \mu_d(\tau_1 - t) - r_d(t) + \frac{1}{2}\sigma_{d1}{}^2(\tau_1 - t)^2 + \sigma_{S1}\sigma_{d1}(\tau_1 - t) \quad (31)$$

Using (28), (30), (31), and $\overline{V}(t) = V(t)S(t)$, strategies (20'') and (25''), respectively, simplify to:

$$\psi(t) = -V(t)\exp\left\{-\int_t^{\tau_i}\rho(s,\tau_i)ds\right\}P_d(t,\tau_1)\frac{\nu_S{}'\nu}{\nu'\nu}$$
$$-\frac{\hat{J}_W}{H(t,\tau_1)\hat{J}_{WW}}\left[\frac{\mu_G - \rho}{\nu'\nu}\right] - \frac{\hat{J}_{Wr_d}}{H(t,\tau_1)\hat{J}_{WW}}\frac{\nu'\sigma_{r_d}}{\nu'\nu} \quad (32)$$

and

$$\phi(t) = -V(t) - \frac{1}{S(t)\kappa}\frac{J_W}{J_{WW}}\left[\mu_G - \nu_d{}'\nu + b_d\left(\frac{\nu_d{}'\nu}{\nu_d{}'\nu_d}\right)\right] \quad (33)$$

In the forward case, the first, pure hedging, term is a one-to-one hedge. In addition, the third, Merton-Breeden hedge, term has vanished since the foreign interest rates are now deterministic, and domestic rates assume a simplified structure. There are however two problems associated with computing directly the overall ratio $\psi(t)/\phi(t)$. First, it depends on both the investor's utility function and the value of the international asset V(t). Sheer inspection of equations (32) and (33) indicates that V(t) is of paramount importance, so that the ratio $\psi(t)/\phi(t)$ crucially depends on its magnitude. The second problem is the presence of the term J_{Wrd}/J_{WW} in the expression for $\psi(t)$. Although a reasonable estimate interval for the relative risk tolerance coefficient $-J_W/J_{WW}$ is known to be [0.5; 1], we have no clue as to what a reasonable estimate could be for $-J_{Wrd}/J_{WW}$ in general. One way to circumvent those two issues is to avoid the computation of the overall ratio $\psi(t)/\phi(t)$ and compute instead the ratio of the two pure hedge components and the ratio of the two speculative components separately, since neither of them depends on the utility function nor on the value of V(t) [5]. Thus the difference between the two strategies can be analyzed piecewise only, not globally. Moreover, the Merton-Breeden term present in the futures strategy, which is deemed small in comparison with the other two elements, will be neglected as a first approximation.

The ratio of the two *pure hedge* components is equal to:

$$\Pi_{ph}(t) = \exp\left\{-\int_t^{\tau_i} \rho(s,\tau_1)ds\right\} P_d(t,\tau_1) \frac{\sigma_{S1}(\sigma_{S1} + \sigma_{d1}(\tau_1 - t)) + \sigma_{S2}^2}{(\sigma_{S1} + \sigma_{d1}(\tau_1 - t))^2 + \sigma_{S2}^2}$$

From equation (28), we have:

$$\int_t^{\tau_i} \rho(s,\tau_i)ds = \frac{1}{2}\sigma_{S1}\sigma_{d1}(\tau_1 - t)^2 + \frac{1}{3}\sigma_{d1}^2(\tau_1 - t)^2$$

We thus obtain:

$$\Pi_{ph}(t) = \exp\left\{-\frac{1}{2}\sigma_{S1}\sigma_{d1}(\tau_1 - t)^2 - \frac{1}{3}\sigma_{d1}^2(\tau_1 - t)^2\right\} P_d(t,\tau_1)$$
$$\times \frac{\sigma_{S1}(\sigma_{S1} + \sigma_{d1}(\tau_1 - t)) + \sigma_{S2}^2}{(\sigma_{S1} + \sigma_{d1}(\tau_1 - t))^2 + \sigma_{S2}^2} \quad (34)$$

The ratio of the two *speculative* components is:

$$\Pi_{spec}(t) = \left(\frac{\hat{J}_W/\hat{J}_{WW}}{J_W/J_{WW}}\right) \exp\left\{-\int_t^{\tau_i} \rho(s,\tau_1)ds\right\} P_d(t,\tau_1) \frac{\kappa}{v'v} \times$$
$$\frac{\mu_G - \rho}{\mu_G - v_d' v + b_d \left(\frac{v_d' v}{v_d' v_d}\right)}$$

Using equations (30) and (31), and setting the ratio of risk tolerances $\left(\frac{\hat{J}_W/\hat{J}_{WW}}{J_W/J_{WW}}\right)$ equal to one (a rather accurate approximation, as $\hat{W}$ must be very close to W) gives:

$$\Pi_{spec}(t) = \exp\left\{-\int^{\tau_1} \rho(s,\tau_1)ds\right\} P_d(t,\tau_1) \frac{\sigma_{S2}{}^2}{\left(\sigma_{S1} + \sigma_{d1}(\tau_1 - t)\right)^2 + \sigma_{S2}{}^2}$$

$$\frac{\mu_S + \mu_d(\tau_1 - t) - r_d(t) - \frac{1}{2}\sigma_{d1}{}^2(\tau_1 - t)^2}{\mu_S - r_d(t) + \frac{\sigma_{S1} + 2\sigma_{d1}(\tau_1 - t)}{\sigma_{d1}(\tau_1 - t)}\mu_d(\tau_1 - t) + \sigma_{d1}(\tau_1 - t)\left(\frac{3}{2}\sigma_{S1} + \sigma_{d1}(\tau_1 - t)\right)} \tag{35}$$

Tables 6.1 to 6.3 present the results of various simulations. Throughout the Tables, the annualized interest rate used to compute the bond price $P_d(t,\tau_1)$ appearing in equations (34) and (35) is set equal to 5% discretely compounded. The volatilities σ_{d1}, σ_{S1} and σ_{S2} are all annualized. Without loss of generality, the current date t is set equal to zero. The time remaining to maturity $(\tau_1 - t) = \tau_1$ is expressed in years. Numerical values for the ratio Π_{ph} of the two pure hedge components appear in Table 6.1.

Table 6.1. The ratio of pure hedging components

The interest rate used to compute the bond price $P_d(t,\tau_1)$ appearing in equations (33) and (34) is equal to 5% discretely compounded. The time remaining to maturity (τ_1 - t) is expressed in years. The volatilities σ_{d1} (of the domestic forward rate), and σ_{S1} and σ_{S2} (relative to the exchange rate) are annualized.

σ_{d1}	σ_{S1}	σ_{S2}	Time to Maturity	Π_{ph}
0,05	0,05	0,05	0,25	**86,73%**
0,05	0,05	0,05	0,5	**75,03%**
0,05	0,05	0,05	0,75	**65,18%**
0,05	0,05	0,05	1	**57,02%**
0,05	0	0,05	0,25	**92,97%**
0,05	0	0,05	0,5	**78,06%**
0,05	0	0,05	0,75	**61,67%**
0,05	0	0,05	1	**47,58%**
0,02	0,05	0,05	0,25	**93,87%**
0,04	0,05	0,05	0,5	**79,10%**
0,06	0,05	0,05	0,75	**60,55%**
0,08	0,05	0,05	1	**44,00%**
0,05	0,02	0,05	0,25	**87,50%**
0,05	0,04	0,05	0,5	**73,97%**
0,05	0,06	0,05	0,75	**66,96%**
0,05	0,08	0,05	1	**63,15%**
0,05	0,05	0,02	0,25	**80,85%**
0,05	0,05	0,04	0,5	**72,23%**
0,05	0,05	0,06	0,75	**68,22%**
0,05	0,05	0,08	1	**66,06%**
0,08	0,05	0,02	0,25	**72,67%**
0,06	0,05	0,04	0,5	**68,27%**
0,04	0,05	0,06	0,75	**73,21%**
0,02	0,05	0,08	1	**83,39%**
0,08	0,02	0,05	0,25	**79,50%**
0,06	0,04	0,05	0,5	**69,85%**
0,04	0,06	0,05	0,75	**71,78%**
0,02	0,08	0,05	1	**79,93%**
			Average =	**72,12%**

Differences in the pure hedging appear to be sizeable in general. The ratio Π_{ph} is always smaller than one, in accordance with the theoretical analysis presented in Section 3, implying that investors will hedge significantly more using forwards than using futures. This ratio ranges between 0.939 and 0.440 and has an average value of 0.722. The reader, however, must bear in mind that this average and the following ones are not meant to be accurate since they depend on the (somewhat arbitrary) set of selected parameters. They simply indicate a reasonable order of magnitude for the relevant ratios.

Numerical estimates for the ratio Π_{spec} of the two speculative components are shown in Tables 6.2 and 6.3. Like all the volatilities and the domestic interest rate, the drifts μ_d and μ_S are annualized. In Table 6.2, all drifts are set equal to 0.05, and in Table 6.3 all volatilities are set equal to 0.05. Results are shown for different sets of volatilities and time to maturity. They are even more striking than in Table 6.1, but the reader has to recall that the absolute values of the speculative components are much smaller than those of the pure hedge elements, so that the same absolute difference between futures and forwards leads to a much smaller ratio. The latter is always much smaller than one and may even be negative in some instances. This *strengthens* the conclusion above that investors will use significantly more forwards than futures, all other things being equal. In Table 6.2, the ratio Π_{spec} ranges from 0.015 to 0.459 and has an average of 0.112, with most values below 0.10.

Table 6.2. The ratio of speculative components

The interest rate used to compute the bond price $P_d(t,\tau_1)$ appearing in equations (33) and (34) is equal to 5% discretely compounded. The time remaining to maturity ($\tau_1 - t$) is expressed in years. The volatilities σ_{d1} (of the domestic forward rate), and σ_{S1} and σ_{S2} (relative to the exchange rate) are annualized. The drifts μ_d (of the domestic forward rate) and μ_S (of the exchange rate), and r_d are all annualized and set to 0.05.

σ_{d1}	σ_{S1}	σ_{S2}	Time to Maturity	Π_{spec}
0,05	0,05	0,05	0,25	**6,29%**
0,05	0,05	0,05	0,5	**7,23%**
0,05	0,05	0,05	0,75	**6,75%**
0,05	0,05	0,05	1	**5,93%**
0,05	0	0,05	0,25	**45,91%**
0,05	0	0,05	0,5	**38,06%**
0,05	0	0,05	0,75	**29,70%**
0,05	0	0,05	1	**22,63%**
0,02	0,05	0,05	0,25	**3,71%**
0,04	0,05	0,05	0,5	**7,14%**
0,06	0,05	0,05	0,75	**6,24%**
0,08	0,05	0,05	1	**3,98%**
0,05	0,02	0,05	0,25	**18,94%**
0,05	0,04	0,05	0,5	**9,72%**
0,05	0,06	0,05	0,75	**5,28%**
0,05	0,08	0,05	1	**3,17%**
0,05	0,05	0,02	0,25	**1,50%**
0,05	0,05	0,04	0,5	**5,20%**
0,05	0,05	0,06	0,75	**8,77%**
0,05	0,05	0,08	1	**11,57%**
0,08	0,05	0,02	0,25	**1,58%**
0,06	0,05	0,04	0,5	**5,05%**
0,04	0,05	0,06	0,75	**9,13%**
0,02	0,05	0,08	1	**11,83%**
0,08	0,02	0,05	0,25	**19,24%**
0,06	0,04	0,05	0,5	**9,40%**
0,04	0,06	0,05	0,75	**5,48%**
0,02	0,08	0,05	1	**3,13%**
			Average:	**11,16%**

Table 6.3 exhibits values for the same ratio under various assumptions regarding the level of the domestic rate, the drifts μ_d and μ_S and the time to maturity. Π_{spec} ranges between -0.190 and 0.681 and averages 0.064, with most values below 0.11. These results, together with those regarding the pure hedge components, strongly suggest that the differences between the two strategies are not negligible and may indeed be substantial.

Table 6.3. The ratio of speculative components

The interest rate used to compute the bond price $P_d(t,\tau_1)$ appearing in equations (33) and (34) is equal to 5% discretely compounded. The time remaining to maturity (τ_1 - t) is expressed in years. The volatilities σ_{d1} (of the domestic forward rate), and σ_{S1} and σ_{S2} (relative to the exchange rate) are annualized and equal to 0.05. The drifts μ_d (of the domestic forward rate) and μ_S (of the exchange rate), and r_d are all annualized.

μ_d	μ_S	r_d	Time to Maturity	Π_{spec}
0	0,05	0,05	0,25	**-2,75%**
0	0,05	0,05	0,5	**-3,75%**
0	0,05	0,05	0,75	**-3,95%**
0	0,05	0,05	1	**-3,80%**
0,05	0	0,05	0,25	**-19,04%**
0,05	0	0,05	0,5	**-7,41%**
0,05	0	0,05	0,75	**-2,42%**
0,05	0	0,05	1	**-0,15%**
0,02	0,05	0	0,25	**68,09%**
0,04	0,05	0	0,5	**25,35%**
0,06	0,05	0	0,75	**14,49%**
0,08	0,05	0	1	**9,94%**
0,05	0,02	0,05	0,25	**-8,90%**
0,05	0,04	0,05	0,5	**4,30%**
0,05	0,06	0,05	0,75	**8,58%**
0,05	0,08	0,05	1	**9,58%**
0,05	0,05	0,02	0,25	**21,49%**
0,05	0,05	0,04	0,5	**10,16%**
0,05	0,05	0,06	0,75	**4,92%**
0,05	0,05	0,08	1	**2,28%**
0,08	0,05	0,02	0,25	**15,89%**
0,06	0,05	0,04	0,5	**9,72%**
0,04	0,05	0,06	0,75	**4,39%**
0,02	0,05	0,08	1	**-3,23%**
0,08	0,02	0,05	0,25	**-3,21%**
0,06	0,04	0,05	0,5	**4,82%**
0,04	0,06	0,05	0,75	**8,94%**
0,02	0,08	0,05	1	**13,99%**
			Average:	**6,37%**

To summarize, in an international economy with stochastic interest and exchange rates, the optimal strategy of a domestic agent investing abroad differs significantly according to which hedging vehicle against exchange rate risk he chooses to adopt. The optimal solution involving forwards is much more complicated than is usually stated and, in particular, than the counterpart solution using futures.

This has theoretical, empirical and practical implications. At the theoretical level, we have exhibited a new hedging term when forwards are used that had been overlooked so far, because under deterministic interest rates it simply does not exist and the difference between futures and forwards is immaterial. Yet it is clear that the additional source of risk brought about by trading forwards must be recognized and properly managed. If markets were complete, the computation of the necessary adjustment would be rather trivial, although still potentially time-consuming. Real markets are not complete, however, and this extra risk cannot be perfectly hedged. Using futures as opposed to forwards thus eliminates the implied residual risk, which is per se valuable for risk averse agents.

At the practical level, the ratio of the pure hedging elements of the optimal strategies is significantly smaller than one in most simulations, and the ratio of the speculative components is dramatically smaller than one in all situations. Our results thus strongly suggest that, even in practice, optimal currency risk hedging strategies using forwards do differ in a sizeable manner from those using futures. The sets of parameters chosen for the simulations were obviously arbitrary to a certain extent, but results appear rather robust to significant changes in these parameters.

Endnotes

[1] This chapter is drawn from Lioui and Poncet (2002).

[2] To avoid repetitions, we mention this assumption only here although it applies to all SDEs.

[3] For instance, in the elementary case where all the components of σ_d are positive constants, $v_d(.)$ writes: $v_d(t,\tau_i) = -(\tau_i - t)\,\sigma_d$.

[4] Under the risk neutral probability measure, the expected rate of change of the spot exchange rate is equal, from the domestic investor's viewpoint, to the difference between the domestic and the foreign spot interest rates. See also the last chapter of part I for the relationship between the forward and the spot exchange rates.

[5] This is true only as a first approximation for the ratio of speculative components. See the text below where we set the ratio $\left(\hat{J}_W/\hat{J}_{WW}\right)/\left(J_W/J_{WW}\right)$ equal to one.

CHAPTER 7: OPTIMAL SPREADING[1]

7.1. INTRODUCTION

We have seen in chapter 3 that an investor constrained to hold a non-traded cash position but allowed to trade futures contracts continuously can achieve his first best optimum if the futures price and the underlying asset price are perfectly correlated. His welfare thus is equal to the level he would have reached had he been allowed to freely trade the cash position.

However, when the correlation coefficient between the futures price and the underlying asset price is not one, the opportunity set generated by *one* futures contract is different than the one generated by the cash asset and the investor cannot reach but his second best optimum. In particular, if he is a pure hedger, a perfect hedge cannot be achieved. The imperfect correlation case is very important in practice since it is most often faced by investors. Two striking examples are i) when the futures is written on an asset related to but different from the non-traded asset, and ii) when interest rates are stochastic.

However, even in such a case of imperfect correlation, an investor can reach her first best optimum if she can trade on various contracts written on the same underlying asset but of different maturities[2]. A strategy that involves a long and a short position in two distinct futures or forward contracts written on the same underlying asset is called a *spread.* Analysis of spreading has mainly been restricted to arbitrage (see Wahab (1995) and references therein). The theoretical analysis of optimal spreading has been limited. Schrock (1971), and then Poitras (1989), analyzed the issue in a traditional mean-variance static framework. Da-Hsiang-Donald (1992) derived a pure hedger's spreading strategy but unfortunately assumed that the yield curve is flat at the zero level and that dividends are deterministic. These assumptions together imply that the futures price and the underlying asset price are perfectly correlated. In addition, the prices of futures with different maturities are also perfectly correlated. Therefore, there is an infinite number of solutions to the spreading strategy of an investor who minimizes the instantaneous risk (variance) of his hedged portfolio.

Assuming the cash assets market is complete and the prices of all derivatives are set by arbitrage, optimal spreading will allow the constrained investor to reach the first best optimum he would attain if he could trade on his cash position. This spanning property can be viewed as a rationale for the simultaneous existence of several futures contracts written on the same underlying with different maturities.

The next Section describes the economic setting and main assumptions. In Section two, we derive the investor's optimal spreading strategy using forward contracts. The effects of marking-to-market on this strategy are analyzed in Section three where futures are introduced.

7.2. SETTING AND ASSUMPTIONS

Non-constrained agents can trade continuously in the frictionless financial market until time τ_E, where τ_E is the horizon of the economy. Three long lived assets are traded, a locally riskless asset, a discount bond and a stock index. These agents follow portfolio strategies that are assumed to be admissible.

The discount bond pays one dollar at maturity $\tau < \tau_E$, and its price $P(t,\tau)$ at date t, $0 \leq t \leq \tau$, is given by:

$$P(t,\tau) = \exp\left\{-\int_t^\tau f(t,T)dT\right\} \tag{1}$$

where $f(t,T)$, the instantaneous forward interest rate for maturity T at time t is the solution to the following stochastic differential equation:

$$df(t,T) = \mu(t,T)dt + v_1 dZ_1(t) + v_2 dZ_2(t) \tag{2}$$

for $0 \leq T < \tau$, where $\mu(t,T)$ satisfies the usual conditions such that (2) has a unique solution and v_1 and v_2 are strictly positive constants. The initial values of the instantaneous forward rates, $f(0,T)$ for all T, are given by the initial term structure of interest rates.

The spot rate is $r(t) = f(t,t)$ and the price of the locally riskless asset (money market account) is equal to:

$$B(t) = \exp\left\{\int_0^t r(s)ds\right\} \tag{3}$$

Substituting for the forward rates (2) into (1) and applying Ito's lemma yields:

$$dP(t,\tau) = P(t,\tau)[[b(t,\tau) + r(t)]dt - v_1(\tau - t)dZ_1(t) - v_2(\tau - t)dZ_2(t)] \quad (4)$$

where $b(t,\tau) = -\int_t^\tau \mu(t,T)dT + \frac{1}{2}v_1^{\,2}(\tau - t)^2 + \frac{1}{2}v_2^{\,2}(\tau - t)$.

The stock index, denoted by I(t), solves the following stochastic differential equation:

$$dI(t) = (\psi(t,I(t)) - \delta)I(t)dt + \sigma_1 I(t)dZ_1(t), \; I(0) = x > 0 \quad (5)$$

where $\psi(t,I(t))$ is the index total return, and δ, its dividend yield, and σ_1, its volatility, are positive constants. $\psi(t,I(t))$ satisfies the usual conditions such that (5) has a unique solution.

In absence of arbitrage, there exists a probability measure such that the discounted (with the appropriate numeraire) stock index price process plus the cumulated discounted dividends is a martingale. Let us choose as numeraire the riskless asset B(t) and define:

$$\kappa(t) \equiv \begin{pmatrix} \kappa_1(t) \\ \kappa_2(t) \end{pmatrix} = \begin{pmatrix} \sigma_1 & 0 \\ -v_1(\tau - t) & -v_2(\tau - t) \end{pmatrix}^{-1} \begin{pmatrix} \psi(t,I(t)) - r(t) \\ b(t,\tau) \end{pmatrix} \quad (6)$$

We further assume that:

$$E^Q\left[\exp\left\{\frac{1}{2}\int_0^\tau \left(\kappa_1^2(t) + \kappa_2^2(t)\right)dt\right\}\right] < \infty$$

The stochastic process:

$$\eta(\tau_D) = \exp\left\{\int_0^{\tau_D} \kappa_1(t)dZ_1(t) + \int_0^{\tau_D} \kappa_2(t)dZ_2(t) - \frac{1}{2}\int_0^{\tau_D} \left(\kappa_1^2(t) + \kappa_2^2(t)\right)dt\right\} \quad (7)$$

then defines the “risk-neutral” probability measure, Q, equivalent to the true measure P.

Applying Girsanov's theorem, the following two processes:

$$\hat{Z}_1(t) = Z_1(t) - \int_0^t \kappa_1(s)ds$$

$$\hat{Z}_2(t) = Z_2(t) - \int_0^t \kappa_2(s)ds$$

are two independent Brownian motions with respect to Q.

The dynamics of the discount bond price and that of the stock index price then become:

$$dP(t,\tau_D)=P(t,\tau_D)\left[r(t)dt-\nu_1(\tau_D-t)d\hat{Z}_1(t)-\nu_2(\tau_D-t)d\hat{Z}_2(t)\right] \quad (8)$$

$$dI(t)=(r(t)-\delta)I(t)dt+\sigma_1 I(t)d\hat{Z}_1(t) \quad (9)$$

Heath et al. (1992, Proposition 3 p. 86) have shown that, for $T \le \tau$:

$$\mu(t,T)=\nu_1^2(T-t)+\nu_2^2(T-t)+\nu_1\kappa_1(t)+\nu_2\kappa_2(t)$$

Substituting for $\mu(t,T)$ in (2), using the new Brownian motions and integrating yields:

$$f(t,T)=f(0,T)+\left(\nu_1^2+\nu_2^2\right)t\left(T-\frac{t}{2}\right)+\nu_1\hat{Z}_1(t)+\nu_2\hat{Z}_2(t) \quad (10)$$

and therefore:

$$r(t)=f(t,t)=f(0,t)+\left(\nu_1^2+\nu_2^2\right)\frac{t^2}{2}+\nu_1\hat{Z}_1(t)+\nu_2\hat{Z}_2(t) \quad (11)$$

Consider now an expected utility maximizing investor endowed with a non-traded cash position of $\pi > 0$ units of a portfolio that replicates the stock index. She continuously trades the riskless asset and two forward or futures contracts written on the stock index with different maturities.

The investor maximizes the expected utility of her terminal wealth at his investment horizon τ_I ($< \tau_E$). As in chapter 5, we assume a logarithmic (Bernoulli) investor, so as to derive an explicit solution even though the market prices of risk associated with the two sources of uncertainty evolve in a stochastic manner:

$$u(W(\tau_I,\omega))=\mathrm{Ln}(W(\tau_I,\omega)),\ \omega\in\Omega \quad (12)$$

The investor's program then writes:

$$\begin{cases}\max\limits_{\alpha,\beta_1,\beta_2} E^P\left[\mathrm{Ln}(W(\tau_I))\right] \\ \text{s.t. The portfolio strategy is admissible and satisfies the budget constraint}\end{cases} \quad (13)$$

We will consider forward contracts first, to assess the impact of stochastic interest rates on the optimal spreading strategy. Then, substituting forwards for futures will allow us to analyze how the marking-to-market mechanism affects this strategy.

7.3. THE SPREADING STRATEGY WITH FORWARDS

According to chapter 2, the price of a forward contract maturing at $\tau_i < \tau$ written on a dividend paying asset is equal to:

$$G(t,\tau_i)=\frac{I(t)\exp\{-\delta(\tau_i-t)\}}{P(t,\tau_i)} \tag{14}$$

Denoting by $\beta_i(t)$ the number of forward contracts and by $\alpha(t)$ the number of units of the money market account held by the investor at time t, her wealth is given by:

$$W(t)=\pi I(t)+P(s,\tau_1)\int_0^t\beta_1(s)dG(s,\tau_1)+P(s,\tau_2)\int_0^t\beta_2(s)dG(s,\tau_2)+\alpha(t)B(t) \tag{15}$$

where the second (third) term is the present value of the gains/losses that have accrued from trades on the forward contract of maturity τ_1 (τ_2).

Since the investor is logarithmic, the solution to her optimization problem is the optimum growth portfolio with initial wealth equal to the initial value of her non-traded position. The value of her wealth at date t will thus be $\pi I(0)\exp\{-\delta\tau_1\}B(t)\eta(t)^{-1}$ where $\eta(t)$ is given by (7). Her optimal strategy is given in the following proposition:

Proposition 1:

The optimal spreading strategy using forward contracts is given by:

$$\begin{pmatrix}\hat\beta_1(t)\\ \hat\beta_2(t)\end{pmatrix}=\begin{pmatrix}\hat\beta_1^s(t)\\ \hat\beta_2^s(t)\end{pmatrix}+\begin{pmatrix}\hat\beta_1^h(t)\\ \hat\beta_2^h(t)\end{pmatrix}+\begin{pmatrix}\hat\beta_1^r(t)\\ \hat\beta_2^r(t)\end{pmatrix} \tag{16}$$

where

$$\begin{pmatrix}\hat\beta_1^s(t)\\ \hat\beta_2^s(t)\end{pmatrix}=\begin{pmatrix}\dfrac{\nu_2(\tau_2-t)\kappa_1(t)-[\sigma_1+\nu_1(\tau_2-t)]\kappa_2(t)}{(\tau_2-\tau_1)\sigma_1\nu_2}\dfrac{W^*(t)}{P(t,\tau_1)G(t,\tau_1)}\\ -\dfrac{\nu_2(\tau_1-t)\kappa_1(t)-[\sigma_1+\nu_1(\tau_1-t)]\kappa_2(t)}{(\tau_2-\tau_1)\sigma_1\nu_2}\dfrac{W^*(t)}{P(t,\tau_2)G(t,\tau_2)}\end{pmatrix}$$

and

$$\begin{pmatrix} \hat{\beta}_1^h(t) \\ \hat{\beta}_2^h(t) \end{pmatrix} = \begin{pmatrix} -\frac{\tau_2 - t}{\tau_2 - \tau_1} \times \frac{\pi I(t)}{P(t,\tau_1)G(t,\tau_1)} \\ \frac{\tau_1 - t}{\tau_2 - \tau_1} \times \frac{\pi I(t)}{P(t,\tau_2)G(t,\tau_2)} \end{pmatrix}$$

$$\begin{pmatrix} \hat{\beta}_1^r(t) \\ \hat{\beta}_2^r(t) \end{pmatrix} = \begin{pmatrix} -\frac{\tau_1 - t}{\tau_2 - \tau_1} \times \frac{P(t,\tau_1)\int_0^t \beta_1(s)dG(s,\tau_1)}{P(t,\tau_1)G(t,\tau_1)} \\ \frac{\tau_1 - t}{\tau_2 - \tau_1} \times \frac{P(t,\tau_1)\int_0^t \beta_1(s)dG(s,\tau_1)}{P(t,\tau_2)G(t,\tau_2)} \end{pmatrix}$$

$$+ \begin{pmatrix} -\frac{\tau_2 - t}{\tau_2 - \tau_1} \times \frac{P(t,\tau_2)\int_0^t \beta_2(s)dG(s,\tau_2)}{P(t,\tau_1)G(t,\tau_1)} \\ \frac{\tau_2 - t}{\tau_2 - \tau_1} \times \frac{P(t,\tau_2)\int_0^t \beta_2(s)dG(s,\tau_2)}{P(t,\tau_2)G(t,\tau_2)} \end{pmatrix}$$

Proof

Since the market is complete, we can use the Cox-Huang (1989, 1991) methodology and reduce the dynamic program (13) to the following static one:

$$\begin{cases} \max_{W(\tau_I)} E^P\left[\operatorname{Ln}(W(\tau_I))\right] \\ \text{s.t.} \qquad E^Q\left[\frac{W(\tau_I)}{B(\tau_I)}\right] = \pi I(0)\exp\{-\delta\tau_I\} \end{cases}$$

the solution to which is unique [Cox-Huang (1991), Proposition 4.2, p. 477] and such that the optimal terminal wealth $W^*(\tau_I)$ solves:

$$\frac{1}{W^*(\tau_I)} - \lambda\frac{1}{B(\tau_I)}\eta(\tau_I) = 0$$

using the fact that $E^Q[F(\tau_I)] = E^P[F(\tau_I)\eta(\tau_I)]$ and where λ (>0) is the Lagrange multiplier associated with the budget constraint. Thus:

$$W^*(\tau_I) = \frac{1}{\lambda}B(\tau_I)\eta^{-1}(\tau_I)$$

. Using the budget constraint to eliminate λ, this becomes:

$$W^*(\tau_I) = \pi I(0)\exp\{-\delta\tau_I\}B(\tau_I)\eta^{-1}(\tau_I) \qquad (17)$$

By construction of the measure Q, the value at t of the investor's wealth is given by:

$$\frac{W^*(t)}{B(t)} = E^Q\left[\frac{W^*(\tau_I)}{B(\tau_I)}\middle|\mathbf{F}_t\right]$$

Using Bayes formula, this rewrites:

$$\frac{W^*(t)}{B(t)} = \eta^{-1}(t)E^P\left[\frac{W^*(\tau_I)}{B(\tau_I)}\eta(\tau_I)\middle|\mathbf{F}_t\right] \tag{18}$$

Substituting for the investor's wealth from (17) yields:

$$W^*(t) = \pi I(0)\exp\{-\delta\tau_I\}B(t)\eta^{-1}(t)$$

Applying Ito's lemma to this equation, one has:

$$dW^*(t) = r(t)W^*(t)dt - W^*(t)\kappa_1(t)d\hat{Z}_1(t) - W^*(t)\kappa_2(t)d\hat{Z}_2(t) \tag{19}$$

Now, this wealth is also generated by a self-financing strategy obeying (15), and thus satisfies:

$$\begin{aligned}
dW^*(t) &= \pi dI(t) + \alpha(t)dB(t)\\
&+P(t,\tau_1)\int_0^t\hat{\beta}_1(s)dG(s,\tau_1)\frac{dP(t,\tau_1)}{P(t,\tau_1)} + P(t,\tau_1)\hat{\beta}_1(t)dG(t,\tau_1)\\
&+P(t,\tau_2)\int_0^t\hat{\beta}_2(s)dG(s,\tau_2)\frac{dP(t,\tau_2)}{P(t,\tau_2)} + \hat{\beta}_2(t)P(t,\tau_2)dG(t,\tau_2)
\end{aligned} \tag{20}$$

Applying Ito's lemma to (14) yields the dynamics of the forward price:

$$dG(t,\tau_i) = (.)dt + G(t,\tau_i)\left[(\sigma_1 + v_1(\tau_i - t))d\hat{Z}_1(t) + v_2(\tau_i - t)d\hat{Z}_2(t)\right] \tag{21}$$

Hence, substituting for the stock index price dynamics from (5) and for the forward price dynamics from (21) into (20), one obtains:

$$\begin{aligned}
dW^*(t) &= r(t)W^*(t)dt\\
&+\begin{bmatrix}\pi I(t)\sigma_1 + \hat{\beta}_1(t)P(t,\tau_1)G(t,\tau_1)(\sigma_1 + v_1(\tau_1 - t))\\ +\hat{\beta}_2(t)P(t,\tau_2)G(t,\tau_2)(\sigma_1 + v_1(\tau_2 - t))\end{bmatrix}d\hat{Z}_1(t)\\
&+\left[\hat{\beta}_1(t)P(t,\tau_1)G(t,\tau_1)v_2(\tau_1 - t) + \hat{\beta}_2(t)P(t,\tau_2)G(t,\tau_2)v_2(\tau_2 - t)\right]d\hat{Z}_2(t)
\end{aligned} \tag{22}$$

Equating the diffusion terms of (19) and (22) yields:

$$\begin{bmatrix} \pi I(t)\sigma_1 \\ +\beta_1(t)P(t,\tau_1)G(t,\tau_1)(\sigma_1+v_1(\tau_1-t))-P(t,\tau_1)\left(\int_0^t\beta_1(s)dG(s,\tau_1)\right)v_1(\tau_1-t) \\ +\beta_2(t)P(t,\tau_2)G(t,\tau_2)(\sigma_1+v_1(\tau_2-t))-P(t,\tau_2)\left(\int_0^t\beta_2(s)dG(s,\tau_2)\right)v_1(\tau_2-t) \end{bmatrix} = -W^*(t)\kappa_1(t)$$

$$\begin{bmatrix} \beta_1(t)P(t,\tau_1)G(t,\tau_1)v_2(\tau_1-t)-P(t,\tau_1)\left(\int_0^t\beta_1(s)dG(s,\tau_1)\right)v_2(\tau_1-t) \\ +\beta_2(t)P(t,\tau_2)G(t,\tau_2)v_2(\tau_2-t)-P(t,\tau_2)\left(\int_0^t\beta_2(s)dG(s,\tau_2)\right)v_2(\tau_2-t) \end{bmatrix} = -W^*(t)\kappa_2(t)$$

(23)

Solving system (23) leads to the desired result (16).

The optimal spreading demand (16) recovers the three usual components: a speculative term denoted by $(\hat{\beta}_1^s(t), \hat{\beta}_2^s(t))$, a minimum-variance hedging term related to the constrained position and denoted by $(\hat{\beta}_1^h(t), \hat{\beta}_2^h(t))$, and a minimum-variance hedging term related to the interest rate risk due to the forward positions themselves and denoted by $(\hat{\beta}_1^r(t), \hat{\beta}_2^r(t))$. There is of course no preference-dependent Merton-Breeden hedging component that would hedge against the random fluctuations of the opportunity set (the riskfree rate here) because of the myopic nature of our Bernoulli investor's behavior.

Consider the minimum-variance hedging terms first. The first hedging term offsets the risk brought about by the non-traded position. Although the price of the non-traded asset is driven by one source of uncertainty only, two forward contracts must be traded to cancel the risk resulting from the non-traded position. This is because, interest rates being stochastic, forward prices are affected by two sources of uncertainty. Therefore, when the investor trades a forward contract for hedging purposes, she introduces a new source of risk into her portfolio. To offset the latter, she trades another forward contract of a different maturity, which is not perfectly correlated with the first one.

This allows the investor to achieve a perfect hedge of her non-traded position (which thus has zero instantaneous variance). This perfect hedge involves spreading, i.e. positions of opposite signs in the two forward contracts. The investor is short the nearby contract (which she would be, had she chosen to trade one contract only) and long the distant contract. Since the volatility of a fixed income instrument is that of the interest rate times its duration, the (relative) duration terms $-\frac{\tau_2 - t}{\tau_2 - \tau_1}$ and $\frac{\tau_1 - t}{\tau_2 - \tau_1}$ appear in a natural way in $\hat{\beta}_1^h(t)$ and $\hat{\beta}_2^h(t)$.

The reason why the investor is short the nearby contract and long the distant one rather than the opposite stems from the nearby forward price having the highest instantaneous correlation with the underlying asset price[3]. One then can interpret the short position in the nearby contract as the traditional term offsetting the non-traded position while the long position in the deferred contract offsets the residual risk.

As to the third term in (16), it hedges against the interest rate risk brought about by the forward positions. This component in fact *characterizes* the use of forward contracts. An analysis similar to that above shows that optimally spreading the two contracts ensures that a perfect hedge is also achieved.

Let us turn now to the first, speculative, component in strategy (16). The latter allows the investor to replicate the optimum growth portfolio. If the expression $v_2(\tau_i - t)\kappa_1(t) - [\sigma_1 + v_1(\tau_i - t)]\kappa_2(t)$ is positive, then this component involves a long position in the nearby contract and a short position in the distant one. If it is negative, then the opposite is true. Note that the expression is nothing but the determinant of the volatility matrix of the optimum growth portfolio value and a (maturity τ_i) forward price. To shed further light on this condition, we derive the following result.

Lemma:

Each forward price is imperfectly negatively correlated with the value of the optimum growth portfolio. If $v_2(\tau_i - t)\kappa_1(t) - [\sigma_1 + v_1(\tau_i - t)]\kappa_2(t) > 0$ *(respectively, <0), then each instantaneous correlation coefficient is an increasing (respectively, decreasing) function, in absolute terms, of the forward contract maturity.*

Proof:

This instantaneous correlation coefficient (for i = 1, 2) is equal to:

$$\frac{-(\sigma_1 + v_1(\tau_i - t))\kappa_1(t) - v_2(\tau_i - t)\kappa_2(t)}{\sqrt{\kappa_1^2(t) + \kappa_2^2(t)}\sqrt{(\sigma_1 + v_1(\tau_i - t))^2 + (v_2(\tau_i - t))^2}} \tag{24}$$

where we have used (19) and (21).

The first order derivative of that expression with respect to the maturity τ_i is:

$$\frac{\sigma_1 \nu_2 [\nu_2(\tau_i - t)\kappa_1(t) - (\sigma_1 + \nu_1(\tau_i - t))\kappa_2(t)]}{(\kappa_1^2(t) + \kappa_2^2(t))((\sigma_1 + \nu_1(\tau_i - t))^2 + (\nu_2(\tau_i - t))^2)}$$

and the result follows since σ_1 and ν_2 are positive. □

If $\nu_2(\tau_i - t)\kappa_1(t) - [\sigma_1 + \nu_1(\tau_i - t)]\kappa_2(t)$ is positive, the speculative term in (16) involves a long position in the nearby contract and a short position in the deferred contract. Since the deferred contract has the highest instantaneous correlation (in absolute terms) with the optimum growth portfolio, the investor shorts this contract to best replicate her optimal wealth. The residual risk that stems from this short position is hedged by a long position in the nearby contract.

If the term $[\nu_2(\tau_i - t)\kappa_1(t) - [\sigma_1 + \nu_1(\tau_i - t)]\kappa_2(t)]$ is negative, then the speculative component involves a short position in the nearby contract and a long position in the distant contract. Hence, in this case, the forward spreading strategy, which, in addition to the speculative and the minimum-variance hedging components, includes a term whose sign depends on whether the contracts have accumulated gains or losses involves a short position in the nearby contract and a long position in the deferred contract if the former has accumulated net gains and the latter net losses. Otherwise, the respective positions in the two contracts is indeterminate.

7.4. THE SPREADING STRATEGY USING FUTURES

We will derive first the futures price, then analyze the investor's problem, and finally assess the impact of the marking-to-market mechanism that characterizes futures on the optimal spreading strategy.

According to the analysis of chapter 2, the price of the futures contract written on the stock index obeys:

$$\frac{H(t,\tau_i)}{B(t)} = E^Q\left[\left.\frac{I(\tau_i)\exp\left\{\int_t^{\tau_i} r(s)ds\right\}}{B(\tau_i)}\right| F_t\right] \tag{25}$$

and

$$H(t,\tau_i) = E^Q[I(\tau_i) | F_t]. \tag{26}$$

Using equation (14) and the relationship (involving the exponential of the covariance between the forward price and the underlying asset price) between the forward and futures prices exhibited at the end of chapter 2, the futures price is equal to:

$$H(t,\tau_i)=\frac{I(t)\exp\{-\delta(\tau_i-t)\}}{P(t,\tau_i)}\exp\left\{\left(v_1^2+v_2^2\right)\frac{(\tau_i-t)^3}{3}+\frac{1}{2}\sigma_1 v_1(\tau_i-t)^2\right\} \quad (27)$$

The value $X_i(t)$ of the margin account at time t associated with the position in futures of maturity τ_i is given by:

$$X_i(t)=\int_0^t \exp\left\{\int_s^t r(s)ds\right\}\beta_i(s)dH(s,\tau_i) \quad (28)$$

The investor's wealth at time t, W(t), comprises four elements, i.e. the non-traded asset, the two margin accounts associated with trading the two futures, and the riskless asset:

$$W(t)=\pi I(t)+X_1(t)+X_2(t)+\alpha(t)B(t) \quad (29)$$

The solution to the investor's program then leads to the following proposition.

Proposition 2:

The optimal spreading strategy using future contracts is given by:

$$\begin{pmatrix}\hat{\beta}_1(t)\\ \hat{\beta}_2(t)\end{pmatrix}=\begin{pmatrix}\hat{\beta}_1^s(t)\\ \hat{\beta}_2^s(t)\end{pmatrix}+\begin{pmatrix}\hat{\beta}_1^h(t)\\ \hat{\beta}_2^h(t)\end{pmatrix} \quad (30)$$

where

$$\begin{pmatrix}\hat{\beta}_1^s(t)\\ \hat{\beta}_2^s(t)\end{pmatrix}=\begin{pmatrix}\dfrac{v_2(\tau_2-t)\kappa_1(t)-[\sigma_1+v_1(\tau_2-t)]\kappa_2(t)}{(\tau_2-\tau_1)\sigma_1 v_2}\dfrac{W^*(t)}{H(t,\tau_1)}\\ -\dfrac{v_2(\tau_1-t)\kappa_1(t)-[\sigma_1+v_1(\tau_1-t)]\kappa_2(t)}{(\tau_2-\tau_1)\sigma_1 v_2}\dfrac{W^*(t)}{H(t,\tau_2)}\end{pmatrix}$$

and

$$\begin{pmatrix} \hat{\hat{\beta}}_1^h(t) \\ \hat{\hat{\beta}}_2^h(t) \end{pmatrix} = \begin{pmatrix} -\dfrac{\tau_2 - t}{\tau_2 - \tau_1} \times \dfrac{\pi I(t)}{H(t,\tau_1)} \\ \dfrac{\tau_1 - t}{\tau_2 - \tau_1} \times \dfrac{\pi I(t)}{H(t,\tau_2)} \end{pmatrix}$$

<u>**Proof**</u>:

Since the financial market is complete, the investor's optimal wealth is still given by (17) and its dynamics by (19).

Since this wealth satisfies the self-financing property, its dynamics is also, from (29):

$$dW^*(t) = \pi dI(t) + \pi\delta I(t)dt + dX_1(t) + dX_2(t) + \alpha(t)dB(t) \tag{31}$$

Applying Ito's lemma to (28) and (27), one obtains, respectively:

$$dX_i(t) = r(t)X_i(t)dt + \beta_i(t)dH(t,\tau_i)$$

$$dH(t,\tau_i) = (.)dt + H(t,\tau_i)\left[(\sigma_1 + v_1(\tau_i - t))d\hat{Z}_1(t) + v_2(\tau_i - t)d\hat{Z}_2(t)\right]$$

Substituting for these values in (31) yields:

$$\begin{aligned} dW^*(t) &= r(t)W^*(t)dt \\ &+ \left[\pi I(t)\sigma_1 + \hat{\hat{\beta}}_1(t)H(t,\tau_1)(\sigma_1 + v_1(\tau_1 - t)) + \hat{\hat{\beta}}_2(t)H(t,\tau_2)(\sigma_1 + v_1(\tau_2 - t))\right]d\hat{Z}_1(t) \\ &+ \left[\hat{\hat{\beta}}_1(t)H(t,\tau_1)v_2(\tau_1 - t) + \hat{\hat{\beta}}_2(t)H(t,\tau_2)v_2(\tau_2 - t)\right]d\hat{Z}_2(t) \end{aligned} \tag{32}$$

Equating the diffusion terms of (19) and (32), one obtains:

$$\begin{aligned} \pi I(t)\sigma_1 + \hat{\hat{\beta}}_1(t)H(t,\tau_1)(\sigma_1 + v_1(\tau_1 - t)) + \hat{\hat{\beta}}_2(t)H(t,\tau_2)(\sigma_1 + v_1(\tau_2 - t)) & \\ = -W^*(t)\kappa_1(t) & \\ \hat{\hat{\beta}}_1(t)H(t,\tau_1)v_2(\tau_1 - t) + \hat{\hat{\beta}}_2(t)H(t,\tau_2)v_2(\tau_2 - t) = -W^*(t)\kappa_2(t) & \end{aligned} \tag{33}$$

and solving system (33) leads to the desired result (30). □

As expected from the previous chapters, the optimal spreading strategy using futures has but two components instead of three: the speculative term $\left(\hat{\hat{\beta}}_1^s(t), \hat{\hat{\beta}}_2^s(t)\right)$ and the minimum-variance hedging term $\left(\hat{\hat{\beta}}_1^h(t), \hat{\hat{\beta}}_2^h(t)\right)$. The second hedging term (against interest rate risk) that characterizes forwards *has vanished* due to the marking-to-market mechanism.

The hedging component present in (30) involves a short position in the nearby futures contract and a long position in the distant one as in the case of forwards. This is because the forward price and the futures price have the same instantaneous volatility. This is also the reason why the adjusting factors $-\frac{\tau_2 - t}{\tau_2 - \tau_1}$ and $\frac{\tau_1 - t}{\tau_2 - \tau_1}$ present in $\hat{\hat{\beta}}_1^h(t)$ and $\hat{\hat{\beta}}_2^h(t)$, respectively, are the same as for $\hat{\beta}_1^h(t)$ and $\hat{\beta}_2^h(t)$, respectively. The only difference lies in the price adjustment factors. For $\hat{\hat{\beta}}_1^h(t)$ and $\hat{\hat{\beta}}_2^h(t)$ they are equal to $\frac{\pi I(t)}{H(t,\tau_1)}$ and $\frac{\pi I(t)}{H(t,\tau_2)}$, and for $\hat{\beta}_1^h(t)$ and $\hat{\beta}_2^h(t)$ they are equal to $\frac{\pi I(t)}{P(t,\tau_1)G(t,\tau_1)}$ and $\frac{\pi I(t)}{P(t,\tau_2)G(t,\tau_2)}$. While in the case of forwards the adjustment involves the present value of the forward price, with futures it involves the futures price itself, for an obvious reason.

The speculative component present in (30) has the same intuitive interpretation as its forward counterpart in (16) and thus its analysis need not be repeated.

A traditional result in hedging theory is that the strategy using forwards and the strategy involving futures differ by the "tailing factor" only. Explicit expressions for the tailing factor, however, are available only in the (very) special case of deterministic interest rates and of a pure hedger[4]. By contrast, we derive the tailing factor under stochastic interest rates and for an expected utility maximizer.

<u>Proposition 3</u>

The relationship between the optimal spreading strategy using futures and that involving forwards obeys:

$$\hat{\hat{\beta}}_i^s(t) = TF_i(t) \times \hat{\beta}_i^s(t)$$
$$\hat{\hat{\beta}}_i^h(t) = TF_i(t) \times \hat{\beta}_i^h(t)$$

where

$$TF_i(t) = P(t,\tau_i) \times \exp\left\{ -\left(v_1^2 + v_2^2\right)\frac{(\tau_i - t)^3}{3} - \frac{1}{2}\sigma_1 v_1 (\tau_i - t)^2 \right\}.$$

This follows directly from sheer inspection of (16) and (30). Note that we cannot compare explicitly the two strategies taken as a whole since the third term in (16) is absent in (30).

The proposition implies that: (i) there exist two tailing factors, one for each leg of the spreading strategy; (ii) these factors are independent of the individual's characteristics, and in particular of his investment horizon (this is a "separation" result); (iii) the number of futures contracts held by the investor (for the speculative and first hedging purposes) is always smaller, in absolute terms, than the corresponding number of forward contracts.

The tailing factors comprise two terms. The first is a discount bond whose maturity is equal to that of the futures contract. Note that this term appears in a deterministic interest rates environment. The second term depends explicitly on the volatility of interest rates. Moreover, it is exactly the ratio of the forward price to the futures price. This does not come as a surprise since the major difference between the two optimal spreading strategies stems from the price adjusting factor.

To summarize, due to the stochastic nature of interest rate variations, and the ensuing imperfect correlation between futures or forward prices and the underlying asset price, investors must trade two distinct contracts to reach their first best optimum.

The optimal spreading strategy using forwards has one more component than the strategy using futures, term that hedges against the interest rate risk brought about by the spreading forward strategy itself. The minimum-variance hedging component (common to both strategies), whose purpose is to offset the risk borne by the investor's non-traded cash position, involves a short position in the nearby contract and a long position in the deferred one. The (common) speculative component, which helps replicate the optimum growth portfolio, involves a short position in the contract most negatively correlated with the latter portfolio and a long position in the other contract. The marking-to-market procedure that characterizes futures leads the investor to hold less futures contracts than he would forward contracts for the pure hedge and the speculative component. Overall, hedging interest rate risk stemming from the forward position may perturb this relationship between the two strategies.

7.5. SIMULATIONS

To shed some light on the results derived in previous sections, some simulations may be helpful. In all cases, and for *each* of the three components taken *separately*, the absolute value of the ratio of the position in the first contract over the position in the second contract has been computed. After easy computations from equation (16), we thus have:

$$\left|\frac{\hat{\beta}_1^s(t)}{\hat{\beta}_2^s(t)}\right| = \frac{\nu_2(\tau_2 - t)\kappa_1(t) - [\sigma_1 + \nu_1(\tau_2 - t)]\kappa_2(t)}{\nu_2(\tau_1 - t)\kappa_1(t) - [\sigma_1 + \nu_1(\tau_1 - t)]\kappa_2(t)} \exp\{-\delta(\tau_2 - \tau_1)\} \quad (34)$$

$$\left|\frac{\hat{\beta}_1^h(t)}{\hat{\beta}_2^h(t)}\right| = \frac{\tau_2 - t}{\tau_1 - t} \exp\{-\delta(\tau_2 - \tau_1)\} \quad (35)$$

$$\left|\frac{\hat{\beta}_{11}^r(t)}{\hat{\beta}_{21}^r(t)}\right| = \exp\{-\delta(\tau_2 - \tau_1)\} \quad (36)$$

Note that the ratio given in (36) is time invariant and therefore will tend to one when the maturities of the two contracts are near to one another and will decrease as the two maturities get far apart.

The base case of the simulations is the following set of parameters:

ν_1	ν_2	κ_1	κ_2	τ_1	τ_2	σ_1	δ
0.1	0.09	0.6	0.7	0.25	0.5	0.2	0.02

Notice in particular that the maturity of the shorter term contract is one quarter. Results for forward contracts appear on Figures 7.1 to 7.5 below.

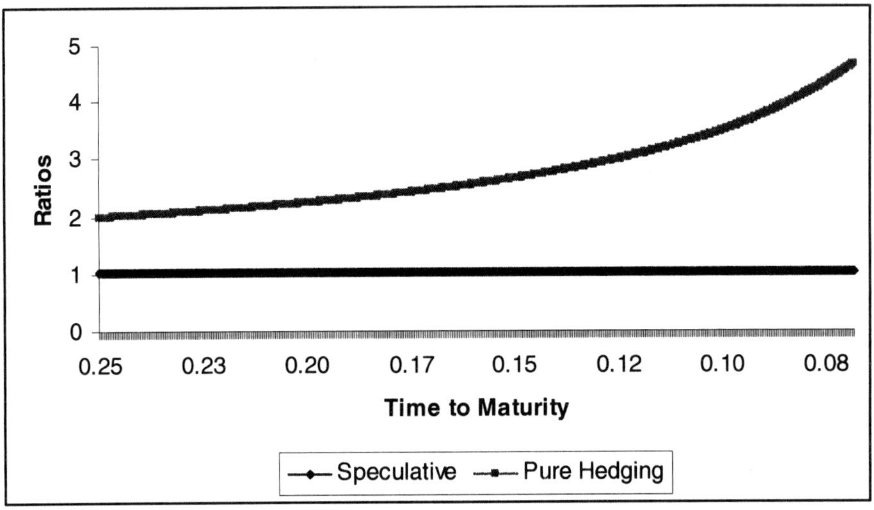

Figure 7.1.

Figure 7.1 exhibits the ratios (i) and (ii) for an investor whose horizon is equal to the maturity of the shortest contract. The ratio for the speculative component turns out to be slightly higher than one (in absolute terms) but very stable over time. As to the hedging ratio, it increases as time goes by, which means that the position in the nearby contract becomes predominant over time. The explanation for this result is that the second forward contract is essentially used to hedge the interest rate risk that affects the first forward position built as a hedge against the risk of the underlying asset. Had interest rate risk be absent, only the nearby forward contract would have been used. Since, as time to maturity decreases, the interest rate risk to be hedged becomes smaller, the second contract becomes less needed.

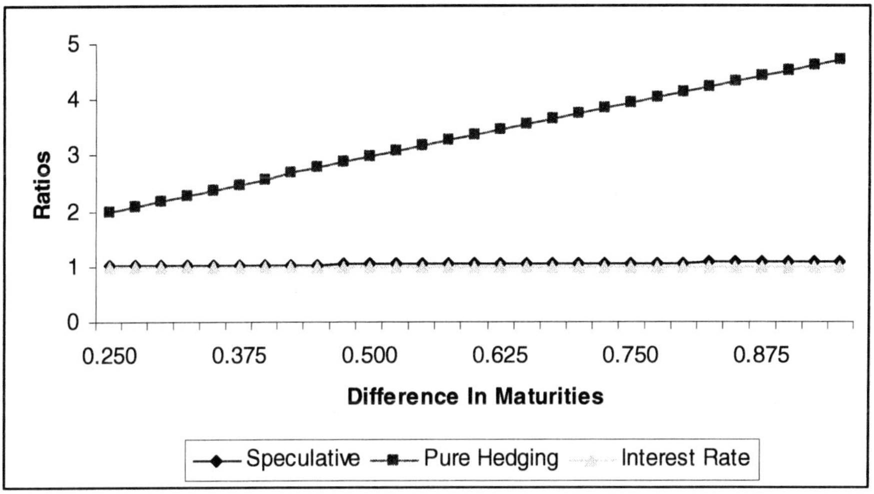

Figure 7.2.

In Figure 7.2 are reported the initial values of the ratios for various differences in maturities (in years) between the two contracts. The pure hedge ratio is by far the most sensitive to this difference in maturities. The relationship is increasing and almost linear: this hedge requires more of the nearby contract relative to the distant one the larger is the difference in maturities. The other two components are much less sensitive to this parameter.

The other parameters that influence the speculative component are the interest rate volatility and the volatility of the underlying asset.

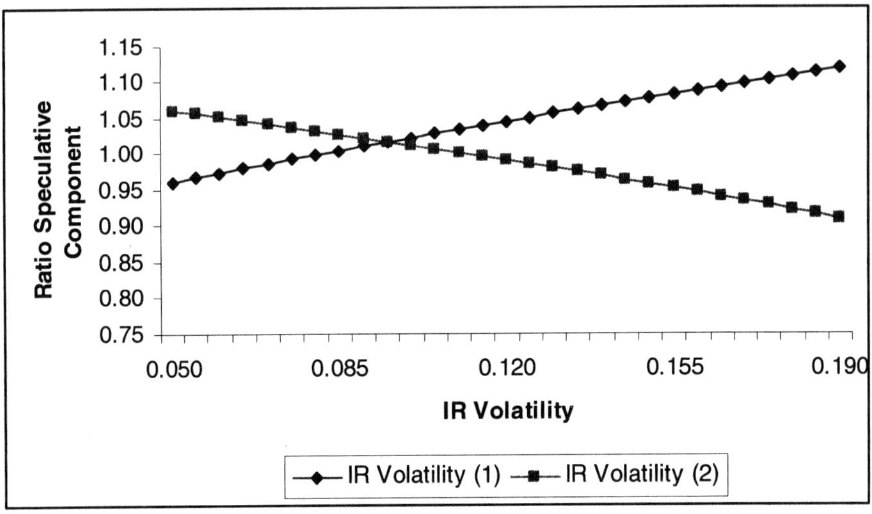

Figure 7.3.

The sensitivity of the speculative ratio with respect to volatility is reported in Figure 7.3. Note that, from (ii) and (iii), the ratios for the two other components do not depend on such volatility. The distinction is made between the volatility (ν_1)related to the first source of risk (Z_1, that affects the stock too), i.e. IR Volatility (1), and the volatility (ν_2) related to the second source of risk, Z_2, that influences interest rates only, i.e. IR Volatility (2). The sensitivity of the speculative ratio varies differently according to which volatility is concerned. The ratio increases with the volatility of the common source of risk (ν_1) and decreases with the pure interest rate volatility (ν_2).

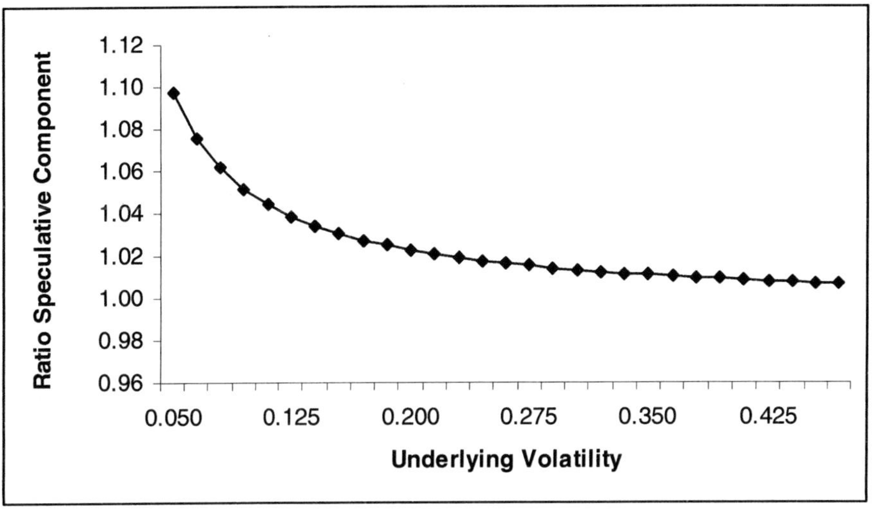

Figure 7.4.

Figure 7.4 reports the sensitivity of the speculative ratio to the level of volatility of the underlying asset (σ_1). Again, the two hedge ratios are left unaffected. The speculative ratio is a decreasing function of this volatility. However, while the relationship between the ratio and the IR volatilities is quasi-linear, here it is markedly convex.

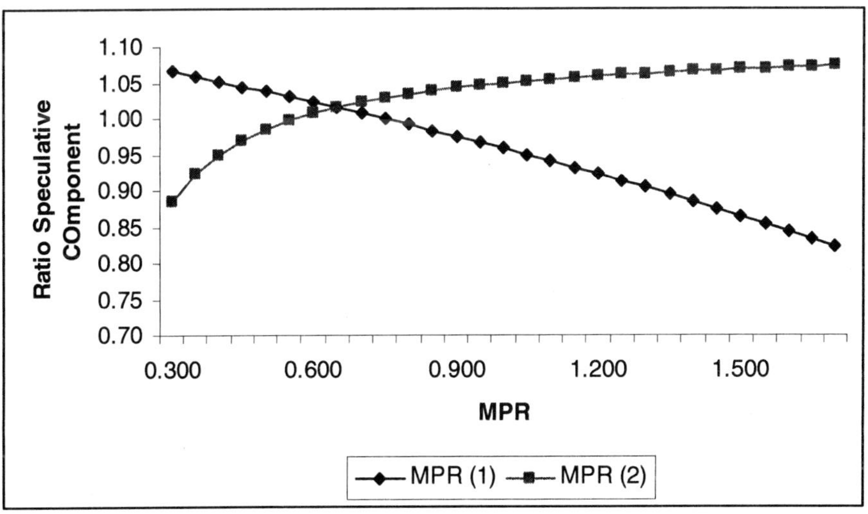

Figure 7.5.

The sensitivity of the speculative component ratio with respect to the market prices of risk (MPR) is shown in Figure 7.5. The ratio is a decreasing function of the MPR associated with the first source of risk, κ_1. The number of nearby contracts held relative to that of the distant contract thus falls with this MPR. The opposite holds true for the MPR associated with the second source of risk, κ_2, although the convexity is much more pronounced at low levels of this MPR.

The preceding simulations show that while the pure hedging component ratio is always greater than one (in fact, two), this is not the case for the other two components. To see where this originates from, note that using Proposition 1 and assuming a zero dividend yield ($\delta = 0$) yields:

$$\hat{\beta}_1^h(t) = -\frac{\tau_2 - t}{\tau_2 - \tau_1}\pi = -\left(1 + \frac{\tau_1 - t}{\tau_2 - \tau_1}\right)\pi = -\pi - \frac{\tau_1 - t}{\tau_2 - \tau_1}\pi = -\pi - \hat{\beta}_2^h(t) \quad (37)$$

and therefore:

$$\left|\frac{\hat{\beta}_1^h(t)}{\hat{\beta}_2^h(t)}\right| = 1 + \frac{\pi}{\hat{\beta}_2^h(t)} \quad (38)$$

Since it is the sum of the two components of the hedge ratios that is equal to $-\pi$, the position in the nearby contract is not (minus) one-to-one vis-à-vis the constrained position (π), a correction being necessary due to the presence of the distant contract: Since the latter contract, used to cancel the interest rate risk brought about by the nearby contract, induces an extra risk on the underlying itself, the position in the nearby contract must be amended accordingly.

As to the speculative component, one has:

$$\hat{\beta}_1^s(t) = \frac{\nu_2\kappa_1 + \nu_1\kappa_2}{\sigma_1\nu_2}\frac{W^*(t)}{S(t)} + \hat{\beta}_2^s(t) \quad (39)$$

$$\left|\frac{\hat{\beta}_1^s(t)}{\hat{\beta}_2^s(t)}\right| = \left|1 + \frac{1}{\hat{\beta}_2^s(t)}\frac{\nu_2\kappa_1 + \nu_1\kappa_2}{\sigma_1\nu_2}\frac{W^*(t)}{S(t)}\right| \quad (40)$$

Since the position in the distant contract may be negative, the speculative ratio may be less than one.

When futures contracts are used instead of forwards, the ratios related to each component are more involved, although there are two components only (no interest rate risk). Proposition 2 in effect implies:

$$\left|\frac{\hat{\hat{\beta}}_1^s(t)}{\hat{\hat{\beta}}_2^s(t)}\right| = \frac{\nu_2(\tau_2 - t)\kappa_1(t) - [\sigma_1 + \nu_1(\tau_2 - t)]\kappa_2(t)}{\nu_2(\tau_1 - t)\kappa_1(t) - [\sigma_1 + \nu_1(\tau_1 - t)]\kappa_2(t)} \frac{P(t,\tau_1)}{P(t,\tau_2)} \exp\left\{-\delta(\tau_2 - \tau_1)\right\}$$
$$\exp\left\{\left(\nu_1^2 + \nu_2^2\right)\left(\frac{(\tau_2 - t)^3}{3} - \frac{(\tau_1 - t)^3}{3}\right) + \frac{1}{2}\sigma_1\nu_1\left((\tau_2 - t)^2 - (\tau_1 - t)^2\right)\right\} \quad (41)$$

and

$$\left|\frac{\hat{\hat{\beta}}_1^h(t)}{\hat{\hat{\beta}}_2^h(t)}\right| = \frac{\tau_2 - t}{\tau_1 - t} \frac{P(t,\tau_1)}{P(t,\tau_2)} \exp\{-\delta(\tau_2 - \tau_1)\}$$
$$\exp\left\{\left(\nu_1^2 + \nu_2^2\right)\left(\frac{(\tau_2 - t)^3}{3} - \frac{(\tau_1 - t)^3}{3}\right) + \frac{1}{2}\sigma_1\nu_1\left((\tau_2 - t)^2 - (\tau_1 - t)^2\right)\right\} \quad (42)$$

Simulations are run under the assumption that all instantaneous forward rates are equal to 5% (these rates are required to compute the zero-coupon bond prices), implying a flat yield curve.

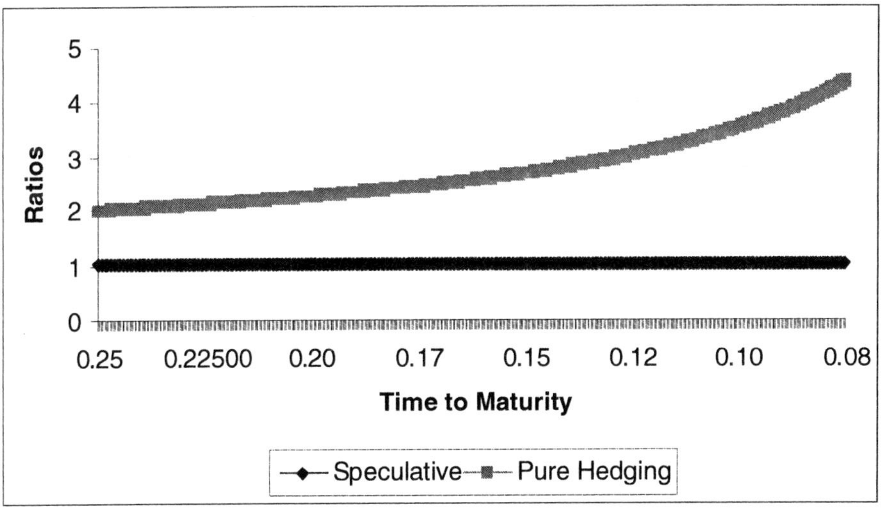

Figure 7.6.

Figure 7.6 shows that, as was the case with forward contracts, the ratio for the speculative component is almost time invariant and that for the pure hedge component increases sharply (with a rather large convexity) as time goes by. For short maturities, the tailing factor that characterizes futures does not alter much the behavior of the ratios relative to that of the forward ratios.

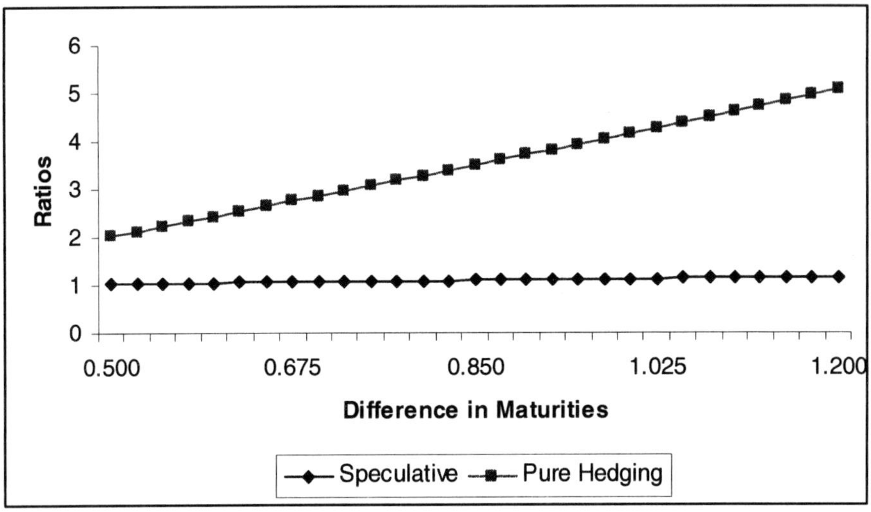

Figure 7.7.

This conclusion carries over to the sensitivity to the difference in maturities (compare Figures 7.7 and 7.2). The pure hedging ratio still is highly sensitive to that parameter, while the speculative ratio still is not.

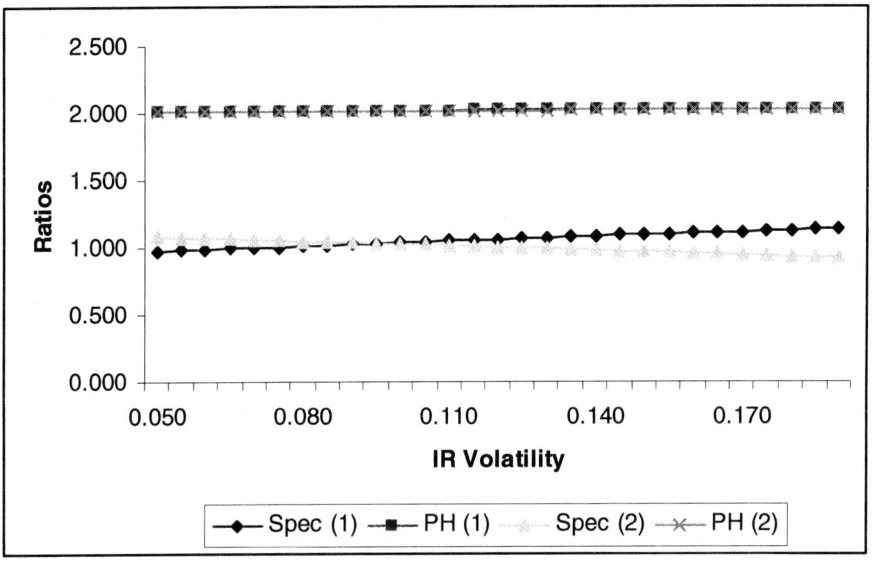

Figure 7.8.

The sensitivities of the speculative ratio and the pure hedge ratio with respect to volatility is reported in Figure 7.8. Note that, from (v), the latter ratio, unlike the case of forwards, does depend on such volatility. As evidenced by Figure 7.8, however, its influence is almost not noticeable (whether ν_1 varies, see PH(1), or ν_2, see PH(2)). The sensitivity of the speculative ratio does vary, and differently according to which volatility is concerned, as with forwards. The ratio increases with the volatility ν_1 of the common source of risk (Spec (1)) and decreases with the pure interest rate volatility ν_2 (Spec (2)).

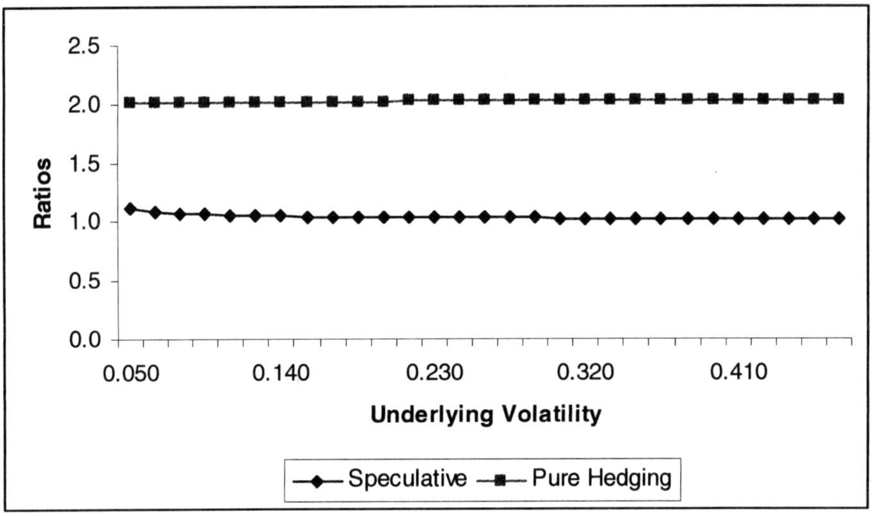

Figure 7.9.

Figure 7.9 reports the sensitivity of the speculative and pure hedge ratios to the level of volatility of the underlying asset (σ_1). Although the latter ratio does now depend on σ_1 (contrast (v) with (ii)), the influence is minimal. The speculative ratio still is a decreasing function of this volatility, with a marked convexity at small values of σ_1.

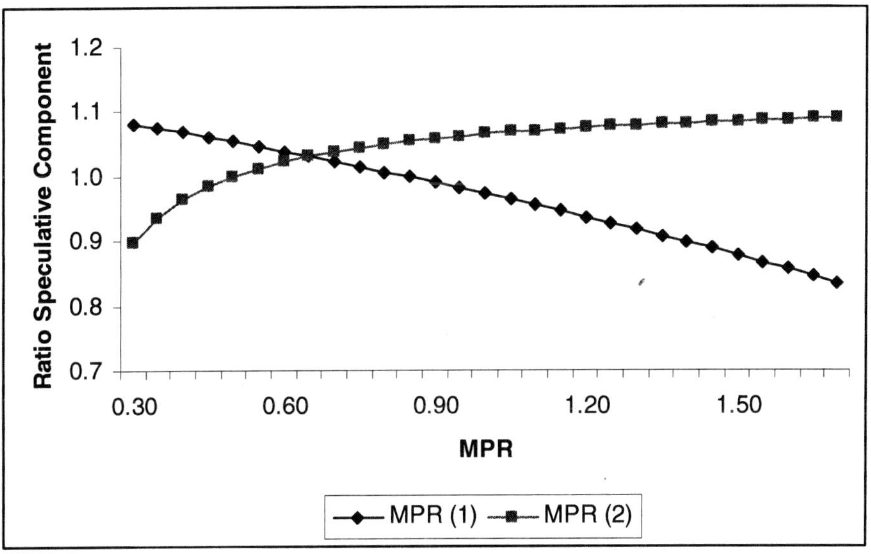

Figure 7.10.

Finally, Figure 7.10 depicts the sensitivity of the speculative ratio with respect to the two market prices of risk, κ_1 and κ_2. The ratio is a decreasing function of the former and an increasing function of the latter. It behaves much like its forward counterpart.

Overall, the ratios using futures and those using forwards are rather similar and react in much the same way to changes in the parameters. However, the reader must bear in mind that we have dealt with each ratio taken separately, not with the overall ratio. This impression thus may be misleading.

Endnotes

[1] The results of this chapter borrow from A. Lioui and R. Eldor (1998).

[2] In a general equilibrium approach, financial innovation aims at completing an initially incomplete market. Redundant contracts are economically useless. For a thorough analysis of non-redundant forward or futures contracts, see Part III below. By contrast, in the literature relative to hedging, futures or forward contracts are used to remove the negative welfare effects of the non-tradability of some primitive assets. Hence, even though they are redundant, such contracts are Pareto improving for *constrained* investors.

[3] The instantaneous correlation between the forward price and its underlying asset price is

equal to $\frac{(\sigma_1 + v_1(\tau_i - t))\sigma_1}{\sigma_1\sqrt{(\sigma_1 + v_1(\tau_i - t))^2 + v_2^2(\tau_i - t)^2}}$. The numerator of the first order derivative of that expression with respect to maturity τ_i is equal to $-\sigma v^2_2(\tau_i - t)$, and thus decreases with τ_i.

[4] Lioui (1997) addressed this issue in the case of interest rates derivatives.

CHAPTER 8: PRICING AND HEDGING UNDER STOCHASTIC DIVIDEND OR CONVENIENCE YIELD

8.1. INTRODUCTION

So far in this book, we have ignored the problem associated with the underlying asset of the forward or futures contract paying a dividend or having a convenience yield. Generally, contingent claim analysis assumes such a dividend away or at best supposes that it is deterministic. In reality, however, and particularly when commodities or stock indices are concerned, dividends are random, which elicits interesting challenges for pricing and hedging derivatives. The main objective of this chapter is to assess the impact of a stochastic dividend or convenience yield on (i) the pricing of forward and futures contracts, and (ii) on the optimal hedging strategy of an investor endowed with a non-tradable position on the underlying asset.

To obtain tractable results, we continue to assume that markets are complete, so that unique prices for contingent claims can be attained by arbitrage arguments and we can concentrate on the issue at hand. However, even in a complete and frictionless market, allowing the dividend yield to be stochastic disrupts most results. Although the random nature of the dividend does not bring about any new source of risk, the market being complete, it complicates dramatically the pricing and hedging of contingent claims.

The main difficulty arises from the fact that the process that must be a martingale given a numeraire under the corresponding probability measure is not the ex dividend price of the underlying asset but its cum dividend price (expressed in term of the numeraire). Given that most contingent claims payoffs at their maturity are a function of the ex dividend price, their price today cannot be obtained trivially even if their payoff is a linear combination of the payoffs of the primitive assets involved. The problem is to find the appropriate martingale measure. A closely related issue is that the market prices of risk will have to be specified, even in a complete market setting, to derive contingent claims prices. Under stochastic dividends, the replicating strategy of even a simple forward contract is not trivial since the usual static strategy is ineffective and must be replaced by a complex dynamic strategy. The cash-and-carry formula that holds even when forward contracts are not redundant[1] fails to hold in such a setting.

One way to overcome part of the above difficulties is to assume that the market prices of risk are constant or deterministic. This is the route generally followed by the literature on commodity derivatives pricing under a stochastic convenience yield[2], in spite of a large empirical evidence on the stochastic nature of the market prices of risk to the contrary (e.g. Lettau and Ludvingson (2004))[3]. To illustrate the difficulties brought about by the stochastic yield assumption, we start with a simple framework in which the market price of risk (MPR hereafter) is deterministic. We then introduce a second source of (interest rate) risk, which will make the MPR stochastic and the problem more realistic but much more involved.

8.2. A ONE-FACTOR MODEL: CONSTANT INTEREST RATE AND MPR

We describe first the economy, then proceed to price the forward and futures contracts, and then solve the hedger's problem.

8.2.1. The Economy.

All agents trade continuously in a frictionless and arbitrage-free financial market until time τ_E, where τ_E is the horizon of the economy. Two long-lived assets are traded, a locally riskless asset (the money market account) yielding a constant instantaneous rate r, and a risky security (e.g. a stock index) or asset (e.g. a commodity). The value B(t) of the former (with B(0) = 1) thus evolves over time as:

$$\frac{dB(t)}{B(t)} = r\,dt \tag{1}$$

The latter is assumed to pay a continuous dividend or convenience yield $\delta(t)$ and its price process is assumed to solve the following stochastic differential equation:

$$\frac{dS(t)}{S(t)} = (\mu_S - \delta(t))dt + \sigma_S dZ(t) \tag{2}$$

where $S(0) > 0$, μ_S is its total return (dividend plus capital gains), σ_S is its constant volatility, both of them being positive, and Z(t) is one-dimensional.

Since we want the financial market to be complete even under stochastic yield, the yield process must be driven by the already existing source of uncertainty, Z(t). Therefore, it is assumed to solve:

$$d\delta(t) = \mu_\delta dt + \sigma_\delta dZ(t) \qquad (3)$$

where $\delta(0) = 0$, and μ_δ and σ_δ are two positive constants.

The main motivation for this (pedagogic) choice is tractability. Unfortunately, the process (3) authorizes negative dividends. In the case of a commodity, however, since $\delta(t)$ is routinely the convenience yield *net* of storage and administration costs, it can become negative and therefore (3) is not an issue.

Agents adopt portfolio strategies that consist of trading on the money market account and the risky asset. These strategies are as usual assumed to be admissible and self-financing. Absence of arbitrage opportunity is equivalent to the existence of a probability measure Q equivalent to P such that the discounted price cum dividend process is a martingale (with the riskless asset as the numeraire). The risk neutral probability Q is defined as:

$$\left.\frac{dQ}{dP}\right|_{F_t} \equiv \eta(t) = \exp\left\{-\kappa Z(t) - \frac{1}{2}\kappa^2 t\right\}$$

where κ is the MPR defined by:

$$\kappa = \frac{\mu_S - r}{\sigma_S} \qquad (4)$$

Under this new measure, the dynamics of the risky asset and that of the dividend process rewrite respectively:

$$\frac{dS(t)}{S(t)} = (r - \delta(t))dt + \sigma_S d\hat{Z}(t) \qquad (5)$$

$$d\delta(t) = (\mu_\delta - \sigma_\delta \kappa)dt + \sigma_\delta d\hat{Z}(t) \qquad (6)$$

where:

$$\hat{Z}(t) = Z(t) + \int_0^t \kappa ds \qquad (7)$$

is a standard Brownian motion under Q.

We derive first the price of forward or futures contracts then consider the hedging problem of an investor endowed with a non-traded position in the risky asset.

8.2.2. Pricing.

Consider a forward contract written on S, with maturity T, whose current price is G(t,T), and an equivalent futures contract, whose price is H(t,T). Since interest rates are constant, these prices are equal and such that:

$$G(t,T)=H(t,T)=E^{Q}\left[S(T)\middle|F_t\right] \tag{8}$$

which leads to the following proposition.

Proposition 1:

The time t price of a maturity T forward, or futures, contract written on a dividend paying risky asset is equal to:

$$\begin{aligned} G(t,T)=H(t,T)=S(t)\exp\left\{(T-t)r\right\} \\ \exp\left\{-\delta(t)(T-t)-\frac{(T-t)^2}{2}\left((\mu_\delta-\sigma_\delta\kappa)+\frac{T-t}{3}\sigma_\delta{}^2-\sigma_\delta\sigma_S\right)\right\} \end{aligned} \tag{9}$$

Proof

Applying Ito's lemma to (5) and (6), respectively, yields:

$$S(t)=S(0)\exp\left\{\left(r-\frac{\sigma_S{}^2}{2}\right)t-\int_0^t\delta(s)ds+\sigma_S\hat{Z}(t)\right\} \tag{10}$$

and

$$\delta(t)=(\mu_\delta-\sigma_\delta\kappa)t+\sigma_\delta\hat{Z}(t) \tag{11}$$

Integrating (11) gives the *cumulative dividend process*:

$$\int_0^t\delta(s)ds=(\mu_\delta-\sigma_\delta\kappa)\frac{t^2}{2}+\sigma_\delta\int_0^t\hat{Z}(s)ds=(\mu_\delta-\sigma_\delta\kappa)\frac{t^2}{2}+\sigma_\delta\int_0^t(t-s)d\hat{Z}(s) \tag{12}$$

Substituting into (10) yields:

$$S(t)=S(0)\exp\left\{\left(r-\frac{\sigma_S{}^2}{2}\right)t-(\mu_\delta-\sigma_\delta\kappa)\frac{t^2}{2}-\sigma_\delta\int_0^t(t-s)d\hat{Z}(s)+\sigma_S\hat{Z}(t)\right\}$$

and, therefore:

$$
\begin{aligned}
H(t,T) &= S(t)E^{Q}\left[\left.\frac{S(T)}{S(t)}\right|F_t\right] \\
&= S(t)\exp\left\{\left(r-\frac{\sigma_S^{\ 2}}{2}\right)(T-t)-(\mu_\delta-\sigma_\delta\kappa)\frac{T^2-t^2}{2}-\sigma_\delta(T-t)\hat{Z}(t)\right\} \\
&\quad E^{Q}\left[\left.\exp\left\{-\sigma_\delta\int_t^T(T-s)d\hat{Z}(s)+\sigma_S\left(\hat{Z}(T)-\hat{Z}(t)\right)\right\}\right|F_t\right]
\end{aligned}
$$

Computing explicitly the conditional expectation using the Laplace transform, one gets:

$$
\begin{aligned}
&H(t,T)=S(t)\exp\left\{r(T-t)\right\} \\
&\exp\left\{-(\mu_\delta-\sigma_\delta\kappa)\frac{T^2-t^2}{2}-\sigma_\delta(T-t)\hat{Z}(t)-\frac{\sigma_\delta^{\ 2}}{2}\frac{(T-t)^3}{3}+\frac{1}{2}\sigma_\delta\sigma_S(T-t)^2\right\}
\end{aligned}
$$

Using equation (11) yields the desired result. □

The introduction of a stochastic dividend or convenience yield has a dramatic impact on derivatives pricing and hedging:

- First, the price of even a contingent claim with a linear payoff (such as a forward or futures contract) cannot be obtained explicitly unless some restrictive assumptions are made as to the dynamics of its underlying asset. In addition, four parameters must be estimated (κ, μ_δ, σ_δ and σ_s).

- Second, even in a complete market, the market price of risk affects the price of any contingent claim and thus need to be specified. In practice, this is often awkward and leads to frequent mispricing.

- Third, even though the volatility of the underlying asset is constant, that of the derivatives, albeit still deterministic in this simple framework, depends on time. Indeed, applying Itô's lemma to (9), the volatility of the contracts (the diffusion parameter of dH(.)/H(.) or dG(.)/G(.)) is equal to:

$$
\sigma_H(t,T)=\sigma_S-\sigma_\delta(T-t) \tag{13}
$$

The two contracts have the same price and volatility. However, the marking-to-market mechanism that characterizes futures will have an impact on the hedger's optimal strategy to which we turn now.

8.2.3. Optimal hedging.

Consider the dynamic strategy a pure hedger endowed with a (at least momentarily) non-tradable position consisting in Π units of asset S. The hedge will involve the riskless asset and either forward or futures contracts.

When forward contracts are used, the investor's wealth at each time t is:

$$W(t)=\Pi S(t)+\alpha(t)B(t)+e^{-r(T-t)}\int_0^t \Theta(s)dG(s,T) \tag{14}$$

where $\alpha(t)$ is the number of units of the riskless asset held, and $\Theta(t)$ the number of forward contracts held at time t. It is worth noting that, implicitly, the dividend yield is reinvested in the money market account.

When futures are involved, the investor's wealth at each time t reads:

$$\overline{W}(t)=\Pi S(t)+\overline{\alpha}(t)B(t)+X(t,T) \tag{15}$$

where the upper bar denotes the use of futures and X(t,T) is the time t value of the margin account:

$$X(t,T)=\int_0^t e^{r(t-s)}\overline{\Theta}(s)dH(s,T) \tag{16}$$

where $\overline{\Theta}(t)$ the number of futures held at time t.

The optimal hedging strategies are gathered in the following proposition:

Proposition 2:

a) The optimal hedging strategy using forwards is given by:

$$\Theta(t)=-\Pi\frac{\sigma_S}{\sigma_S-\sigma_\delta(T-t)}\exp\left\{\delta(t)(T-t)+\frac{(T-t)^2}{2}\left((\mu_\delta-\sigma_\delta\kappa)+\frac{T-t}{3}\sigma_\delta^{\,2}-\sigma_\delta\sigma_S\right)\right\} \tag{17}$$

b) and the optimal strategy using futures is:

$$\overline{\Theta}(t)=-\Pi\frac{\sigma_S}{\sigma_S-\sigma_\delta(T-t)}e^{-r(T-t)}\exp\left\{\delta(t)(T-t)+\frac{(T-t)^2}{2}\left((\mu_\delta-\sigma_\delta\kappa)+\frac{T-t}{3}\sigma_\delta^{\,2}-\sigma_\delta\sigma_S\right)\right\} \tag{18}$$

Proof

a) Applying Ito's lemma to (14) knowing that the strategy is self-financing yields:

$$dW(t) = \Pi dS(t) + \alpha(t)dB(t)$$
$$+\left(\int_0^t \Theta(s)dG(s,T)\right)e^{-r(T-t)}rdt + \Theta(t)e^{-r(T-t)}dG(t,T)$$

Using (1), (2) and (9), this becomes:

$$dW(t) = (.)dt + (\Pi S(t)\sigma_S + \Theta(t)P(t,T)G(t,T)(\sigma_S - \sigma_\delta(T-t)))dZ(t)$$

Setting the diffusion term equal to zero gives the desired result (17).

b) Applying Ito's lemma to (15), and using (16), one gets:

$$d\overline{W}(t) = \Pi dS(t) + \Pi S(t)\delta(t)dt + \overline{\alpha}(t)dB(t) + rX(t,T)dt + \overline{\Theta}(t)dH(t,T)$$

Therefore, using (1), (2) and (9), it follows that:

$$d\overline{W}(t) = (.)dt + \left(\Pi S(t)\sigma_S + \overline{\Theta}(t)H(t,T)(\sigma_S - \sigma_\delta(T-t))\right)dZ(t)$$

Equating the diffusion term to zero yields the desired result (18). □

Since the dividend yield $\delta(t)$ appearing in results (17) and (18) is stochastic, the hedge ratios $\Theta(t)/\Pi$ and $\overline{\Theta}(t)/\Pi$ evolve randomly through time, even in this simple setting. Note that in both cases the investor can achieve a perfect hedge since the market is complete. The increased complexity of the formulas is due to the time dependence brought about by the dividend yield itself and the parameters of its dynamics. We recover nonetheless the usual and simple difference between the two strategies, namely the presence of the « tailing factor » $e^{-r(T-t)}$ in the expression (18) using futures. This was expected, as interest rates are constant in this setting. This will not be the case in the more complicated framework we consider now.

8.3. A TWO-FACTOR MODEL: STOCHASTIC INTEREST RATES AND MPR

This section generalizes the preceding results to the case of stochastic interest rates and MPR.

8.3.1. The economy

We will now assume that two fundamental sources of risk affect the economy, Z_1 and Z_2, which are one-dimensional and independent of each other.

We continue to assume that the risky asset is influenced by Z_1 alone. However, its drift is now time dependent, so we rewrite (2) as:

$$\frac{dS(t)}{S(t)} = (\mu_S(t,S(t)) - \delta(t))dt + \sigma_S dZ(t) \tag{19}$$

To make interest rates stochastic, we assume, as in Heath et al. (1992), that the instantaneous forward rate f(t, T) is driven by both $Z_1(t)$ and $Z_2(t)$, i.e.

$$df(t,T) = \mu_f(t,T)dt + \sigma_{f1}dZ_1(t) + \sigma_{f2}dZ_2(t) \tag{20}$$

where μ_f is a constant. We thus adopt a two-factor model of the yield curve.

The value at time t of the money market account now evolves as:

$$\frac{dB(t)}{B(t)} = r(t)dt \tag{21}$$

where r(t) is the spot rate defined as r(t) = f(t, t).

Since we want to retain the complete market assumption even though dividends are stochastic, the dividend yield process must be driven by (at most) the already existing sources of uncertainty. Therefore, the dividend yield process is supposed to solve:

$$d\delta(t) = \mu_\delta dt + \sigma_{\delta 1}dZ_1(t) + \sigma_{\delta 2}dZ_2(t) \tag{22}$$

8.3.2. Pricing forward and futures contracts

Given the dynamics of instantaneous forward rates (20), the dynamics of a discount bond price P(t, τ) maturing at time τ ($t < \tau \le \tau_E$) is:

$$\frac{dP(t,\tau)}{P(t,\tau)} = [b(t,\tau) + r(t)]dt - (\tau - t)\sigma_{f1}dZ_1(t) - (\tau - t)\sigma_{f2}dZ_2(t)$$

where the b(t, τ) part of the drift, i.e. the risk premium, is deterministic.

The martingale measure Q, with the riskless asset chosen as numeraire, is now defined as:

$$\left.\frac{dQ}{dP}\right|_{F_t} \equiv \eta(t) = \exp\left\{-\int_0^t \kappa(s)' dZ(s) - \frac{1}{2}\int_0^t \kappa(s)' \kappa(s) ds\right\} \tag{23}$$

where:

$$\kappa(t) = \begin{pmatrix} \sigma_S & 0 \\ -(\tau - t)\sigma_{f1} & -(\tau - t)\sigma_{f2} \end{pmatrix}^{-1} \begin{pmatrix} \mu_S(t, S(t) - r(t)) \\ b(t,\tau) \end{pmatrix} \tag{24}$$

is the vector of the market prices of risk. The latter fluctuates randomly due to the presence of the spot rate, which is at a crucial variance with the preceding section, and will drive new results.

The time t price G(t, T) of a maturity T forward contract written on S is such that:

$$E^Q\left[\frac{S(T) - G(t,T)}{B(T)}\middle| F_t\right] = 0$$

or else:

$$G(t,T) E^Q\left[\frac{1}{B(T)}\middle| F_t\right] = E^Q\left[\frac{S(T)}{B(T)}\middle| F_t\right]$$

and thus, since P(T,T) =1:

$$G(t,T)\frac{P(t,T)}{B(t)} = E^Q\left[\frac{S(T)}{B(T)}\middle| F_t\right] \tag{25}$$

As seen in Chapter 2, the time t price H(t,T) of a futures contract written on S and maturing at time T is given by:

$$H(t,T) = E^Q\left[S(T)\middle| F_t\right] \tag{26}$$

Equations (25) and (26) lead to the following two propositions.

<u>Proposition 3:</u>

The time t price of a maturity T forward contract written on a dividend paying asset is equal to:

$$G(t,T)=\frac{S(t)}{P(t,T)}g(t)\exp\left\{-(T-t)\delta(t)-\frac{(T-t)^2}{2}\left(\mu_\delta-\sigma_\delta{}'\kappa(t)\right)\right\} \qquad (27)$$

where g(t) is the deterministic function:

$$g(t)=\exp\left\{\frac{1}{2}\int_t^T(T-s)^2 d\Psi_\delta(s)+\frac{1}{2}\Lambda_\delta\int_t^T(T-s)^2\left(\mu_f(s,t)-\Psi_f(s)\right)ds-\frac{1}{2}\sigma_S{}^2(T-t\right.$$

$$\exp\left\{\frac{1}{2}\int_t^T\left(\begin{array}{l}\left[\sigma_S-(T-s)\sigma_{\delta 1}+\frac{1}{2}\Lambda_\delta\sigma_{f1}(T-s)^2\right]^2\\ -\left[(T-s)\sigma_{\delta 2}-\frac{1}{2}\Lambda_\delta\sigma_{f2}(T-s)^2\right]^2\end{array}\right)ds\right\}$$

Proof

The solution, under the martingale measure Q, to equation (19) is:

$$S(t)=S(0)\exp\left\{\int_0^t\left(r(s)-\delta(s)-\frac{1}{2}\sigma_S{}^2\right)ds+\sigma_S\hat{Z}_1(t)\right\}$$

so that we also have:

$$\frac{S(T)}{S(t)}=\exp\left\{\int_t^T\left(r(s)-\delta(s)-\frac{1}{2}\sigma_S{}^2\right)ds+\sigma_S\left(\hat{Z}_1(T)-\hat{Z}_1(t)\right)\right\}$$

Rewriting (25) as

$$G(t,T)=\frac{S(t)}{P(t,T)}E^Q\left[\frac{S(T)B(t)}{S(t)B(T)}\middle|F_t\right]$$

one obtains:

$$G(t,T)=\frac{S(t)}{P(t,T)}E^Q\left[\exp\left\{-\int_t^T\left(\delta(s)+\frac{1}{2}\sigma_S{}^2\right)ds+\sigma_S\left(\hat{Z}_1(T)-\hat{Z}_1(t)\right)\right\}\middle|F_t\right] \qquad (28)$$

where the task consists in computing explicitly the conditional expectation on the RHS.

Integrating the dividend stream $\delta(s)$ between t and T yields:

$$\int_t^T\delta(s)ds=(T-t)\delta(t)+\int_t^T(T-s)d\delta(s) \qquad (29)$$

Under the martingale measure Q, we have:

$$d\delta(t) = \left(\mu_\delta - \sigma_\delta{}'\kappa(t)\right)dt + \sigma_{\delta 1} d\hat{Z}_1(t) + \sigma_{\delta 2} d\hat{Z}_2(t)$$

Substituting for $d\delta(s)$ into (29), it follows that:

$$\begin{aligned}\int_t^T \delta(s)ds &= (T-t)\delta(t) + \int_t^T (T-s)\left(\mu_\delta - \sigma_\delta{}'\kappa(s)\right)ds \\ &\quad + \int_t^T (T-s)\sigma_{\delta 1} d\hat{Z}_1(s) + \int_t^T (T-s)\sigma_{\delta 2} d\hat{Z}_2(s) \\ &= (T-t)\delta(t) + \frac{(T-t)^2}{2}\left(\mu_\delta - \sigma_\delta{}'\kappa(t)\right) \\ &\quad - \frac{1}{2}\int_t^T (T-s)^2 \sigma_\delta{}' d\kappa(s) + \int_t^T (T-s)\sigma_{\delta 1} d\hat{Z}_1(s) + \int_t^T (T-s)\sigma_{\delta 2} d\hat{Z}_2(s)\end{aligned} \tag{30}$$

Using (24), define:

$$\kappa(t) \equiv \begin{pmatrix} \kappa_1(t) \\ \kappa_2(t) \end{pmatrix} = \begin{pmatrix} \dfrac{\mu_S(t, S(t) - r(t))}{\sigma_S} \\ -\dfrac{\sigma_{f1}\left[\mu_S(t, S(t) - r(t))\right]}{\sigma_{f2}\sigma_S} - \dfrac{b(t,\tau)}{(\tau - t)\sigma_{f2}} \end{pmatrix} \tag{31}$$

Therefore, using (22) yields:

$$\sigma_\delta{}'\kappa(t) = \Psi_\delta(t) + \Lambda_\delta r(t) \tag{32}$$

where:

$$\Psi_\delta(t) \equiv \left(\frac{\sigma_{\delta 1}}{\sigma_S} - \frac{\sigma_{\delta 2}\sigma_{f1}}{\sigma_{f2}\sigma_S}\right)\mu_S(t, S(t)) - \frac{\sigma_{\delta 2} b(t,\tau)}{\sigma_{f2}(\tau - t)}$$

$$\Lambda_\delta \equiv -\frac{\sigma_{\delta 1}}{\sigma_S} + \frac{\sigma_{\delta 2}\sigma_{f1}}{\sigma_{f2}\sigma_S}$$

It follows that,

$$\sigma_\delta{}' d\kappa(t) = d\Psi_\delta(t) + \Lambda_\delta dr(t) \tag{33}$$

Under Q, we also have:

$$df(t,T) = \left(\mu_f(t,T) - \sigma_f{}'\kappa(t)\right)dt + \sigma_{f1} d\hat{Z}_1(t) + \sigma_{f2} d\hat{Z}_2(t)$$

Using (31), it follows that:

$$df(t,T) = \left(\mu_f(t,T) - \Psi_f(t)\right)dt + \sigma_{f1} d\hat{Z}_1(t) + \sigma_{f2} d\hat{Z}_2(t)$$

where:

$$\Psi_f(t) = -\frac{b(t,\tau)}{(\tau - t)}$$

Integrating df(t,T) yields:

$$f(t,T)=f(0,T)+\int_0^t(\mu_f(s,T)-\Psi_f(s))ds+\sigma_{f1}\hat{Z}_1(t)+\sigma_{f2}\hat{Z}_2(t)$$

Therefore, we have:

$$r(t)=f(t,t)=f(0,t)+\int_0^t(\mu_f(s,t)-\Psi_f(s))ds+\sigma_{f1}\hat{Z}_1(t)+\sigma_{f2}\hat{Z}_2(t)$$

Applying Ito's lemma yields:

$$dr(t)=(\mu_f(t,t)-\Psi_f(t))dt+\sigma_{f1}d\hat{Z}_1(t)+\sigma_{f2}d\hat{Z}_2(t)$$

Substituting into (33), one has:

$$\begin{aligned}\sigma_\delta' d\kappa(t)&=d\Psi_\delta(t)+\Lambda_\delta dr(t)\\&=d\Psi_\delta(t)+\Lambda_\delta(\mu_f(t,t)-\Psi_f(t))dt+\Lambda_\delta\sigma_{f1}d\hat{Z}_1(t)+\Lambda_\delta\sigma_{f2}d\hat{Z}_2(t)\end{aligned}$$

Substituting into (30) yields:

$$\begin{aligned}\int_t^T\delta(s)ds&=(T-t)\delta(t)+\frac{(T-t)^2}{2}(\mu_\delta-\sigma_\delta'\kappa(t))\\&-\frac{1}{2}\int_t^T(T-s)^2 d\Psi_\delta(s)-\frac{1}{2}\Lambda_\delta\int_t^T(T-s)^2(\mu_f(s,t)-\Psi_f(s))ds\\&+\int_t^T\left[(T-s)\sigma_{\delta 1}-\frac{1}{2}\Lambda_\delta\sigma_{f1}(T-s)^2\right]d\hat{Z}_1(s)\\&+\int_t^T\left[(T-s)\sigma_{\delta 2}-\frac{1}{2}\Lambda_\delta\sigma_{f2}(T-s)^2\right]d\hat{Z}_2(s)\end{aligned}$$

Substituting into (28), we finally get:

$$\begin{aligned}G(t,T)&=\frac{S(t)}{P(t,T)}\exp\left\{-(T-t)\delta(t)-\frac{(T-t)^2}{2}(\mu_\delta-\sigma_\delta'\kappa(t))\right\}\\&\exp\left\{\frac{1}{2}\int_t^T(T-s)^2 d\Psi_\delta(s)+\frac{1}{2}\Lambda_\delta\int_t^T(T-s)^2(\mu_f(s,t)-\Psi_f(s))ds-\frac{1}{2}\sigma_S{}^2(T-t)\right\}\\&E^Q\left[\exp\left\{\begin{aligned}&+\int_t^T\left[\sigma_S-(T-s)\sigma_{\delta 1}+\frac{1}{2}\Lambda_\delta\sigma_{f1}(T-s)^2\right]d\hat{Z}_1(s)\\&-\int_t^T\left[(T-s)\sigma_{\delta 2}-\frac{1}{2}\Lambda_\delta\sigma_{f2}(T-s)^2\right]d\hat{Z}_2(s)\end{aligned}\right\}\middle|F_t\right]\end{aligned}\tag{34}$$

Explicit computation of the conditional expectation in the RHS of (34) completes the proof. □

In brief, two decisive properties of complete markets (explicit prices for derivatives and absence of the market price(s) of risk in the solution) break down when dividends are stochastic: i) even if the derivative's payoff at maturity is linear in the price of its underlying asset, no explicit expression for its price is reachable in general, unless, *as here*, strong assumptions are made as to the parameters of the processes driving the underlying asset price, the forward rates and the market prices of risk, and ii) to value any derivative asset, the dynamics of the market price(s) of risk need be specified explicitly.

Consequently, the replicating strategy is far more involved than usually assumed. The strategy implicitly contains three hedging demands *in addition to* the standard hedge of the risk brought about by the underlying asset. The first component hedges the interest rate risk of the forward position from one period to the next. The cumulative gains/losses from the position being discounted with stochastic interest rates, their value changes randomly over time. The second component hedges against the risk stemming from the dividend yield. The third component hedges the randomness of the market price(s) of risk. Even in the case of a plain forward contract, the relationship between the spot and the forward price turns out disappointingly to be much more complex than the simple and appealing cash-and-carry formula.

Proposition 4:

The time t settlement price of a maturity T futures contract written on a dividend paying asset is such that:

$$\frac{H(t,T)}{G(t,T)} = \exp\left\{ \int_t^T \left((T-s)\sigma_{f1}\sigma_S - (T-s)^2 (\sigma_{f1}\sigma_{\delta 1} + \sigma_{f2}\sigma_{\delta 2}) + \left((T-s)^2 + \frac{(T-s)^3}{2}\Lambda_\delta \right) (\sigma_{f1}{}^2 + \sigma_{f2}{}^2) \right) ds \right\} \tag{35}$$

Proof

From chapter 2, and given deterministic volatilities, we have:

$$\frac{H(t,T)}{G(t,T)} = \exp\left[-\int_t^T \operatorname{cov}\left(\frac{dG(u,T)}{G(u,T)}, \frac{dP(u,T)}{P(u,T)} \right) du \right]$$

From (20) we have:

$$\frac{dP(t,T)}{P(t,T)} = (.)dt - (T-t)\sigma_{f1}dZ_1(t) - (T-t)\sigma_{f2}dZ_2(t) \tag{36}$$

Applying Ito's lemma to (25) yields:

$$\begin{aligned}\frac{dG(t,T)}{G(t,T)} = (.)dt &+ \left(\sigma_S + (T-t)\sigma_{f1} - (T-t)\sigma_{\delta 1} + \frac{(T-t)^2}{2}\Lambda_\delta \sigma_{f1}\right)dZ_1(t) \\ &+ \left((T-t)\sigma_{f2} - (T-t)\sigma_{\delta 2} + \frac{(T-t)^2}{2}\Lambda_\delta \sigma_{f2}\right)dZ_2(t)\end{aligned} \tag{37}$$

Using (36) and (37), it follows that:

$$\begin{aligned}\frac{1}{dt}\mathrm{cov}\left(\frac{dG(t,T)}{G(t,T)}, \frac{dP(t,T)}{P(t,T)}\right) = \\ &-(T-t)\sigma_{f1}\left(\sigma_S + (T-t)\sigma_{f1} - (T-t)\sigma_{\delta 1} + \frac{(T-t)^2}{2}\Lambda_\delta \sigma_{f1}\right) \\ &-(T-t)\sigma_{f2}\left((T-t)\sigma_{f2} - (T-t)\sigma_{\delta 2} + \frac{(T-t)^2}{2}\Lambda_\delta \sigma_{f2}\right)\end{aligned}$$

Rearranging terms yields:

$$\begin{aligned}&\frac{1}{dt}\mathrm{cov}\left(\frac{dG(t,T)}{G(t,T)}, \frac{dP(t,T)}{P(t,T)}\right) = \\ &-\left((T-t)\sigma_{f1}\sigma_S - (T-t)^2(\sigma_{f1}\sigma_{\delta 1} + \sigma_{f2}\sigma_{\delta 2}) + \left((T-t)^2 + \frac{(T-t)^3}{2}\Lambda_\delta\right)(\sigma_{f1}^{\ 2} + \sigma_{f2}^{\ 2})\right)\end{aligned}$$

Substituting into (36) yields the result. □

Since the exponential in (35) is deterministic, the instantaneous volatilities of the forward price and futures price are identical, even though these prices are different for all $t < T$.

8.3.3. Perfect hedging

Since the financial market is complete, a perfect hedge can be achieved, provided two different contracts (of respective maturities τ_1 and τ_2) are traded, in addition to the riskless asset.

Proposition 5:

When *forwards* are used, the investor's spreading strategy is:

$$\begin{aligned}\begin{bmatrix}\theta_1(t)\\ \theta_2(t)\end{bmatrix} = &-\begin{bmatrix}\sigma_{G1}(t,\tau_1) & \sigma_{G1}(t,\tau_2)\\ \sigma_{G2}(t,\tau_1) & \sigma_{G2}(t,\tau_2)\end{bmatrix}^{-1}\begin{bmatrix}\sigma_S\\ 0\end{bmatrix}\pi_S(t)\\ &-\begin{bmatrix}\sigma_{G1}(t,\tau_1) & \sigma_{G1}(t,\tau_2)\\ \sigma_{G2}(t,\tau_1) & \sigma_{G2}(t,\tau_2)\end{bmatrix}^{-1}\begin{bmatrix}\sigma_{P1}(t,\tau_1)\\ \sigma_{P2}(t,\tau_1)\end{bmatrix}\pi_{\theta_1}(t)\\ &-\begin{bmatrix}\sigma_{G1}(t,\tau_1) & \sigma_{G1}(t,\tau_2)\\ \sigma_{G2}(t,\tau_1) & \sigma_{G2}(t,\tau_2)\end{bmatrix}^{-1}\begin{bmatrix}\sigma_{P1}(t,\tau_2)\\ \sigma_{P2}(t,\tau_2)\end{bmatrix}\pi_{\theta_2}(t)\end{aligned} \tag{38}$$

and when *futures* are used, the spreading strategy is:

$$\begin{bmatrix}\overline{\theta}_1(t)\\ \overline{\theta}_2(t)\end{bmatrix} = -\begin{bmatrix}\sigma_{H1}(t,\tau_1) & \sigma_{H1}(t,\tau_2)\\ \sigma_{H2}(t,\tau_1) & \sigma_{H2}(t,\tau_2)\end{bmatrix}^{-1}\begin{bmatrix}\sigma_S\\ 0\end{bmatrix}\overline{\pi}_S(t) \tag{39}$$

Proof

a) When *forwards* are used, the investor's wealth writes:

$$W(t) = \Pi S(t) + \Gamma(t)B(t) + P(t,\tau_1)\int_0^t \Theta_1(s)dG(s,\tau_1) + P(t,\tau_2)\int_0^t \Theta_2(s)dG(s,\tau_2)$$

so that:

$$\begin{aligned}dW(t) = {} & \Pi dS(t) + \Gamma(t)dB(t) + P(t,\tau_1)\int_0^t \Theta_1(s)dG(s,\tau_1)\frac{dP(t,\tau_1)}{P(t,\tau_1)}\\ &+P(t,\tau_1)\Theta_1(t)dG(t,\tau_1) \quad +P(t,\tau_2)\int_0^t \Theta_2(s)dG(s,\tau_2)\frac{dP(t,\tau_2)}{P(t,\tau_2)}\\ &+P(t,\tau_2)\Theta_2(t)dG(t,\tau_2)\end{aligned}$$

or else:

$$\begin{aligned}\frac{dW(t)}{W(t)} &= (.)dt\\ &+\left(\pi_S(t)\sigma_S + \theta_1(t)\sigma_{G1}(t,\tau_1) + \theta_2(t)\sigma_{G1}(t,\tau_2) + \pi_{\theta_1}(t)\sigma_{P1}(t,\tau_1) + \pi_{\theta_2}(t)\sigma_{P1}(t,\tau_2)\right)dZ_1(t)\\ &+\left(\theta_1(t)\sigma_{G2}(t,\tau_1) + \theta_2(t)\sigma_{G2}(t,\tau_2) + \pi_{\theta_1}(t)\sigma_{P2}(t,\tau_1) + \pi_{\theta_2}(t)\sigma_{P2}(t,\tau_2)\right)dZ_2(t)\end{aligned}$$

where:

$$\pi_S(t) = \frac{\Pi S(t)}{W(t)}$$

$$\theta_i(t) = \frac{P(t,\tau_i)\Theta_i(t)G(t,\tau_i)}{W(t)}$$

$$\pi_{\theta_i}(t) = \frac{P(t,\tau_i)\int_0^t \Theta_i(s)dG(s,\tau_i)}{W(t)}$$

$$\sigma_{G1}(t,\tau_i) = \sigma_S + (\tau_i - t)\sigma_{f1} - (\tau_i - t)\sigma_{\delta 1} + \frac{(\tau_i - t)^2}{2}\Lambda_\delta \sigma_{f1}$$

$$\sigma_{G2}(t,\tau_i) = (\tau_1 - t)\sigma_{f2} - (\tau_1 - t)\sigma_{\delta 2} + \frac{(\tau_1 - t)^2}{2}\Lambda_\delta \sigma_{f2}$$

$$\sigma_{P1}(t,\tau_i) = -(\tau_i - t)\sigma_{f1}$$

$$\sigma_{P2}(t,\tau_i) = -(\tau_i - t)\sigma_{f2}$$

To reach a perfect hedge, the two forward positions must obey:

$$0 = \pi_S(t)\sigma_S + \theta_1(t)\sigma_{G1}(t,\tau_1) + \theta_2(t)\sigma_{G1}(t,\tau_2) + \pi_{\theta_1}(t)\sigma_{P1}(t,\tau_1) + \pi_{\theta_2}(t)\sigma_{P1}(t,\tau_2)$$

$$0 = \theta_1(t)\sigma_{G2}(t,\tau_1) + \theta_2(t)\sigma_{G2}(t,\tau_2) + \pi_{\theta_1}(t)\sigma_{P2}(t,\tau_1) + \pi_{\theta_2}(t)\sigma_{P2}(t,\tau_2)$$

Solving for this system yields (38).

b) When *futures* are used, the investor's wealth is such that:

$$\overline{W}(t) = \Pi S(t) + \overline{\Gamma}(t)B(t) + X(t,\tau_1) + X(t,\tau_2)$$

and its dynamics reads:

$$\frac{d\overline{W}(t)}{\overline{W}(t)} = \Pi dS(t) + \overline{\Gamma}(t)dB(t) + dX(t,\tau_1) + dX(t,\tau_2)$$

or else:

$$\frac{d\overline{W}(t)}{\overline{W}(t)} = (.)dt + \left(\overline{\pi}_S(t)\sigma_S + \overline{\theta}_1(t)\sigma_{H1}(t,\tau_1) + \overline{\theta}_2(t)\sigma_{H1}(t,\tau_2)\right)dZ_1(t)$$
$$+ \left(\overline{\theta}_1(t)\sigma_{H2}(t,\tau_1) + \overline{\theta}_2(t)\sigma_{H2}(t,\tau_2)\right)dZ_2(t)$$

where

$$\overline{\pi}_S(t) = \frac{\Pi S(t)}{\overline{W}(t)}$$

$$\overline{\theta}_i(t) = \frac{\Theta_i(t)H(t,\tau_i)}{\overline{W}(t)}$$

$$\sigma_{H1}(t,\tau_i) = \sigma_{G1}(t,\tau_i)$$

$$\sigma_{H2}(t,\tau_i) = \sigma_{G1}(t,\tau_i)$$

To achieve a perfect hedge, the futures strategy must solve:

$$0 = \overline{\pi}_S(t)\sigma_S + \overline{\theta}_1(t)\sigma_{H1}(t,\tau_1) + \overline{\theta}_2(t)\sigma_{H1}(t,\tau_2)$$

$$0 = \overline{\theta}_1(t)\sigma_{H2}(t,\tau_1) + \overline{\theta}_2(t)\sigma_{H2}(t,\tau_2)$$

and this yields (39). □

As compared to (38), only one term remains in the hedging strategy using futures since the two extra terms due to the interest rate risks brought about by the two forward positions here vanish.

8.3.4. Imperfect hedging

We consider now the case of imperfect hedging. Suppose the hedger trades on one contract only, and, in the case of forwards, does not use the riskless asset either to simplify the analysis without much loss of generality.

The investor's wealth then writes:

$$W(t) = \Pi S(t) + P(t,T)\int_0^t \Theta(s)dG(s,T) \tag{40}$$

or:

$$\overline{W}(t) = \Pi S(t) + X(t,T) \tag{41}$$

with:

$$X(t,T) = \int_0^t e^{\int_s^t r(u)du}\overline{\Theta}(s)dH(s,T) \tag{42}$$

depending on whether the forward or the futures contract is used.

This assumption then leads to the following proposition:

Proposition 6:

a)The dynamic strategy using forwards that must be followed to hedge the constrained position is:

$$\theta(t) = -\frac{\sigma_{G1}(t,T)\sigma_S}{\sigma_{G1}(t,T)^2 + \sigma_{G2}(t,T)^2}\pi_S(t) - \frac{\sigma_{G1}(t,T)\sigma_{f1} + \sigma_{G2}(t,T)\sigma_{f2}}{\sigma_{G1}(t,T)^2 + \sigma_{G2}(t,T)^2}(T-t)(1-\pi_S(t)) \tag{43}$$

b) and its counterpart using futures is:

$$\overline{\theta}(t) = -\frac{\sigma_{H1}(t,T)\sigma_S}{\sigma_{H1}(t,T)^2 + \sigma_{H2}(t,T)^2}\overline{\pi}_S(t) \tag{44}$$

where:

$$\pi_S(t) \equiv \frac{\Pi S(t)}{W(t)}$$

$$\overline{\pi}_S(t) \equiv \frac{\Pi S(t)}{\overline{W}(t)},$$

$$\theta(t) \equiv \frac{P(t,T)\Theta(t)G(t,T)}{W(t)}$$

$$\overline{\theta}(t) \equiv \frac{\overline{\Theta}(t)H(t,T)}{\overline{W}(t)}$$

Proof

a) Applying Ito's lemma to (40), one has:

$$\frac{dW(t)}{W(t)} = (.)dt + (\pi_S(t)\sigma_S + (1-\pi_S(t))(T-t)\sigma_{f1} + \theta(t)\sigma_{G1}(t,T))dZ_1(t) + ((1-\pi_S(t))(T-t)\sigma_{f2} + \theta(t)\sigma_{G2}(t,T))dZ_2(t)$$

Computing the instantaneous variance gives:

$$(\pi_S(t)\sigma_S + (1-\pi_S(t))(T-t)\sigma_{f1} + \theta(t)\sigma_{G1}(t,T))^2 + ((1-\pi_S(t))(T-t)\sigma_{f2} + \theta(t)\sigma_{G2}(t,T))^2$$

Minimizing this expression yields result (43)

b) Applying Ito's lemma to (41) using (42), one has:

$$\frac{d\overline{W}(t)}{\overline{W}(t)} = (.)dt + (\overline{\pi}_S(t)\sigma_S + \overline{\theta}(t)\sigma_{H1}(t,T))dZ_1(t) + \overline{\theta}(t)\sigma_{H2}(t,T)dZ_2(t)$$

Computing the instantaneous variance gives:

$$\left(\overline{\pi}_S(t)\sigma_S + \overline{\theta}(t)\sigma_{H1}(t,T)\right)^2 + \left(\overline{\theta}(t)\sigma_{H2}(t,T)\right)^2$$

Minimizing this expression yields result (44). □

It turns out that the imperfect hedge ratio is nothing but the standard minimum-variance hedging ratio when futures contracts are used. With forward contracts, the optimal solution is as usual more involved as an additional term accounting for the interest rate risk related to the present value of the gain or loss is present. The dividend or convenience yield risk is present everywhere since it influences the volatilities of the hedging instruments.

Endnotes

[1] See chapters 10 and 11.
[2] See for example Korn (2004).
[3] An interesting exception is Schroder (1999) who uses as numeraire the reinvested asset price process.

PART III

GENERAL EQUILIBRIUM PRICING

Part II was concerned by individual agents' optimal behavior, given the price or the price process of the forward or futures contracts. This final Part is about general equilibrium pricing. Indeed, when these contracts are not redundant instruments, their introduction completes (partially or fully) the originally incomplete financial market. Consequently, the usual no-arbitrage arguments are not sufficient per se to establish their prices and the general equilibrium of the entire economy must be derived in which all prices are endogenous. Three types of economy, ranked by increasing order of generality, are examined.

Chapter 9 is set in a pure exchange (endowment) economy. It shows how the various capital asset pricing models (CAPM) which have become common knowledge must be amended to adequately account for the introduction of non-redundant contracts. In particular, since all portfolio allocations and all asset prices are affected, traditional results regarding the mean-variance efficiency of the market portfolio become invalid.

Chapter 10 extends the previous analysis to the case of a stochastic production economy a la Cox, Ingersoll and Ross (1985a). The various CAPMs that then obtain differ from the ones derived in Chapter 9. In addition, the traditional cash-and-carry relationship which is grounded on the usual absence of arbitrage opportunity argument is shown not to hold in general. In situations where it does hold, it must be grounded on equilibrium considerations which are more demanding than the usual no-arbitrage condition.

Finally, to the production economy of Chapter 10, we add in Chapter 11 a monetary sector in which the money supply by the Central Bank is an exogenous stochastic process. Consequently, we obtain a genuine monetary economy affected by both real and monetary shocks. The stochastic process followed by the general price level (or Consumer Price Index, CPI) can thus be derived as an endogenous process. Since the general price level is obviously not a traded asset, a general equilibrium analysis, as opposed to the weaker no-arbitrage condition, is required to evaluate forward and futures contracts written on the CPI.

CHAPTER 9: EQUILIBRIUM ASSET PRICING IN AN ENDOWMENT ECONOMY WITH NON-REDUNDANT FORWARD OR FUTURES CONTRACTS[1]

9.1. INTRODUCTION

The aim of this chapter is to derive an equilibrium asset pricing model in an endowment (no production) economy where the initially incomplete financial market is completed, partially or totally, by introducing non-redundant futures or forward contracts. As a by-product, it will assess the validity of the various capital asset pricing models (CAPM) that are widely used in finance.

It is well known that this validity is closely related to the mean-variance efficiency of the market portfolio. An important distinction, however, has to be made between the standard one-period model of Sharpe (1964) and Lintner (1965) and multi-period models, such as the intertemporal models (ICAPM thereafter) of Merton (1973) and Breeden (1979, 1984). The static, one-factor, CAPM has long been the dominant paradigm in financial theory including portfolio allocation, corporate investment decisions and fund manager performance evaluation. Recent empirical research, however, reveals that, in contrast with a long tradition of results, expected asset returns are not explained by their sensitivity to the market return only but are influenced by other factors as well[2]. This suggests that dynamic or multi-factor models could perform better in practical applications[3].

In the static CAPM, mean-variance efficiency of the market portfolio is a necessary and sufficient condition for an exact linear relationship to exist between the expected return on an asset and its risk measured by its beta. Roll's (1977) critique that the market portfolio is not observable, hence not measurable, initiated a flood of research that mainly focused on developing econometric tests of the market portfolio mean-variance efficiency. Kandel and Stambaugh (1995) carefully distinguished the two theoretical implications of the model, i.e. market portfolio efficiency and the linear risk-return relationship. They showed that, if the market portfolio is not exactly efficient, "either (implication) can hold nearly perfectly while the other fails grossly"[4]. The main thrust of their result obviously holds in Merton-Breeden's more general multi-period framework. Here, no a priori assumption will be made as to whether the market portfolio is approximately efficient or not.

In the dynamic ICAPM, some economic state variables are assumed to drive the investment opportunity set. Investors' optimal demands for risky assets then include, in addition to the usual mean-variance components, hedging components. Those hedging terms protect investors against unfavorable shifts in their opportunity set brought about by random changes in the state variables. The market portfolio then need not be mean-variance efficient [Fama (1996)]. Yet, a special case arises when investors are endowed with time-additive logarithmic utility functions. Indeed, Bernoulli investors are myopic in the sense that they do not hedge against the random fluctuations of their opportunity set. In that case as in the static CAPM, the market portfolio *must* be mean–variance efficient for the (simplified) ICAPM to hold. In this chapter, we derive a new ICAPM in which, regardless of whether investors are myopic or not, mean-variance efficiency of the market portfolio is neither a necessary nor a sufficient condition for a linear risk-return relationship.

The economy we consider is more general than that of the usual ICAPM. The investment opportunity set is driven by an arbitrary number (K) of state variables, investors are endowed with general Von Neuman-Morgenstern utility functions, and they can trade non-redundant futures or forward contracts in addition to primitive risky assets and a riskless asset. Such contracts are written neither on financial assets nor on storable commodities but, for example, on non-storable goods such as electricity, or on non-tradable variables such as the weather, natural catastrophes, the Consumer Price Index, the Gross National Product or the like. The contracts are long lived, are not perfectly correlated with the state variables, and the financial market remains in general incomplete[5]. Financial markets and institutions have been under pressure in recent periods to design such contracts [see, for instance, Shiller (1993), Sumner (1997) or Athanasoulis, Shiller and van Wincoop (1999)]. A good example is the discussion surrounding forward contracts written on the Consumer Price Index which could be launched by various Central Banks as a substitute to inflation targeting [see Cowen (1997), Dowd (1994) and Sumner (1997)]. It has also been suggested that the forward price targeting system be expanded to other macro-economic aggregates, such as GNP and monetary aggregates [Sumner (1995)].

Theoretical work on financial innovation has mainly dealt with the welfare effects of adding non-redundant contracts to a set of primitive assets that forms an incomplete market. Surprisingly, however, little attention has been paid to the pricing of such non-redundant contracts at equilibrium. Cox, Ingersoll and Ross (1981) provided a comprehensive study of the pricing of *redundant* forward and futures contracts. Subsequent research focused on developing pricing models for futures contracts, particularly with stochastic interest rates, while redundant forward contracts continued to be priced according to the cash-and-carry formula. Richard and Sundaresan (1981) derived general equilibrium pricing of *non-redundant* forward contracts. They showed in particular that the simple cash-and-carry pricing equation that characterizes redundant forward contracts still holds for non-redundant ones in special cases. However, their work has three limitations. First, they did not provide a CAPM-like equation for the forwards. Second, the cash-and-carry relationship does not hold when the underlying asset pays stochastic dividend(s) and/or provides a stochastic convenience yield. To derive their results, they assumed these stochastic features away. Third, they considered only the case of forward contracts with linear pay-offs for which the cash-and-carry pricing relationship holds at equilibrium.

Similarly, although the issue of the endogenous determination of the optimal number of contracts to be created, and the nature of their underlying assets, has been investigated [6], little if any attention has been paid to the portfolio re-allocation effects brought about by the trading of such new instruments. Optimal portfolio allocations and thus market equilibrium yet are likely to be significantly affected, particularly in a dynamic environment.

The chapter is organized as follows. Section II describes the economy and presents the main assumptions and notations. Section III derives an investor's wealth dynamics in a possibly incomplete market and provides the optimal demands for all risky assets. Section IV establishes two mutual-fund separation theorems. Section V characterizes the market portfolio and derives the ICAPM that applies to cash assets on the one hand and to non-redundant futures or forward contracts on the other. The last section concludes.

9.2. THE ECONOMIC FRAMEWORK.

In this section, we describe the pure exchange economy under scrutiny. Particular attention is devoted to the investor's profit-and-loss process generated by trading forward contracts and to the investor's margin account resulting from trading futures.

9.2.1. The Economy

The general assumptions regarding the characteristics of the financial market and the strategies followed by individual agents are the same as throughout the book. Agents can trade on primitive risky assets and on forward or futures contracts, and can lend or borrow at an instantaneous riskless rate.

N primitive (cash) risky assets are traded in the economy. The N asset prices evolve through time according to the following system of SDEs:

$$dS(t) = I_S \mu_S(t, Y(t))dt + I_S \Sigma_S(t, Y(t))dZ(t) \tag{1}$$

where I_S is an $(N \times N)$ diagonal matrix valued function of S(t) whose i^{th} diagonal element is $S_i(t)$, the price of asset i (i = 1,…, N), $\mu_S(t, Y(t))$ is an $(N \times 1)$-dimensional vector whose i^{th} component is $\mu_{S_i}(t, Y(t))$, a bounded function of t and Y, $\Sigma_S(t, Y(t))$ is a $(N \times (N+K))$ matrix valued function whose i^{th} element is $\sigma_{S_i}(t, Y(t))$, a bounded $((K+N) \times 1)$ vector valued function of t and Y, Z(t) is an $((N+K) \times 1)$ - dimensional Wiener process in R^{N+K}, defined on the usual complete probability space $(\mathbf{\Omega}, \mathbf{F}, \mathbf{P})$, and Y(t) is a $(K \times 1)$ - dimensional vector of state variables.

The dynamics of the K state variables is determined by the following system of SDEs:

$$dY(t) = \mu_Y(t, Y(t))dt + \Sigma_Y(t, Y(t))dZ(t) \tag{2}$$

where $\mu_Y(t, Y(t))$ is a bounded $(K \times 1)$ vector valued function of t and Y and $\Sigma_Y(t, Y(t))$ is a bounded $(K \times (N + K))$ matrix valued function of t and Y.

There are H non-redundant derivatives, futures *or* forwards, also available for trade in this economy. These are "long-lived" assets, i.e. do not have instantaneous maturity. They are written on non-tradable but observable variables that are variously affected by the state variables, such as GNP and the like. The net supply of these instruments is zero.

When *futures* are traded, the maturity dates of all contracts are assumed, without loss of generality, to extend beyond the representative investor's horizon date, denoted by τ. When *forwards* are available for trade, all contracts are supposed, to simplify notation, to have the same maturity. The latter, without loss of generality, equals the investors' horizon (τ).

The prices of these derivatives are denoted by $F_j(t, T_j) \equiv F_j(t)$, with all $T_j > \tau$ for futures and all $T_j = \tau$ for forwards. The settlement price of the jth contract solves the following SDE:

$$dF_j(t) = F_j(t)\mu_{F_j}(t, Y(t))dt + F_j(t)\sigma_{F_j}(t, Y(t))' dZ(t)$$

where $\mu_{F_j}(t, Y(t))$ is a bounded function of t and Y, and $\sigma_{F_j}(t, Y(t))$ is a bounded $((N+K) \times 1)$ vector valued function of t and Y. In vector notation, the process of these prices then writes:

$$dF(t) = I_F\mu_F(t, Y(t))dt + I_F\Sigma_F(t, Y(t))dZ(t) \tag{3}$$

where I_F is a $(H \times H)$ diagonal matrix valued function of F(t) whose j^{th} diagonal element is $F_j(t)$, $\mu_F(t, Y(t))$ is a $(H \times 1)$-dimensional vector whose j^{th} component is $\mu_{F_j}(t, Y(t))$ and $\Sigma_F(t, Y(t))$ is a $(H \times (N+K))$ matrix valued function whose j^{th} element is $\sigma_{F_j}(t, Y(t))$.

We assume that $H \leq K$. Together with the primitive assets, the contracts form the basis of the financial market. Assets in the basis have linearly independent cash flows. Therefore, in the extreme case where H is equal to K, the financial market is complete. In general, however, the market is incomplete (H < K). Regardless of whether the market is complete or not, futures or forwards are not redundant, and the correlation of their prices with those of the cash assets is arbitrary.

The variance-covariance matrices $\Sigma_S\Sigma_S^{'}$ and $\Sigma_F\Sigma_F^{'}$ are assumed to be positive definite. The variance-covariance matrix of the percent changes in all asset prices[7], i.e. $\Sigma\Sigma^{'}$ where $\Sigma \equiv \begin{bmatrix} \Sigma_S \\ \Sigma_F \end{bmatrix}$, is also assumed to be positive definite.

Investors have access to an instantaneously riskless asset (money market account) yielding the rate r(t) at which they can lend or borrow. The diffusion process followed by r(t) is completely general and need not be made explicit. It determines endogenously the evolution of the whole yield curve. In particular, one of the N cash securities is a pure discount bond whose maturity (τ) coincides with that of all forward contracts when the latter exist[8].

Let P(t), short for P(t, τ), be its price at time t. Its dynamics then obeys the following SDE (for t positive and smaller than or equal to τ):

$$dP(t) = P(t)\mu_P(t, Y(t))dt + P(t)\sigma_P(t, Y(t))^{'} dZ(t) \tag{4}$$

where $\mu_P(t, Y(t))$ is a bounded function of t and Y, and $\sigma_P(t, Y(t))$ is a bounded ((N+K) $\times$ 1) vector valued function of t and Y.

9.2.2. The value process for the futures or forward position

We now turn to an investor's cumulative cash or gain process X(t) generated by her trading on futures or forward contracts.

When futures are traded, margins are lent or borrowed at the instantaneously riskless rate r(t). Assuming a continuous (rather than daily) marking to market, the value of the investor's margin account at time t writes:

$$X(t) = \int_0^t \exp\left[\int_s^t r(u)du\right]\Theta(s)' dF(s) \tag{5}$$

where $\Theta(t)$ is the $(H \times 1)$ vector of the number of futures held (not traded) at time t.

If forwards are traded, the total value at time t of the investor's forward position is equal to:

$$X(t) = P(t)\int_0^t \Theta(u)' dF(u) \tag{6}$$

where $\Theta(t)$ is the $(H \times 1)$ vector of the number of forward contracts held at time t. The RHS of (6) is the current value of the profits and losses incurred from the forward position. Since these cumulative (algebraic) gains are cashed-in or -out at the contract maturity date only, the discount factor P(t) is required.

9.3. OPTIMAL DEMANDS

The dynamics of an investor's wealth is derived first. We then derive this investor's optimal demands for all risky assets.

9.3.1. Wealth dynamics

To ease the analysis and the technical derivations without real loss of generality, the investor is assumed, as in Merton (1973), to finance his continuous consumption through continuous selling of a fraction of his portfolio.

a) Futures. Let α be the $(N \times 1)$ vector of the proportions of his wealth invested in the primitive asset and C his instantaneous consumption rate. Dropping for convenience the explicit time dependence of all processes, his budget constraint writes:

$$dW = W\alpha' I_S^{-1} dS + dX - Cdt$$

Changes in wealth are due to fluctuations in cash asset prices, to variations in the margin account or forward position value, and to consumption. Using equations (1), (3) and (5) and applying Itô's lemma yields the following wealth dynamics:

$$dW = \left[W\alpha'\mu_S + rX + \Theta' I_F\, \mu_F - C \right] dt + \left[W\alpha'\Sigma_S + \Theta' I_F\, \Sigma_F \right] dZ$$

Using the definition of wealth $W \equiv W\alpha' 1_N + X$ to eliminate X, the wealth dynamics can be rewritten as:

$$dW = \left[W\alpha'(\mu_S - r\mathbf{1}_N) + Wr + \Theta' I_F\, \mu_F - C \right] dt + \left[W\alpha'\Sigma_S + \Theta' I_F\, \Sigma_F \right] dZ$$

To further simplify the notations, we denote by θ the (H x 1) vector of the ratios of the futures nominal positions (not their values) to the investor's wealth, i.e. $\theta \equiv \frac{1}{W}\Theta' I_F$. Consequently, the investor's wealth dynamics is given by:

$$dW = \left[W\alpha'(\mu_S - r\mathbf{1}_N) + Wr + W\theta'\mu_F - C \right] dt + \left[W\alpha'\Sigma_S + W\theta'\Sigma_F \right] dZ \quad (7)$$

b) Forwards. In addition to the previous notation, let γ be the proportion of wealth invested in the riskless asset. This is required as X(t) here is not the position in the money market account but the value of the forward position. The budget constraint then writes:

$$dW = W\alpha' I_S^{-1} dS + dX + W\gamma r dt - C dt$$

Using equations (1), (3), (6) and (4) and applying Itô's lemma yields the following wealth dynamics:

$$dW = \begin{bmatrix} W\alpha'\mu_S + \left(P\int_0^t \Theta' dF \right)\mu_P + P\Theta' I_F \mu_F \\ + P\Theta' I_F \Sigma_F \sigma_P + W\gamma r - C \end{bmatrix} dt$$
$$+ \left[W\alpha'\Sigma_S + \left(P\int_0^t \Theta' dF \right)\sigma_P' + P\Theta' I_F \Sigma_F \right] dZ$$

Using the definition of wealth $W \equiv W\gamma + W\alpha' 1_N + P\int_0^{t} \Theta' dF$ to eliminate the term involving the cumbersome integral, the wealth dynamics rewrites, after some rearranging, as:

$$dW = \left[W\alpha'(\mu_S - \mu_P \mathbf{1}_N) + W\mu_P + P\Theta' I_F(\mu_F + \Sigma_F \sigma_P) + W\gamma(r - \mu_P) - C \right] dt$$
$$+ \left[W\alpha'(\Sigma_S - \mathbf{1}_N \sigma_P') + W(1-\gamma)\sigma_P' + P\Theta' I_\Gamma \Sigma_\Gamma \right] dZ$$

Using $\theta \equiv \frac{1}{W} P\Theta' I_F$ as above, the investor's wealth dynamics is finally given by:

$$dW = \left[W\alpha'(\mu_S - \mu_P \mathbf{1}_N) + W\mu_P + W\theta'(\mu_F + \Sigma_F \sigma_P) + W\gamma(r - \mu_P) - C \right] dt$$
$$+ \left[W\alpha'(\Sigma_S - \mathbf{1}_N \sigma_P') + W(1-\gamma)\sigma_P' + W\theta' \Sigma_F \right] dZ \qquad (7')$$

9.3.2. Optimal demand for risky assets

Assume an investor endowed with a Von Neuman-Morgenstern utility function who maximizes the expected utility of her consumption flow under a budget constraint, i.e. solves:

$$E_t\left[\int_t^\tau U(s, C(s))ds \right] \qquad (8)$$

subject to equation (7) or (7')
and to positive consumption **P**-a.s.

U is a well-behaved utility function. Let $J(t, W(t), Y(t))$ be her indirect utility of wealth function defined by $J(.) \equiv \text{Max } E_t\left[\int_t^\tau U(s, C(s))ds \right]$. J(.) is assumed to be an increasing and strictly concave function of W[9]. The obvious notation J_i (respectively, J_{ii}) stands for the first (respectively, second) partial derivative of J(.) with respect to its argument i. Since the financial market may remain incomplete, we will use the traditional stochastic dynamic programming approach. Using the standard technique, the solution to program (8) leads to the following

Proposition 1:

a) Under the present set of assumptions, and when futures are traded, an investor's optimal demand for risky assets is expressed as:

$$\begin{pmatrix}\hat{\alpha}\\ \hat{\theta}\end{pmatrix}=(\Sigma\Sigma')^{-1}\begin{pmatrix}\mu_S-r\mathbf{1}_N\\ \mu_F\end{pmatrix}\left(-\frac{J_W}{WJ_{WW}}\right)+(\Sigma\Sigma')^{-1}\Sigma\Sigma_Y'\left(-\frac{J_{WY}}{WJ_{WW}}\right) \quad (9)$$

b) If forwards are traded, the optimal demand for risky assets is given by:

$$\begin{pmatrix}\hat{\alpha}\\ \hat{\theta}\end{pmatrix}=(\Sigma\Sigma')^{-1}\begin{pmatrix}\mu_S-\mathbf{1}_N r\\ \mu_F+\Sigma_F\sigma_P\end{pmatrix}\left(-\frac{J_W}{WJ_{WW}}\right)$$
$$+(\Sigma\Sigma')^{-1}\Sigma\Sigma_Y'\left(-\frac{J_{WY}}{WJ_{WW}}\right)-(\Sigma\Sigma')^{-1}\Sigma\sigma_P\frac{X}{W} \quad (10)$$

Proofs

a) Let L(t) be the differential generator of J(.) defined under equation (8). Letting $\psi \equiv LJ + U$, the Hamilton-Jacobi-Bellman equation writes:

Max $\psi(C, \alpha, \theta)$ =

$$\text{Max}\left[U+J_W\mu_W+J_Y\mu_Y+\frac{1}{2}J_{WW}\sigma_W'\sigma_W+\frac{1}{2}J_{YY}\Sigma_Y\Sigma_Y'+J_{WY}\Sigma_Y\sigma_W\right]=0$$

where μ_W is the drift of the wealth process given by equation (7).

The necessary and sufficient conditions for optimality are derived from this equation by computing its first derivatives with respect to the control variables C, α and θ:

$$\psi_C=U_C-J_W\leq 0$$

$$\hat{C}\psi_C=0$$

$$\psi_\alpha = (\mu_S - r\mathbf{1}_N)WJ_W + \Sigma_S\Sigma_Y{}'WJ_{WY} + \left[\Sigma_S\Sigma_S{}'\hat{\alpha} + \Sigma_S\Sigma_F{}'\hat{\theta}\right]W^2J_{WW} = 0 \quad (11)$$

$$\psi_\theta = \mu_F WJ_W + \Sigma_F\Sigma_Y{}'WJ_{WY} + \left[\Sigma_F\Sigma_S{}'\hat{\alpha} + \Sigma_F\Sigma_F{}'\hat{\theta}\right]W^2J_{WW} = 0 \quad (12)$$

The hat ^ above a variable denotes an optimal value. The first two (Kuhn and Tucker) equations concern consumption and follow from the non-negativity constraint imposed on the optimal consumption path. Combining equations (11) and (12) leads to equation (9).

b) The necessary and sufficient conditions for optimality that are derived from the Hamilton-Jacobi-Bellman equation using (7') in lieu of (7) write as follows:

$$\psi_C = U_C - J_W \le 0$$

$$\hat{C}\psi_C = 0$$

$$\begin{aligned}\psi_\alpha = {} & (\mu_S - \mathbf{1}_N\mu_P)WJ_W + (\Sigma_S - \mathbf{1}_N\sigma_P{}')\Sigma_Y{}'WJ_{WY} + \\ & \begin{bmatrix}(\Sigma_S - \mathbf{1}_N\sigma_P{}')(\Sigma_S - \mathbf{1}_N\sigma_P{}')'\hat{\alpha} + (1-\hat{\gamma})(\Sigma_S - \mathbf{1}_N\sigma_P{}')\sigma_P \\ + (\Sigma_S - \mathbf{1}_N\sigma_P{}')\Sigma_F{}'\hat{\theta}\end{bmatrix} W^2J_{WW} = 0\end{aligned} \quad (13)$$

$$\begin{aligned}\psi_\theta = {} & (\mu_F + \Sigma_F\sigma_P)WJ_W + \Sigma_F\Sigma_Y{}'WJ_{WY} \\ & + \begin{bmatrix}\Sigma_F(\Sigma_S - \mathbf{1}_N\sigma_P{}')'\hat{\alpha} + (1-\hat{\gamma}) \\ \Sigma_F\sigma_P + \Sigma_F\Sigma_F{}'\hat{\theta}\end{bmatrix} W^2J_{WW} = 0\end{aligned} \quad (14)$$

$$\begin{aligned}\psi_\gamma = {} & (r - \mu_P)WJ_W - \sigma_P{}'\Sigma_Y{}'WJ_{WY} \\ & - \begin{bmatrix}\hat{\alpha}'(\Sigma_S - \mathbf{1}_N\sigma_P{}')\sigma_P + (1-\hat{\gamma})\sigma_P{}'\sigma_P \\ + \hat{\theta}'\Sigma_F\sigma_P\end{bmatrix} W^2J_{WW} = 0\end{aligned} \quad (15)$$

Combining the last three equations to eliminate the proportion $\hat{\gamma}$ of wealth held in the riskless asset leads to result (10).

9.3.3 Discussion

- We start with the simpler case involving *futures*, expression (9). The demand for (both primitive and derivative) risky assets retains its two familiar components. The first term on the RHS of (9) is the mean-variance speculative component and the second term is the dynamic Merton-Breeden hedging component.

Before commenting on the economic interpretation of this result, it is instructive first to compare it with a previous result due to Breeden (1984) in the case of a complete market where each and every state variable is perfectly correlated with each and every futures contract of instantaneous maturity. Equation (9) resembles that in Breeden, but is actually different in two essential ways.

To see this, let us write, using our notation, Breeden's demand for risky assets for an individual k in absence of futures:

$$\hat{\alpha}W^k = (\Sigma\Sigma')^{-1}(\mu_S - r\mathbf{1}_N)\left(-\frac{J_W^k}{WJ_{WW}^k}\right) + (\Sigma\Sigma')^{-1}\Sigma\Sigma_Y'\left(-\frac{J_{WY}^k}{WJ_{WW}^k}\right)$$

Aggregating across investors then leads to, again for an individual k:

$$\hat{\alpha}W^k = \frac{\dfrac{J_W^k}{WJ_{WW}^k}}{\sum_k \dfrac{J_W^k}{WJ_{WW}^k}}\hat{\alpha}_M M + (\Sigma\Sigma')^{-1}\Sigma\Sigma_Y'\left(\frac{J_{WY}^k}{WJ_{WW}^k} - \frac{\dfrac{J_W^k}{WJ_{WW}^k}}{\sum_k \dfrac{J_W^k}{WJ_{WW}^k}}\sum_k \frac{J_{WY}^k}{WJ_{WW}^k}\right)$$

where M stands for the value of the market portfolio. The first part is the market portfolio and the second is the demand for hedging

Then, introducing instantaneous futures, he obtains:

$$\hat{\alpha} = \frac{\dfrac{J^k_W}{WJ^k_{WW}} M}{\displaystyle\sum_k \frac{J^k_W}{WJ^k_{WW}}} \hat{\alpha}_M$$

$$\hat{\theta} = \frac{J^k_{WY}}{WJ^k_{WW}} - \frac{\dfrac{J^k_W}{WJ^k_{WW}}}{\displaystyle\sum_k \frac{J^k_W}{WJ^k_{WW}}} \sum_k \frac{J^k_{WY}}{WJ^k_{WW}} \qquad (9')$$

The second equation expresses the demand for instantaneous futures. Note that the futures being perfectly correlated to the state variables, the usual covariance/variance ratio has vanished. Breeden thus obtains a (K+2) separation theorem: the riskless asset, the market portfolio and K instantaneous futures. It is essential to notice that the speculative demand for cash assets has remained unchanged after the introduction of futures.

Our results are different. First, both the demands for cash assets ($\hat{\alpha}$) and for futures ($\hat{\theta}$) involve a speculative term and a hedging term, while in Breeden's economy the demand for futures is governed by hedging motives only, and the demand for cash assets by speculative motives only. Second, both the speculative and hedging components depend on the full [(N+H) × (N+H)] covariance matrix $\Sigma\Sigma'$ of all risky assets. In contrast, Breeden's speculative term depends on the [N × N] covariance matrix $\Sigma_S\Sigma_S'$ of primitive assets only, and the hedging term depends on the [N x K] matrix $\Sigma_S\Sigma_Y'$ of covariances of cash assets with the state variables only.

The reason for this difference is that, in Breeden's framework, futures of *instantaneous* maturities complete the market, and each and every contract is *perfectly* correlated with each and every state variable. The investor thus is able to reach her first-best optimum. Her strategy comprises a perfect hedge against unfavorable changes in each state variable and this perfect hedge is trivially obtained by trading futures only. In contrast, in our more general (in this respect) setting, futures contracts have *finite*, not infinitesimal, maturities, and their variance-covariance matrix is completely arbitrary. In particular, no futures contract is perfectly correlated with a particular state variable, except by chance. This is true even though a given futures contract may happen to be more positively correlated with a particular state variable than any cash asset, a likely assumption that would justify its adoption by market participants. Furthermore, since the market is incomplete, perfect hedges cannot be achieved and the investor's first-best optimum cannot be reached. Therefore, although the excess return terms present in the speculative component of (9), $(\mu_S - r\mathbf{1}_N)$ and μ_F respectively, do differ, the optimal demands for primitive and derivative instruments are *formally* identical and depend in the same way on the whole structure of correlations. Note that this is true whether the market is incomplete (H < K) or just complete (H = K).

- The economic interpretation of the second term on the RHS of equation (9) is straightforward. It is composed of information-based elements whose purpose is, as usual, to hedge wealth against unfavorable changes in the K economic state variables. The rational investor constructs his portfolio comprising all available risky assets so as to protect himself against decreases in wealth due to shifts in the investment opportunity set brought about by these changes. This component, present in both demands for primitive and derivative assets, is preference-dependent as J_{WY} ($\equiv \partial J_W/\partial Y$) is the cross-partial derivative that represents the effect of the state variable Y on the investor's wealth marginal value. The terms $-J_{WY}/WJ_{WW}$ reflect that dependence, each one of them being interpreted as a coefficient of relative risk tolerance with respect to the relevant state variable along the wealth's optimal path. It is recalled from previous chapters that if utility were logarithmic, the Bernoulli investor would be myopic to changes in his investment opportunity set (all cross partial derivatives J_{WY} vanish) so that this Merton-Breeden hedge component would disappear.

- The first term on the RHS of (9) is the speculative component, the product of a mean-variance term by the investor's relative risk tolerance coefficient $\left(-\dfrac{J_W}{WJ_{WW}}\right)$. It can be interpreted as the demand for risky assets expressed by a logarithmic investor. It is "speculative" in the sense that an individual exhibiting zero risk tolerance would set it equal to zero. To gain further insight and make comparisons with known results, let us rewrite this component as follows (neglecting the risk tolerance coefficient, or setting it to 1 if the investor has log utility):

$$\left(\Sigma\Sigma^{'}\right)^{-1}\begin{pmatrix}\mu_S - r\mathbf{1}_N \\ \mu_F\end{pmatrix} = \begin{bmatrix} A & -\left(\Sigma_S\Sigma_S^{'}\right)^{-1}\Sigma_S\Sigma_F^{'}B \\ -\left(\Sigma_F\Sigma_F^{'}\right)^{-1}\Sigma_F\Sigma_S^{'}A & B \end{bmatrix}\begin{bmatrix}\lambda_S \\ \lambda_F\end{bmatrix} \quad (16)$$

where:

$$\lambda_S \equiv \left(\Sigma_S\Sigma_S^{'}\right)^{-1}\left(\mu_S - \mathbf{1}_N r\right)$$

$$\lambda_F = \left(\Sigma_F\Sigma_F^{'}\right)^{-1}\mu_F$$

and:

$$A = \left[\Sigma_S\Sigma_S^{'} - \Sigma_S\Sigma_F^{'}\left(\Sigma_F\Sigma_F^{'}\right)^{-1}\Sigma_F\Sigma_S^{'}\right]^{-1}\left(\Sigma_S\Sigma_S^{'}\right)$$
$$B = \left[\Sigma_F\Sigma_F^{'} - \Sigma_F\Sigma_S^{'}\left(\Sigma_S\Sigma_S^{'}\right)^{-1}\Sigma_S\Sigma_F^{'}\right]^{-1}\left(\Sigma_F\Sigma_F^{'}\right)$$

Two basic sets of market prices of risk, λ_S and λ_F, are identified. The first one is traditional and concerns cash assets only, while the second involves futures contracts only. Note that, in contrast with λ_S, the numerator of λ_F is not expressed in excess return form (the riskless rate r is absent). This is because there is no actual investment involved with a futures contract, i.e. the cost-of-carry is nil (note that this is the case too when forwards are traded).

Given equation (16), the speculative part of equation (9) rewrites as:

$$\begin{pmatrix}\hat{\alpha}_{Spec} \\ \hat{\theta}_{Spec}\end{pmatrix} \equiv \left(-\frac{J_W}{WJ_{WW}}\right)\begin{bmatrix} A\lambda_S - \left(\Sigma_S\Sigma_S^{'}\right)^{-1}\Sigma_S\Sigma_F^{'}B\lambda_F \\ B\lambda_F - \left(\Sigma_F\Sigma_F^{'}\right)^{-1}\Sigma_F\Sigma_S^{'}A\lambda_S \end{bmatrix} \quad (17)$$

Now consider the two portfolios $A\lambda_S$ and $B\lambda_F$. Assume for a while that the cash asset prices and the futures prices are not correlated $[\Sigma_S\Sigma_F^{'} = \mathbf{0}_{N\times H}]$. Then, A and B are mere identity matrices and equation (14) simplifies to:

$$\begin{pmatrix} \hat{\alpha}_{Spec} \\ \hat{\theta}_{Spec} \end{pmatrix} = \left(-\frac{J_W}{WJ_{WW}} \right) \begin{bmatrix} \lambda_S \\ \lambda_F \end{bmatrix}$$

The speculative part of the investor's portfolio then consists of two basic, *mean-variance efficient*, and *well separated,* portfolios: the first one is the traditional efficient portfolio containing primitive assets only and the second is the efficient portfolio containing futures contracts only. Note however that this economy is neither Merton's (1973) nor Breeden's (1984), in which the speculative part of the investor's portfolio consists of a mean-variance efficient portfolio of cash assets only. The difference is due to the fact that futures contracts in the present setting are not redundant (spanning property).

More generally, however, in presence of (imperfect) correlation between cash assets and futures contracts [$\Sigma_S \Sigma_F^{'} \neq \mathbf{0}_{N \times H}$], the speculative part of the demands for risky assets is given by equation (17) where A and B are no longer identity matrices. It immediately follows that *neither* $A\lambda_S$ *nor* $B\lambda_F$ are mean-variance efficient. Furthermore, in the demand for cash assets, an extra term is subtracted from $A\lambda_S$ that depends on $B\lambda_F$ and thus accounts for cross-hedging (with futures) effects. Similarly, in the demand for futures, an extra term is subtracted from $B\lambda_F$ that depends on $A\lambda_S$ and accounts for cross hedging with the cash assets. Consequently, the two portfolios α_{spec} and θ_{spec} are severely perturbed and loose their separation property between cash assets only on the one hand and futures only on the other. They both depend on the whole variance-covariance matrix of cash and derivative asset returns and on the expected excess returns on all these assets. Even more crucially, it turns out that both are mean-variance *inefficient.*

- Turning now to the case where *forward* contracts are traded, note that the first two terms of the RHS of solution (10) have exactly the same interpretation as their counterpart in (9). There is but one difference, the presence of the term $\Sigma_F \sigma_P$ that is added to μ_F in the part of the speculative component due to forwards, because of an extra risk fully discussed below. Also note that, in spite of the presence of X in the last term of the RHS of equation (10), the latter is a closed form expression. This is because X(t) depends on the holdings $\hat{\alpha}(t)$ and $\hat{\theta}(t)$ of time t^{-}, and is therefore known at date t when the new holdings are chosen. For instance, at date t = 0, $\hat{\alpha}(0)$ and $\hat{\theta}(0)$ are selected with X(0) equal to zero.

- The demand for risky assets (10) thus contains an extra element vis-à-vis the solution (9) involving futures. It is a hedging component and results specifically from trading in forward contracts. It is equal to the fraction of wealth X/W corresponding to the forward position value times a covariance/variance ratio. This term however, unlike the second term on the RHS of (10), does not qualify as a Merton-Breeden component for two reasons. First, it is not a hedge against the future level of any state variable. Second, it does not depend on the utility parameter ($-J_{WY}/J_{WW}$). However, it is not preference free since both optimal X and W do depend on the investor's utility. Rather, this second hedging component is due to the forward position not being marked-to-market, hence inducing an interest rate risk on the cumulative gains/losses that have accrued so far.

As in several previous chapters, the source of this additional risk is to be found in the forward trading strategy itself. Because she anticipates that one period ahead the current value of her forward position will have changed, the investor will optimally hedge against the interest rate risk brought about by her strategy. Thus, this hedging component is not due to the presence of an exogenous source of non-diversifiable risk but results from the risk brought about by the particular nature of the strategy involving forward contracts. In addition, as intuition suggests, it depends on the fraction of wealth X/W that has been generated by the forward strategy.

- It must be emphasized that this component being independent of J_{WY} ($\equiv \partial J_W/\partial Y$), it will appear in the optimal strategy of even a myopic Bernoulli investor, contrary to the first hedging component. Incidentally, it also appears in a pure hedger's optimal strategy, as was shown in chapter 3. This result is reminiscent of the strategy of a logarithmic investor endowed with a non-traded position who maximizes his expected utility of wealth by adding to the usual speculative component two hedging terms, one preference dependent and one preference free, as demonstrated in chapter 4. In the same way, our investor includes a hedging component in his strategy because forward trading creates a risky position in the maturity τ discount bond.

9.4. MUTUAL-FUND SEPARATION THEOREMS

The above framework involving non-redundant futures or forward contracts generates interesting mutual-fund separation theorems. Merton's (1973) traditional separation result states that, at equilibrium, all investors divide their investment between the riskless asset, the market portfolio and the K funds that are most correlated with the K state variables. Therefore, a (K + 2) fund separation obtains. Here, the case of futures must be distinguished from that of forwards since two different separation theorems obtain.

9.4.1. Futures.

Under the present set of assumptions, the introduction of non-redundant futures contracts leads to the following

__**Proposition 2 (futures)**__:

Investors are indifferent to the reduction of their investment opportunity set from the riskless asset, N primitive assets and H futures contracts to (K+2) mutual funds: the riskless asset, a speculative portfolio providing the optimal risk-return trade-off, and K funds hedging against random shifts in the K state variables. The optimal demand for risky assets can be expressed as:

$$\begin{pmatrix} \hat{\alpha} \\ \hat{\theta} \end{pmatrix} = \omega_0 \lambda_0 + \sum_{j=1}^{K} \omega_j \lambda_j + \omega_{K+1} \lambda_{K+1} \tag{18}$$

with:

$$\lambda_0 = \left(\left((\Sigma\Sigma')^{-1} \begin{pmatrix} \mu_S - \mathbf{1}_N r \\ \mu_F \end{pmatrix} \right)' \begin{pmatrix} \mathbf{1}_N \\ \mathbf{0}_H \end{pmatrix} \right)^{-1} (\Sigma\Sigma')^{-1} \begin{pmatrix} \mu_S - \mathbf{1}_N r \\ \mu_F \end{pmatrix}$$

$$\lambda_j = \left(\left((\Sigma\Sigma')^{-1} \Sigma\Sigma_Y' \right)_j' \begin{pmatrix} \mathbf{1}_N \\ \mathbf{0}_H \end{pmatrix} \right)^{-1} \left((\Sigma\Sigma')^{-1} \Sigma\Sigma_Y' \right)_j \qquad j = 1,.., K$$

where $\left((\Sigma\Sigma')^{-1}\Sigma\Sigma_Y'\right)_j$ *is the* j^{th} $(N+H \times 1)$ *column vector of the matrix* $(\Sigma\Sigma')^{-1}\Sigma\Sigma_Y'$*, and the* ω*'s are weights defined by:*

$$\omega_0 = \left((\Sigma\Sigma')^{-1} \begin{pmatrix} \mu_S - \mathbf{1}_N r \\ \mu_F \end{pmatrix} \right)' \begin{pmatrix} \mathbf{1}_N \\ \mathbf{0}_H \end{pmatrix} \left(-\frac{J_W}{WJ_{WW}} \right)$$

$$\omega_j = \left((\Sigma\Sigma')^{-1}\Sigma\Sigma_Y'\right)_j' \begin{pmatrix} \mathbf{1}_N \\ \mathbf{0}_H \end{pmatrix} \left(-\frac{J_{WY_j}}{J_{WW}} \right)$$

Merton's theorem is recovered. The first fund is of course the riskless asset. The next K funds are the traditional Merton-Breeden hedging funds (λ_j, j = 1,…, K) from the second term on the RHS of equation (18). These portfolios hedge against the fluctuations in the opportunity set brought about by the state variables. Fund (K+2) is a portfolio of risky cash assets and futures contracts constructed as usual to provide optimal diversification. It stems from the first term on the RHS of equation (9), the traditional speculative component of the optimal dynamic strategy of an intertemporal expected utility maximizer. However, while Merton's corresponding fund is a mean-variance efficient fund of cash assets, our λ_0 is the growth optimum portfolio generated by risky cash assets and futures contracts.

In order to further characterize this speculative portfolio, consider the case of a Bernoulli investor. Using the fact that J_{WY} then is equal to zero and the relative risk tolerance coefficient is equal to one, the demand for risky assets (9) simplifies to

$$\begin{pmatrix} \hat{\alpha}_{spec} \\ \hat{\theta}_{spec} \end{pmatrix} = \begin{bmatrix} A & -(\Sigma_S\Sigma_S')^{-1}\Sigma_S\Sigma_F' B \\ -(\Sigma_F\Sigma_F')^{-1}\Sigma_F\Sigma_S' A & B \end{bmatrix} \begin{bmatrix} \lambda_S \\ \lambda_F \end{bmatrix} \tag{19}$$

Summing over all investors yields:

$$\begin{pmatrix} \alpha_M \\ \mathbf{0}_H \end{pmatrix} = \begin{bmatrix} A & -(\Sigma_S\Sigma_S')^{-1}\Sigma_S\Sigma_F' B \\ -(\Sigma_F\Sigma_F')^{-1}\Sigma_F\Sigma_S' A & B \end{bmatrix} \begin{bmatrix} \lambda_S \\ \lambda_F \end{bmatrix} \tag{20}$$

Eliminating B by using the second row of (20), the first row becomes:

$$\alpha_M = \left(I_N - \left(\Sigma_S \Sigma_S^{'}\right)^{-1} \Sigma_S \Sigma_F^{'} \left(\Sigma_F \Sigma_F^{'}\right)^{-1} \Sigma_F \Sigma_S^{'}\right) A \lambda_S \tag{21}$$

where α_M is the vector of weights in the market portfolio.

Equation (21) clearly implies that the *market portfolio* differs from the usual one in a crucial way: it is not proportional to a mean-variance efficient portfolio of cash assets. It immediately follows that it need not be mean-variance efficient. Thus, the first, and major, difference between our more general separation result and Merton's is that not only does the speculative component contain futures contracts, but also the portfolio of risky cash assets that is part of this component is not necessarily mean-variance efficient within the set of portfolios comprising cash assets only. In Merton's framework, the speculative component is homothetic to the portfolio tangent to the instantaneous efficient frontier of risky cash assets (more on this below when forwards are considered). Therefore, the market portfolio in an economy populated by myopic investors is mean-variance efficient at equilibrium. When futures contracts are included in the investment opportunity set, the market portfolio is mean-variance efficient only when cash asset prices and futures prices are not correlated. Now, recall that this result was derived for Bernoulli investors. When individuals are not myopic and hedge against random shifts in the state variables, Fama (1996) has shown that the market portfolio need not be efficient. Equation (21) thus extends that result to even logarithmic investors who do not hedge against state variables. Therefore, in the present economy, and in contrast with standard analysis without non-redundant futures, the non-necessarily efficient nature of the market portfolio is *not* due to Merton-Breeden hedging activity. This result may have important implications when testing the ICAPM, because the linear relationship between expected return and beta will be shown (in section V) to hold for primitive assets despite the (possible) inefficiency of the market portfolio.

The second difference with Merton is that the speculative portfolio providing the optimal risk-return trade-off and the K funds hedging against random shifts in the K state variables contain all risky cash assets *and* all futures contracts.

Restating now the optimal demand for risky assets as

$$\begin{pmatrix} \hat{\alpha} \\ \hat{\theta} \end{pmatrix} = \begin{bmatrix} I_N & 0 \\ -\left(\Sigma_F \Sigma_F'\right)^{-1} \Sigma_F \Sigma_S' & B - \left(\Sigma_F \Sigma_F'\right)^{-1} \Sigma_F \Sigma_S' \left(\Sigma_S \Sigma_S'\right)^{-1} \Sigma_S \Sigma_F' B \end{bmatrix} \begin{bmatrix} \alpha_M \\ \lambda_F \end{bmatrix} \quad (22)$$

recovers the usual finding that optimal investment in the risky cash assets is proportional to the market portfolio. However, in this framework, it is not necessarily mean-variance efficient. Furthermore, the portfolio of futures contracts in which part of the wealth is invested is not necessarily mean-variance efficient either.

9.4.2. Forwards.

Under the present set of assumptions, the introduction of non-redundant forward contracts leads to the following

Proposition 3 (forwards):

Investors are indifferent to the reduction of their investment opportunity set from the riskless asset, N primitive assets and H forward contracts to (K+3) mutual funds: the riskless asset, a speculative portfolio providing the optimal risk-return trade-off, K funds hedging against random shifts in the state variables, and a hedge portfolio against the interest rate risk generated by the forward position. All these portfolios comprise both risky cash assets and forward contracts. The optimal demand for risky assets is given by:

$$\begin{pmatrix} \hat{\alpha} \\ \hat{\theta} \end{pmatrix} = \omega_0 \lambda_0 + \sum_{j=1}^{K} \omega_j \lambda_j + \omega_{K+1} \lambda_{K+1} \quad (23)$$

with:

$$\lambda_0 = \left(\left((\Sigma\Sigma')^{-1} \begin{pmatrix} \mu_S - \mathbf{1}_N r \\ \mu_F + \Sigma_F \sigma_P \end{pmatrix} \right)' \begin{pmatrix} \mathbf{1}_N \\ \mathbf{0}_H \end{pmatrix} \right)^{-1} (\Sigma\Sigma')^{-1} \begin{pmatrix} \mu_S - \mathbf{1}_N r \\ \mu_F + \Sigma_F \sigma_P \end{pmatrix}$$

$$\lambda_j = \left(\left((\Sigma\Sigma')^{-1} \Sigma\Sigma_Y' \right)_j' \begin{pmatrix} \mathbf{1}_N \\ \mathbf{0}_H \end{pmatrix} \right)^{-1} \left((\Sigma\Sigma')^{-1} \Sigma\Sigma_Y' \right)_j \qquad j = 1,.., K$$

$$\lambda_{K+1} = \left(\left((\Sigma\Sigma')^{-1} \Sigma\sigma_P \right)' \begin{pmatrix} \mathbf{1}_N \\ \mathbf{0}_H \end{pmatrix} \right)^{-1} (\Sigma\Sigma')^{-1} \Sigma\sigma_P$$

where $\left((\Sigma\Sigma')^{-1} \Sigma\Sigma_Y' \right)_j$ *is the* j^{th} *(N+H × 1) column vector of the matrix* $(\Sigma\Sigma')^{-1} \Sigma\Sigma_Y'$, *and the ω's are weights defined by:*

$$\omega_0 = \left((\Sigma\Sigma')^{-1} \begin{pmatrix} \mu_S - \mathbf{1}_N r \\ \mu_F + \Sigma_F \sigma_P \end{pmatrix} \right)' \begin{pmatrix} \mathbf{1}_N \\ \mathbf{0}_H \end{pmatrix} \left(-\frac{J_W}{W J_{WW}} \right)$$

$$\omega_j = \left((\Sigma\Sigma')^{-1} \Sigma\Sigma_Y' \right)_j' \begin{pmatrix} \mathbf{1}_N \\ \mathbf{0}_H \end{pmatrix} \left(-\frac{J_{WY_j}}{J_{WW}} \right)$$

$$\omega_{K+1} = -\left((\Sigma\Sigma')^{-1} \Sigma\sigma_P \right)' \begin{pmatrix} \mathbf{1}_N \\ \mathbf{0}_H \end{pmatrix} \frac{X}{W}$$

The first major difference with Merton's separation theorem is that, as in the case of futures, the speculative term contains forward contracts and the cash asset component of this portfolio is not necessarily efficient. The second difference with Merton's result lies in the presence of an extra fund, number (K+3), given by the third term on the RHS of equation (10). As already explained, this fund λ_{K+1} allows investors to hedge against the interest rate risk generated by their forward strategies. It contains both forward contracts and primitive assets. Since this component is independent of J_{WY} ($\equiv \partial J_W/\partial Y$), it will be present even in a Bernoulli investor's portfolio, unlike the K Merton-Breeden hedging portfolios. However, for the same reason, it will *not* lead to any additional risk premium in equilibrium neither for forward contracts nor for cash assets, since it cancels out by aggregation. Consequently, the reason why the traditional ICAPM will not hold in equilibrium for forward contracts [see Section V] is *not* due to the presence of this extra fund.

Comparing expressions (18) and (23) thus highlights an important difference between forward and futures contracts. Since financial markets are not complete in general, the additional interest rate risk that is inherent in forward contracts cannot be perfectly hedged. Hence the marking-to-market mechanism that characterizes futures and allows for the complete elimination of this risk is valuable to risk-averse agents. Under stochastic interest rates and incomplete markets, not only the pricing of forwards and futures is different but the optimal allocation of risk and, therefore, the social welfare also differ since perfect hedging of interest rate risk cannot be achieved when only forward contracts are traded.

As in the case of futures, the speculative component of equation (10) can be split in two distinct funds, one comprising cash assets only, and the other forward contracts only. Fully characterizing these portfolios will allow a better understanding of the changes in the standard optimal dynamic strategy brought about by the introduction of forward contracts.

The speculative component in equation (10) can be rewritten as follows, dropping the risk aversion coefficient (or setting it to one, if utility is logarithmic):

$$\left(\Sigma\Sigma'\right)^{-1}\begin{pmatrix}\mu_S - \mathbf{1}_N r\\ \mu_F + \Sigma_F\sigma_P\end{pmatrix} = \begin{bmatrix} A\lambda_S - \left(\Sigma_S\Sigma_S'\right)^{-1}\Sigma_S\Sigma_F{}'B\lambda_F \\ B\lambda_F - \left(\Sigma_F\Sigma_F'\right)^{-1}\Sigma_F\Sigma_S{}'A\lambda_S \end{bmatrix} \tag{24}$$

where:

$$\lambda_S \equiv \left(\Sigma_S\Sigma_S'\right)^{-1}\left(\mu_S - \mathbf{1}_N r\right) \tag{25}$$

$$\lambda_F \equiv \left(\Sigma_F\Sigma_F'\right)^{-1}\left(\mu_F + \Sigma_F\sigma_P\right) \tag{26}$$

and:

$$A = \left[\Sigma_S\Sigma_S' - \Sigma_S\Sigma_F'\left(\Sigma_F\Sigma_F'\right)^{-1}\Sigma_F\Sigma_S'\right]^{-1}\left(\Sigma_S\Sigma_S'\right)$$
$$B = \left[\Sigma_F\Sigma_F' - \Sigma_F\Sigma_S'\left(\Sigma_S\Sigma_S'\right)^{-1}\Sigma_S\Sigma_F'\right]^{-1}\left(\Sigma_F\Sigma_F'\right)$$

Consider the vectors λ_S and λ_F. The former is traditional and concerns risky cash assets *only*. The latter involves forward contracts *only*. The vector λ_S is nothing but the tangency portfolio[10] that is mean-variance efficient. Now it is clear that any portfolio other than the tangency portfolio times some multiple will result in a mean-variance inefficient portfolio of cash assets being held by individuals for the speculative component. Sheer inspection of the matrix denoted by A shows that investors will hold the tangency portfolio only if changes in the forward prices are uncorrelated with cash asset returns, making A an identity matrix. In general, however, A will not be an identity matrix. Therefore, exactly as with futures, although one can separate the speculative component fund into two funds, one with cash assets and the other with forward contracts, only in the case where primitive and derivative assets are uncorrelated does one obtain the tangency portfolio for this speculative component. In general, the latter will be mean-variance inefficient.

Incidentally, one could ask whether the (K+1) portfolios hedging against the state variables and interest rate risk can, like the speculative portfolio, each be split into a portfolio of cash assets and one of forward contracts. This decomposition is in fact irrelevant for the hedging portfolios, since investors will construct, from both the cash and forward assets, the (unique) portfolio that is best correlated with each and every source of uncertainty to be hedged. It may so happen that, for some given source of risk, the best hedging portfolio contains only some cash assets, only some forwards or a combination of some, not all, of them.

To ease the comparison with futures (equations (19)-(21) above), prepare the ground for the derivation of the ICAPM, and fully characterize the market portfolio, consider the behavior of logarithmic investors. The extension to other types of utility functions is straightforward. Using the fact that J_{WY} then is equal to zero and the relative risk tolerance coefficient is equal to one, the demand for risky assets (10) simplifies to:

$$\begin{pmatrix} \hat{\alpha}_{spec} \\ \hat{\theta}_{spec} \end{pmatrix} = \begin{bmatrix} A & -\left(\Sigma_S \Sigma_S'\right)^{-1} \Sigma_S \Sigma_F' B \\ -\left(\Sigma_F \Sigma_F'\right)^{-1} \Sigma_F \Sigma_S' A & B \end{bmatrix} \begin{bmatrix} \lambda_S \\ \lambda_F \end{bmatrix} - \left(\Sigma \Sigma'\right)^{-1} \Sigma \sigma_P \frac{X}{W} \quad (27)$$

Since the aggregate value of X is zero, summing over all investors yields:

$$\begin{pmatrix} \alpha_M \\ \mathbf{0}_H \end{pmatrix} = \Lambda \begin{bmatrix} A & -\left(\Sigma_S \Sigma_S{'}\right)^{-1} \Sigma_S \Sigma_F{'} B \\ -\left(\Sigma_F \Sigma_F{'}\right)^{-1} \Sigma_F \Sigma_S{'} A & B \end{bmatrix} \begin{bmatrix} \lambda_S \\ \lambda_F \end{bmatrix} \tag{28}$$

where α_M is the vector of weights in the market portfolio.

Eliminating B by using the second row of (28), the first row becomes:

$$\alpha_M = \Lambda \left(I_N - \left(\Sigma_S \Sigma_S{'}\right)^{-1} \Sigma_S \Sigma_F{'} \left(\Sigma_F \Sigma_F{'}\right)^{-1} \Sigma_F \Sigma_S{'} \right) A \lambda_S \tag{29}$$

Equation (29) clearly implies that the market portfolio is not proportional to a mean-variance efficient portfolio of primitive assets since the matrix A is not equal to a constant times the identity matrix I_N. It immediately follows that the market portfolio need not be mean-variance efficient. The implications as to the empirical tests of the ICAPM are evidently the same as in the case of futures.

9.5. MARKET EQUILIBRIUM

The ICAPM for the cash assets and the non-redundant futures or forward contracts can now be derived. Utility functions are no longer restricted to be logarithmic.

To characterize market equilibrium, we retain the classic assumption that a representative investor exists. If the financial market is complete, this is innocuous as such an investor exists and is unique. If the market is incomplete, existence is not guaranteed, except trivially if all individuals are identical. Accordingly, aggregate wealth and individual wealth are equal. We further impose the usual market clearing conditions. Net positions in the futures or forward contracts are set equal to zero $\left(\hat{\theta} = \mathbf{0}_H\right)$ as well as the sum of all margin accounts (X = 0, if futures) or the net investment in the riskless asset ($\hat{\gamma} = 0$, if forwards). Total wealth thus is invested in the primitive assets only $\left(\hat{\alpha}{'}\mathbf{1_N} = 1\right)$. Combining these conditions and the optimality conditions yields the following

Proposition 4 (ICAPM):

Under the present set of assumptions, the equilibrium expected returns on cash assets satisfy

$$\mu_{S_i} = r + \beta_{i,M}(\mu_M - r) + \sum_{k=1}^{K} \beta_{i,Y_k}(\mu_{Y_k} - r) \tag{30}$$

when futures are traded, the equilibrium expected percent changes in futures prices satisfy

$$\mu_{F_j} = \beta_{j,M}(\mu_M - r) + \sum_{k=1}^{K} \beta_{j,Y_k}(\mu_{Y_k} - r) \tag{31}$$

and, when forwards are traded, the expected percent changes in forward prices satisfy

$$\mu_{F_j} = -\sigma_{F_j}^{'} \sigma_P + \beta_{j,M}(\mu_M - r) + \sum_{k=1}^{K} \beta_{j,Y_k}(\mu_{Y_k} - r) \tag{32}$$

where $\beta_{l,U}$ stands for the sensitivity of the return on asset l to the excess return on the market portfolio (U = M) or to the (adjusted for the riskless rate) drift of a state variable process (U = Y_k).

Proofs.

a) *Futures.*

Using equations (11) and (12), one can easily show that, at equilibrium,

$$\begin{pmatrix} \mu_S - \mathbf{1}_N r \\ \mu_F \end{pmatrix} = V_{SF,W}\left(-\frac{WJ_{WW}}{J_W}\right) + V_{SF,Y}\left(-\frac{J_{WY}}{J_W}\right) \tag{33}$$

where $V_{SF,W} = \begin{pmatrix} \Sigma_S \Sigma_S^{'} \hat{\alpha} \\ \Sigma_F \Sigma_S^{'} \hat{\alpha} \end{pmatrix}$ and $V_{SF,Y} = \begin{pmatrix} \Sigma_S \Sigma_Y^{'} \\ \Sigma_F \Sigma_Y^{'} \end{pmatrix}$.

Pre-multiplying (33) by $\left(\hat{\alpha}^{'} \quad \mathbf{0}_H^{'}\right)$ yields the equilibrium risk-return trade-off for total wealth (equal to the market portfolio value):

$$\mu_W - r = V_{W,W}\left(-\frac{WJ_{WW}}{J_W}\right) + V_{W,Y}'\left(-\frac{J_{WY}}{J_W}\right) \tag{34}$$

where μ_W is the expected return on total wealth, $V_{W,W}$ is the variance of total wealth and $V_{W,Y}$ the (K×1) vector of covariances between total wealth and the state variables.

Also, pre-multiplying (33) by $\Sigma_Y(\Sigma'\Sigma)^{-1}\Sigma'$ gives:

$$\mu_Y - \mathbf{1}_H r \equiv \Sigma_Y(\Sigma'\Sigma)^{-1}\Sigma'\begin{pmatrix}\mu_S - \mathbf{1}_N r \\ \mu_F\end{pmatrix} = V_{Y,W}\left(-\frac{WJ_{WW}}{J_W}\right) + V_{Y,Y}\left(-\frac{J_{WY}}{J_W}\right) \tag{35}$$

where $V_{Y,W}$ (=$V_{W,Y}$) is a (K × 1) covariance vector and $V_{Y,Y}$ is a (K × K) variance-covariance matrix.

Combining (34) and (35) yields:

$$\begin{pmatrix}\mu_W - r \\ \mu_Y - \mathbf{1}_H r\end{pmatrix} = \begin{pmatrix} V_{W,W} & V_{W,Y}' \\ V_{Y,W} & V_{Y,Y}\end{pmatrix}\begin{pmatrix} -\frac{WJ_{WW}}{J_W} \\ -\frac{J_{WY}}{J_W}\end{pmatrix}$$

Defining $\Sigma_{WY} \equiv \begin{pmatrix} V_{W,W} & V_{W,Y} \\ V_{Y,W} & V_{Y,Y}\end{pmatrix}$, we obtain:

$$\begin{pmatrix} -\frac{WJ_{WW}}{J_W} \\ -\frac{J_{WY}}{J_W}\end{pmatrix} = (\Sigma_{WY})^{-1}\begin{pmatrix}\mu_W - r \\ \mu_Y - \mathbf{1}_H r\end{pmatrix} \tag{36}$$

Substituting (36) into (33) and defining $V_{SF,WY} \equiv (V_{SF,W} \quad V_{SF,Y})$ yields:

$$\begin{pmatrix}\mu_S - \mathbf{1}_N r \\ \mu_F\end{pmatrix} = V_{SF,WY}(V_{WY})^{-1}\begin{pmatrix}\mu_W - r \\ \mu_Y - \mathbf{1}_H r\end{pmatrix} \tag{37}$$

Results (30) and (31) follow from (37) since the value of primitive assets represents total wealth at equilibrium so that W is the value of the market portfolio M. □

b) *Forwards.*

The proof is similar. Using (13), (14) and (15), one easily shows that, in equilibrium,

$$\begin{pmatrix} \mu_S - \mathbf{1}_N r \\ \mu_F + \Sigma_F \sigma_P \end{pmatrix} = V_{SF,W}\left(-\frac{WJ_{WW}}{J_W}\right) + V_{SF,Y}\left(-\frac{J_{WY}}{J_W}\right) \tag{38}$$

where $V_{SF,W}$ and $V_{SF,Y}$ are defined as in (33).

Now pre-multiplying (38) by $\begin{pmatrix}\hat{\alpha}' & \mathbf{0}_H'\end{pmatrix}$ yields:

$$\mu_W - r = V_{W,W}\left(-\frac{WJ_{WW}}{J_W}\right) + V_{W,Y}'\left(-\frac{J_{WY}}{J_W}\right) \tag{39}$$

Also, pre-multiplying (38) by $\Sigma_Y(\Sigma'\Sigma)^{-1}\Sigma'$ gives:

$$\mu_Y - \mathbf{1}_H r \equiv \Sigma_Y(\Sigma'\Sigma)^{-1}\Sigma'\begin{pmatrix} \mu_S - \mathbf{1}_N r \\ \mu_F + \Sigma_F \sigma_P \end{pmatrix} = V_{Y,W}\left(-\frac{WJ_{WW}}{J_W}\right) + V_{Y,Y}\left(-\frac{J_{WY}}{J_W}\right) \tag{40}$$

where $V_{Y,W}$ and $V_{Y,Y}$ are as in (35).

Combining (39) and (40) yields:

$$\begin{pmatrix} \mu_W - r \\ \mu_Y - \mathbf{1}_H r \end{pmatrix} = \begin{pmatrix} V_{W,W} & V_{W,Y}' \\ V_{Y,W} & V_{Y,Y} \end{pmatrix}\begin{pmatrix} -\dfrac{WJ_{WW}}{J_W} \\ -\dfrac{J_{WY}}{J_W} \end{pmatrix}$$

Using $\Sigma_{WY} \equiv \begin{pmatrix} V_{W,W} & V_{W,Y} \\ V_{Y,W} & V_{Y,Y} \end{pmatrix}$, we get:

$$\begin{pmatrix} -\dfrac{WJ_{WW}}{J_W} \\ -\dfrac{J_{WY}}{J_W} \end{pmatrix} = \left(\Sigma_{WY}\right)^{-1} \begin{pmatrix} \mu_W - r \\ \mu_Y - \mathbf{1}_H r \end{pmatrix} \tag{41}$$

Substituting (41) into (38) and using $V_{SF,WY} \equiv \left(V_{SF,W} \quad V_{SF,Y}\right)$ yields:

$$\begin{pmatrix} \mu_S - \mathbf{1}_N r \\ \mu_F + \Sigma_F \sigma_P \end{pmatrix} = V_{SF,WY} \left(V_{WY}\right)^{-1} \begin{pmatrix} \mu_W - r \\ \mu_Y - \mathbf{1}_H r \end{pmatrix} \tag{42}$$

Results (30) and (32) follow from (42) since the value of primitive assets represents total wealth at equilibrium so that W is the value of the market portfolio M.

Whether futures or forward contracts are traded, the excess return on a cash asset is expressed in the usual Merton's ICAPM form (expression (30)). This result is striking because we have found the market portfolio not to be necessarily efficient. In a dynamic model where the risk generated by the state variables is priced by the market, a multi-beta ICAPM thus obtains *regardless of whether the market portfolio is mean-variance efficient or not.* This results from the availability of non-redundant futures or forward contracts for trading. Moreover, this result carries over even to Bernoulli investors who do not price the risks associated with the state variables. In short, the market portfolio may not be mean-variance efficient because of the presence of futures or forwards, but the traditional one-beta CAPM for cash assets still holds for myopic investors.

As to futures prices, result (31) is not really surprising since the marking-to-market mechanism makes futures contracts similar to cash assets. Therefore, except for the obvious absence of the riskless rate of interest r (since there is no cost of carry), the ICAPM must equally hold for futures.

Now, the ICAPM in its standard form does not hold for forward contracts, as evidenced by equation (32). The expected percent change in the price of a forward contract comprises not only the usual premiums on the market portfolio and the state variables but also an additional term (the riskless rate r is of course absent from the expected return equation, for the same reason as for futures). The latter includes the instantaneous covariance between the forward price and the pure discount bond price of identical maturity. The intuition behind the negative sign that affects this component is the following. According to the cash-and-carry relationship, the forward price of an asset is its spot price (possibly deflated by a dividend rate) divided by the price of the relevant pure discount bond. Consequently, for any asset whose spot price is not positively correlated with the discount bond price, the correlation between its forward price and the discount bond price is negative[11]. Result (32) implies that the expected percent change in the price of a forward contract contains an additional element of compensation for the risk of the portfolio strategy itself. We call this additional term a *strategy risk premium*. Consequently, holding a forward contract is rewarded also for the systematic risk that results from the covariance between the contract and its associated discount bond. Trading on forward contracts implies that investors are bound to have non-tradable discount bond positions. Being unable to diversify the corresponding systematic risk, they must be compensated for it at equilibrium.

Finally, it is worth stressing that knowing the cash-and-carry relationship between the forward price and the underlying spot price, on the one hand, and the ICAPM for the underlying cash asset and the relevant discount bond, on the other hand, does not make trivial the derivation of the corresponding ICAPM equation for the forward. First, the cash-and-carry relationship in general does not hold for forward contracts because of the stochastic nature of the dividend or convenience yield on the underlying asset or because the latter is not traded and the market is incomplete. Second, this method would assume away the issue of how the introduction of forwards in an incomplete market economy affects the equilibrium prices of existing cash assets. Third, one could not provide a convincing economic interpretation of the result since the precise mechanism that makes the traditional ICAPM invalid for forwards would not be exhibited. By contrast, none of the previous results is grounded on the cash-and-carry relationship.

9.6. CONCLUSIONS

In an incomplete market in which non-redundant futures or forward contracts contribute to span (totally or not) the uncertainty, some standard results of portfolio theory must be amended. Introducing such contracts modifies the way investors optimally allocate their wealth. When futures are traded, their portfolios comprise the riskless asset, a perturbed mean-variance efficient portfolio of cash assets and futures contracts. Furthermore, a (K+2) mutual fund separation is obtained, with K the number of state variables driving the investment opportunity set, as Merton's fund separation. However, the composition of the optimal speculative element and of the Merton-Breeden hedging terms differs from that in Merton as they both include all the available derivatives. When forward contracts are traded, a (K+3), rather than a (K+3) mutual fund separation theorem is obtained. The additional fund is a portfolio that hedges the interest rate risk brought about by the optimal portfolio strategy itself. In addition, the pricing equation for a forward contract is shown to contain an extra term relative to that for a cash asset, namely a strategy risk premium.

The latter finding helps clarify the intuition that, when investors trade forward contracts, they bear an additional, interest rate related, risk. More fundamentally, the presence of this forward trading strategy risk has been shown, in an incomplete markets economy, to affect the expected percent change in the forward contract prices only, the equilibrium expected returns on the cash assets remaining unchanged. Another finding is that the covariance term present (uniquely) in the ICAPM for forwards does not stem from the additional term in the investor's optimal dynamic strategy, since the latter cancels out in equilibrium. Therefore, the ICAPM for forward contracts holds regardless of whether interest rate risk can be perfectly hedged or not.

Irrespective of whether futures or forwards are traded, the mean-variance efficiency of the market portfolio of cash assets is not required and, in particular, is neither a necessary nor a sufficient condition for the linear relationship between expected return and beta to hold. This result holds whether individuals exhibit a myopic behavior or not. Since derivative assets have enriched the opportunity set of direct investors and fund managers alike, this finding is important for the practical aspects of asset allocation, risk control and management, and performance measurement. Moreover, this result may have important implications for empirical tests of the ICAPM, because the linear relationship between expected return and beta continues to hold for risky assets in spite of the possible inefficiency of the market portfolio.

These results have been derived within the simple framework of a frictionless, albeit possibly incomplete, financial market. However, their basic insight should remain useful in more complicated situations. In particular, the equations for the optimal demands and market equilibrium are tractable yet reasonably realistic, so that the model should be applicable to the analysis of a variety of theoretical and empirical issues. Introducing some market frictions such as transaction costs, portfolio composition restrictions and default or counter-party risk may lead to a further understanding of the particularities of forward and futures markets. This is left to further research.

Endnotes

[1] This chapter is grounded on both Lioui and Poncet (2001a) and Lioui and Poncet (2003b).
[2] See Chen, Roll and Ross (1986), Jegadeesh and Titman (1993), Fama and French (1996), or Cochrane (1997), among many others.
[3] See Fama (1996) for a lucid analysis of the relationship between ICAPM and multifactor efficiency.
[4] The quote is from their abstract, on p. 157.
[5] Breeden (1984) was the first to introduce futures in an intertemporal equilibrium framework à la Merton. In his model, the number of futures contracts is equal to the number K of state variables, which thus makes his financial market complete. In addition, each and every futures contract is of instantaneous maturity and perfectly correlated with each and every state variable. His main objective was to examine under what conditions an initially incomplete market can be completed by introducing instantaneous futures contracts and to characterize the (Pareto) optimal allocation that ensues.
[6] See, among others, Ohashi (1995, 1997).
[7] The phrase "rates of return" would be somewhat misleading since futures or forward contracts are included in the portfolio.
[8] An equivalent assumption is that this zero-coupon bond is spanned by the existing cash securities.
[9] Cox et al. (1985a) provides necessary conditions for J to have these properties.
[10] See for instance Ingersoll (1987), Chapter 4, or Huang and Litzenberger (1988), Chapter 3.
[11] This however does not rule out the possibility of a positive covariance $\sigma_{F_j}'\sigma_P$ in the case where the asset spot price is positively enough correlated with the discount bond price.

CHAPTER 10: EQUILIBRIUM ASSET PRICING IN A PRODUCTION ECONOMY WITH NON-REDUNDANT FORWARD OR FUTURES CONTRACTS[1]

10.1. INTRODUCTION

The preceding chapter considered a pure endowment economy. The objective of this chapter is to asses to what extent the previous results carry over to a more general economy in which production exists and follows a stochastic process. We again derive an equilibrium asset pricing model for an initially incomplete financial market that is completed, totally or not, by introducing non-redundant futures or forward contracts. And we establish new separation theorems in the spirit of those of the previous chapter. We derive both a Breeden-like Consumption based CAPM (CCAPM) and a Merton-like multi-beta ICAPM for various primitive assets, non-redundant forwards and futures and offer an intuitive economic interpretation of the results. The difference between forwards and the other assets is again explicitly related to the additional (interest rate) risk that stems from the very portfolio strategy involving forward contracts.

The remainder of the chapter is organized as follows. In Section II, we present the economic framework and describe an investor's wealth dynamics in an incomplete financial market. Section III derives the CCAPM and the multi-beta ICAPM that apply to forward contracts and compares them with the usual ones valid for cash assets and futures. Our results are shown not to depend on the usual cash-and-carry relationship, which in general does not hold. We nevertheless show in Section IV that, in the special case due to CIR (1985a), it does hold. The last section concludes.

10.2. ECONOMIC FRAMEWORK

We provide first a description of the economy and then an explicit expression for the value process generated by trading continuously on forward or futures contracts. Finally, we derive the investors' wealth dynamics. Note that trading in technologies and all financial assets takes place continuously in a frictionless market and only at equilibrium prices. The only (albeit important) restriction is that the real assets (technologies) defined below cannot be shorted.

10.2.1. Real and financial assets

Following CIR (1985a), we assume an economy in which there is a single physical good, the numeraire, which may be allocated to consumption or investment. We assume that there are N technological investment opportunities in the economy, all producing the same good. When an amount $\eta_i(t)$ of this consumption good is invested in technology i, (i = 1,…., N), the change in its value over time is governed by the following stochastic differential equation (SDE):

$$d\eta_i(t) = \eta_i(t)\mu_{\eta_i}(t, Y(t))dt + \eta_i(t)\sigma_{\eta_i}(t, Y(t))' dZ(t) \qquad (1)$$

where Z(t) is an (N + K) × 1 dimensional Wiener process in R^{N+K}, Y(t) is a K × 1 dimensional vector of state variables, $\mu_{\eta_i}(t, Y(t))$ is a bounded valued function of t and Y, and $\sigma_{\eta_i}(t, Y(t))$ is a bounded (K + N) × 1 vector valued function of t and Y. The Wiener process is defined on the usual complete probability space (**Ω**, F, P). Like in CIR (1985a), equation (1) specifies the growth of an initial investment when the output of the process is continually reinvested in that same process.

When convenient, we will write the dynamics of the N technological processes in the following form:

$$d\eta(t) = I_\eta \mu_\eta(t, Y(t))dt + I_\eta \Sigma_\eta(t, Y(t))dZ(t) \qquad (2)$$

where I_η is an N × N diagonal matrix valued function of η(t) whose i^{th} diagonal element is $\eta_i(t)$, $\mu_\eta(t, Y(t))$ is an N × 1 dimensional vector whose i^{th} component is $\mu_{\eta_i}(t, Y(t))$ and finally $\Sigma_\eta(t, Y(t))$ is a (K × N) + K matrix valued function whose i^{th} element is $\sigma_{\eta_i}(t, Y(t))$.

The movement of the K state variables is determined by the following system of SDEs:

$$dY(t) = \mu_Y(t, Y(t))dt + \Sigma_Y(t, Y(t))dZ(t) \tag{3}$$

where $\mu_Y(t, Y(t))$ is a bounded K × 1 vector valued function of t and Y and $\Sigma_Y(t, Y(t))$ is a bounded K × (N + K) matrix valued function of t and Y.

In addition to these real assets, individuals can also lend or borrow at the instantaneously riskless real rate r(t) expressed in the numeraire good. This money market account is in zero net supply. The diffusion process followed by r(t) is endogenous and will not be made explicit until the special case examined at the end of Section III.

Non-redundant forward or futures contracts, which are contingent claims to a specified amount of the physical good at a given maturity, are also available for trade in this economy. These financial claims are in zero net supply. Since there is a single good in this economy, we assume without real loss of generality that there exists one forward (or futures) contract only that, together with the N technologies and the riskless asset, forms the basis of our financial market[2]. It is a claim to a payoff that is any deterministic function, not necessarily linear, of some units of the physical good, with maturity T. The latter extends at least to the representative investor's horizon date, which will be denoted by τ.

Hence investors have access to (N+2) trading instruments. It is important to realize that none of our results depends on whether the financial market is incomplete or not, provided the forward or futures contract we are interested in is not redundant.

The price of the forward or futures contract solves the following SDE:

$$dF(t) = F(t)\mu_F dt + F(t)\sigma_F' dZ(t) \tag{4}$$

where the notation F(t) is short for F(t, T); μ_F and σ_F, respectively, are assumed a bounded valued function of t and Y, and a bounded (N + K) × 1 vector valued function of t and Y. The explicit dependence of the drift and diffusion parameters on t and Y(t) has been omitted for simplicity. Part of the problem at hand is to determine these functions endogenously in equilibrium. As usual in this book, F = G will denote a forward contract and F = H will denote a futures.

The variance-covariance matrix $\Sigma_\eta \Sigma_\eta^{'}$ is assumed to be positive definite. The variance-covariance matrix of the percent changes in all risky asset prices (technologies and forward or futures contract), i.e. $\Sigma\Sigma^{'}$ where $\Sigma \equiv \begin{bmatrix} \Sigma_\eta \\ \sigma_F^{'} \end{bmatrix}$, is also assumed to be positive definite.

In this CIR-like economy, we assume for simplicity that no bond is actually traded. This assumption is used only to ease the interpretation of the investor's optimal strategy and is completely innocuous. Relaxing it would not affect the results significantly. Indeed, the price of any risky cash asset, bonds included, will be shown to obey the usual CCAPM and ICAPM. Thus, the only difference, apart from a slightly more complicated optimal strategy on the investor's part, is that, if the number of such bonds were large enough to make the market complete, some optimal hedge to be defined later on would be perfect as opposed to imperfect, as here.

Nevertheless, the process r(t) for the riskless asset determines an *implicit* yield curve the characteristics of which are endogenous. In particular, denote by P(t, T), or P(t) for short, the price at time t of an implicit pure discount bond the maturity T of which coincides with that of the forward or futures contract. Its dynamics then obeys the following SDE (for t such that $0 \leq t < T$):

$$dP(t) = P(t)\mu_P(t, Y(t))dt + P(t)\sigma_P(t, Y(t))^{'} dZ(t) \tag{5}$$

Since the implicit yield curve is endogenous, so are the parameters of SDE (5), like those of SDE (4).

10.2.2. Wealth dynamics

To derive the investor's wealth dynamics, we need first to know the value of the position X(t) that results from her trading in the forward or futures contract. Let Θ be the number of contracts held (not traded) at time t ($t \leq T$).

The profit-and-loss account from trading on the forward contracts is equal to:

$$X(t) = P(t)\int_0^t \Theta(u)dF(u) \tag{6}$$

As before, this cumulative algebraic gain being cashed-in or -out at the contract maturity date T only, it must bc discounted using P(t).

When futures are traded, margins are lent or borrowed at the instantaneously riskless rate r(t) so that the value of the investor's margin account at time t writes:

$$X(t) = \int_0^t \exp\left[\int_s^t r(u)du\right]\Theta(s)'dF(s) \tag{6'}$$

Now, let α be the vector of proportions of wealth invested in the technologies, γ the proportion of wealth invested in the riskless asset and C the instantaneous consumption rate.

a) Forwards. Given equation (6), an investor's wealth dynamics writes:

$$\begin{aligned} dW = &\left[W\alpha'\mu_\eta + \left(P\int_0^t \Theta dF\right)\mu_P + P\Theta F\mu_F + P\Theta F\sigma_F{}'\sigma_P + W\gamma r - C\right]dt \\ &+\left[W\alpha'\Sigma_\eta + \left(P\int_0^t \Theta dF\right)\sigma_P{}' + P\Theta F\sigma_F{}'\right]dZ \end{aligned} \tag{7}$$

As shown in the previous chapter, this dynamics can be rewritten:

$$\begin{aligned} dW = &\begin{bmatrix} W\alpha'(\mu_\eta - \mu_P \mathbf{1}_N) + W\mu_P + W\theta(\mu_F + \sigma_F{}'\sigma_P) \\ + W\gamma(r - \mu_P) - C \end{bmatrix}dt \\ &+\left[W\alpha'(\Sigma_\eta - \mathbf{1}_N\sigma_P{}') + W(1-\gamma)\sigma_P{}' + W\theta\sigma_F{}'\right]dZ \end{aligned} \tag{8}$$

where we have used the definition of wealth $W \equiv W\gamma + W\alpha' 1_N + P\int_0^t \Theta dF$, and, to simplify notations, have denoted by θ the ratio of the present value of the forward position to the investor's wealth, i.e. $\theta \equiv \frac{1}{W}P\Theta F$.

b) Futures. Given equation (6'), the investor's wealth dynamics reads:

$$dW = \left[W\alpha'\mu_\eta + rX + \Theta F\mu_F + W\gamma r - C\right]dt + \left[W\alpha'\Sigma_\eta + \Theta F\sigma_F{}'\right]dZ \quad (8')$$

We are now fully equipped to derive the two general equilibrium pricing models of interest.

10.3. GENERAL EQUILIBRIUM MODELS

Let us assume, like CIR (1985a) and numerous followers, that a representative investor exists[3]. The latter maximizes the expected utility of his intertemporal consumption stream subject to his budget constraint. Thus, his optimal consumption and portfolio rules must solve (see the previous chapter):

$$\text{Max } E\left[\int_t^\tau U(s, C(s))ds\right] \quad (9)$$

subject to equation (8)and to positive consumption P -a.s.

Recall from the previous section that, without loss of generality, the investor's horizon τ is assumed to be smaller than or equal to the forward or future contract expiration date T.

Although Cox-Ingersoll-Ross (1981) have shown that neither Merton's multi-beta ICAPM nor Breeden's CCAPM hold for non-redundant forward contracts, they did not produce alternative equations. To provide them, we impose first that the following two market-clearing conditions hold in equilibrium:

i) the total amount invested in the technologies equals total wealth (i.e., $\hat{\alpha}'\mathbf{1}_N = 1$), and ii) the net positions in the forward (or future) market and the riskless asset are zero (i.e., $\hat{\gamma} = 0$ and $\hat{\theta} = 0$).

Note that we need not derive again the individual's optimal demand for risky assets that have been formally obtained and economically interpreted in the previous chapter.

10.3.1. Consumption-based CAPM

A cash asset of particular relevance is the *implicit* cash bond of maturity T that is part of the representative investor's wealth when she uses forward contracts. Thus the first proposition contrasts the CCAPM for the implicit cash bond and for the forward contract.

Proposition 1: *The consumption-based CAPM for the implicit pure discount bond P(t) is expressed as:*

$$\mu_P = r - \frac{\hat{C}U_{\hat{C}\hat{C}}}{U_{\hat{C}}}\sigma_P{}'\sigma_{\hat{C}} \tag{10}$$

where $\sigma_{\hat{C}}$ is the instantaneous volatility of the relative changes in aggregate consumption,

and the consumption-based CAPM for the forward contract F(t) writes:

$$\mu_F = -\sigma_F{}'\sigma_P - \frac{\hat{C}U_{\hat{C}\hat{C}}}{U_{\hat{C}}}\sigma_F{}'\sigma_{\hat{C}} \tag{11}$$

Proof:

Let $J(t, W(t), Y(t))$ be the value (indirect utility) function at date $t \leq T$ and let L(t)J be the differential generator of J. We assume that J exists and is an increasing and strictly concave function of W. This assumption encompasses several of the assumptions made by CIR (1985a). Let $\psi \equiv LJ + U$. Then the necessary and sufficient conditions for optimality are:

$$\psi_{\hat{C}} = U_{\hat{C}} - J_W \leq 0 \tag{12}$$

$$\hat{C}\psi_{\hat{C}} = 0 \tag{13}$$

$$\begin{aligned}\psi_{\hat{\alpha}} &= W(\mu_\eta - \mu_P \mathbf{1}_N)J_W + W(\Sigma_\eta - \mathbf{1}_N \sigma_P')\Sigma_Y' J_{WY} + \\ &\begin{bmatrix}(\Sigma_\eta - \mathbf{1}_N\sigma_P')(\Sigma_\eta - \mathbf{1}_N\sigma_P')'\hat{\alpha} + (1-\hat{\gamma})(\Sigma_\eta - \mathbf{1}_N\sigma_P')\sigma_P \\ + (\Sigma_\eta - \mathbf{1}_N\sigma_P')\sigma_F\hat{\theta}\end{bmatrix} W^2 J_{WW} \le 0\end{aligned} \tag{14}$$

$$\hat{\alpha}'\psi_{\hat{\alpha}} = 0 \tag{15}$$

$$\begin{aligned}\psi_{\hat{\theta}} &= W(\mu_F + \sigma_F'\sigma_P)J_W + W\sigma_F'\Sigma_Y' J_{WY} \\ &\quad + [\sigma_F'(\Sigma_\eta - \mathbf{1}_N\sigma_P')'\hat{\alpha} + (1-\hat{\gamma})\sigma_F'\sigma_P + \sigma_F'\sigma_F\hat{\theta}]W^2 J_{WW} = 0\end{aligned} \tag{16}$$

$$\begin{aligned}\psi_{\hat{\gamma}} &= W(r - \mu_P)J_W - W\sigma_P'\Sigma_Y' J_{WY} \\ &\quad - [\hat{\alpha}'(\Sigma_\eta - \mathbf{1}_N\sigma_P')\sigma_P + (1-\hat{\gamma})\sigma_P'\sigma_P + \hat{\theta}\sigma_F'\sigma_P]W^2 J_{WW} = 0\end{aligned} \tag{17}$$

with usual notations for partial derivatives of the value function with respect to each of its arguments. The hat ^ above a variable denotes an optimal value. Equation (12) is the standard envelope condition while equations (13) and (15) guarantee that the optimal value for the consumption process and the proportions of wealth invested in the technologies are non-negative.

Using the market clearing conditions and (16) yields:

$$\mu_F = -\sigma_F'\sigma_P - \sigma_F'\left(\frac{WJ_{WW}}{J_W}\hat{\alpha}'\Sigma_\eta + \frac{J_{WY}'}{J_W}\Sigma_Y\right)' \tag{18}$$

Using the market clearing conditions, the aggregate wealth dynamics writes:

$$dW = [W\hat{\alpha}'\mu_\eta - \hat{C}]dt + [W\hat{\alpha}'\Sigma_\eta]dZ \tag{19}$$

This setting being Markovian, the control variables may be written in a feedback form. Therefore, the optimal consumption process $\hat{C}(t,.)$ writes $\hat{C}(t, W, Y)$. Applying Ito's lemma then yields:

$$\frac{d\hat{C}}{\hat{C}} = \mu_{\hat{C}} dt + \sigma_{\hat{C}}' dZ \tag{20}$$

where:

$$\sigma_{\hat{C}} = \frac{W\hat{C}_W \Sigma_\eta' \hat{\alpha} + \Sigma_Y' \hat{C}_Y}{\hat{C}} \tag{21}$$

The envelope condition (12) implies:

$$U_{\hat{C}} = J_W \text{ , } \hat{C}_W U_{\hat{C}\hat{C}} = J_{WW} \text{ and } \hat{C}_Y U_{\hat{C}\hat{C}} = J_{WY} \tag{22}$$

and therefore:

$$\hat{C}_W \frac{U_{\hat{C}\hat{C}}}{U_{\hat{C}}} = \frac{J_{WW}}{J_W} \text{ and } \hat{C}_Y \frac{U_{\hat{C}\hat{C}}}{U_{\hat{C}}} = \frac{J_{WY}}{J_W} \tag{23}$$

Using this, one gets:

$$\frac{WJ_{WW}}{J_W} \hat{\alpha}' \Sigma_\eta + \frac{J_{WY}'}{J_W} \Sigma_Y = \frac{U_{\hat{C}\hat{C}}}{U_{\hat{C}}} \left(W\hat{C}_W \hat{\alpha}' \Sigma_\eta + \hat{C}_Y' \Sigma_Y \right) \tag{24}$$

Using this and (18) yields the second part of Proposition 1.

The first part of the proposition follows from the same approach applied to (17) instead of (16). □

As expected, Breeden's traditional CCAPM holds for the cash bond (equation (10)). Investors are fairly compensated by the market for the systematic risk they bear from holding (in positive or negative amounts) the implicit discount bond generated by their forward position. In addition, this CCAPM of course holds for the technologies themselves, because these are in effect cash assets.

However, the CCAPM for the forward contract is different (equation (11)). As noted in the previous chapter, investors must be compensated for the two risks they bear. The risk associated with the random fluctuations of the forward price itself gives rise to the usual premium $-\frac{\hat{C}U_{\hat{C}\hat{C}}}{U_{\hat{C}}}\sigma_F' \sigma_{\hat{C}}$. The risk associated with the forward trading strategy generates a premium, previously dubbed the *strategy risk premium*, equal to minus the instantaneous covariance between the relative changes in the forward contract and the relative changes in the discount bond whose maturity is equal to that of the forward contract $\left(-\sigma_F{}'\sigma_P\right)$. It is interesting to remark that the sign of this covariance term is indeterminate. This is not necessarily at variance with equation (10) since the interest rate r is a real rate in the moneyless economy considered here and thus could actually be negative in equilibrium. Therefore, in all rigor, both r and $(-\sigma_F{}'\sigma_P)$ have indeterminate signs.

Thus, the "return"[4] on a forward contract compensates also for the systematic risk that results from the covariance between the contract and its associated discount bond. When trading on forward contracts, the investor generally has an implicit discount bond position and, being unable to diversify the corresponding systematic risk, she must be compensated for it. An important feature of this additional premium is that, in contrast to the premium related to the consumption risk of the forward price, it is preference free. This not so intuitive result can be explained as follows. First, at equilibrium the accumulated profit or loss X(t), which is preference-dependent, is obviously zero for the set of all investors (or the representative individual). Second, under the assumption of homogeneous beliefs, the covariance $\left(-\sigma_F{}'\sigma_P\right)$ is common to all investors (or is the belief of the representative agent). This term thus plays to some extent the role of a riskless interest rate. In effect, rewriting equation (11) under an "excess return" form yields:

$$\mu_F - \left(-\sigma_F{}'\sigma_P\right) = -\frac{\hat{C}U_{\hat{C}\hat{C}}}{U_{\hat{C}}}\sigma_F{}'\sigma_{\hat{C}}$$

Thus, the RHS of the rewritten equation has exactly the same structure as the RHS of equation (10). This RHS does of course depend on the investor's utility function.

The relationship between CCAPM (11) and the classic cash-and-carry relationship deserves a comment. One can show that if the cash-and-carry relationship is *assumed* to hold, then equation (11) follows essentially from Itô's lemma.

Proof:

Assuming the price of a forward contract of maturity T written on a technology satisfies the cash-and-carry relationship implies:

$$F(t,T) = \frac{\eta(t)}{P(t,T)} \tag{25}$$

Using:

$$\begin{aligned} \frac{dF}{F} &= \mu_F dt + \sigma_F' dZ \\ \frac{d\eta}{\eta} &= \mu_\eta dt + \sigma_\eta' dZ \\ \frac{dP}{P} &= \mu_P dt + \sigma_P' dZ \end{aligned} \tag{26}$$

and since the CCAPM holds for cash assets, we have:

$$\begin{aligned} \mu_P - r &= -\frac{\hat{C}U_{\hat{C}\hat{C}}}{U_{\hat{C}}} \sigma_P' \sigma_{\hat{C}} \\ \mu_S - r &= -\frac{\hat{C}U_{\hat{C}\hat{C}}}{U_{\hat{C}}} \sigma_S' \sigma_{\hat{C}} \end{aligned} \tag{27}$$

Applying Itô's lemma to (25), one gets:

$$\frac{dF}{F} = \left(\mu_\eta - \mu_P - \sigma_\eta' \sigma_P + \sigma_P' \sigma_P\right) dt + \left(\sigma_\eta - \sigma_P\right)' dZ \tag{28}$$

and therefore:

$$\begin{aligned} \mu_F &= \mu_\eta - \mu_P - \sigma_\eta' \sigma_P + \sigma_P' \sigma_P \\ \sigma_F &= \sigma_\eta - \sigma_P \end{aligned} \tag{29}$$

Using the preceding results, one gets:

$$
\begin{aligned}
\mu_F &= \mu_\eta - \mu_P - \sigma_\eta{}'\sigma_P + \sigma_P{}'\sigma_P \\
&= r - \frac{\hat{C}U_{\hat{C}\hat{C}}}{U_{\hat{C}}}\sigma_\eta{}'\sigma_{\hat{C}} - r + \frac{\hat{C}U_{\hat{C}\hat{C}}}{U_{\hat{C}}}\sigma_P{}'\sigma_{\hat{C}} - (\sigma_\eta - \sigma_P)'\sigma_P \\
&= -\frac{\hat{C}U_{\hat{C}\hat{C}}}{U_{\hat{C}}}(\sigma_\eta - \sigma_P)'\sigma_{\hat{C}} - (\sigma_\eta - \sigma_P)'\sigma_P \\
&= -\frac{\hat{C}U_{\hat{C}\hat{C}}}{U_{\hat{C}}}\sigma_F{}'\sigma_{\hat{C}} - \sigma_F{}'\sigma_P
\end{aligned}
\tag{30}
$$

which is equation (11). □

Therefore, result (11) holds for both redundant and non-redundant forwards and does not depend on whether the cash-and-carry equation holds or not. However, the previous derivation is not grounded on this assumption and thus is more general. In this setting, the extra term emerges from Itô's lemma applied to the present value of the profit and loss account. In addition, a clear economic interpretation of the result can be provided in terms of trading strategy risk, interpretation that is impossible from the cash-and-carry formula.

10.3.2. Multi-beta ICAPM

The one-to-one relationship that is known to exist in general equilibrium between the CCAPM and the multi-beta ICAPM seems on a priori grounds to make the derivation of the latter useless. Yet the volatilities of financial assets appearing in equations (10) and (11) are endogenously determined, so that it is useful to characterize them as a function of the volatilities of the state variables and aggregate wealth. This leads to the multi-beta ICAPM that (i) is novel, thus interesting at the theoretical level, (ii) has obvious implications as to the current hotly debated issue of financial asset predictability, and (iii) is easier to submit to empirical testing. The second observation is motivated by the currently very active empirical research on the extent to which asset returns are predictable, in spite of the early efficient market hypothesis. It is clear that if systematic factors affect expected returns, and some of these factors are at least partially observable or predictable, asset returns will be partially predictable themselves. Regarding the last point, it is indeed well known that testing the CCAPM is very difficult due to severe practical and empirical problems. For instance, one has to measure the "representative individual's" utility and its relevant derivatives, available consumption data are too infrequent, their accuracy depends on the quality of the samples that are used, and expenses rather than consumption itself are actually measured. Proposition 2 provides the ICAPM for the implicit discount bond and the non-redundant forward contract.

Proposition 2: *The general equilibrium expected return on the discount bond P(t) is given by:*

$$\mu_P = r + \frac{W}{P} P_W \lambda_W + \sum_{j=1}^{K} \frac{W}{P} P_{Y_j} \lambda_{Y_j} \tag{31}$$

and the general equilibrium expected percent change in the forward contract is equal to:

$$\mu_F = \frac{W}{F} F_W \left(\lambda_W - \sigma_P{}' \sigma_W\right) + \sum_{j=1}^{K} \frac{F_{Y_j}}{F} \left(W\lambda_{Y_j} - \sigma_P{}' \sigma_{Y_j}\right) \tag{32}$$

where σ_W *is the instantaneous volatility of aggregate wealth,* P_x *and* F_x *denote partial derivatives of the two asset prices, and where:*

$$\lambda_W = \left(-\frac{WJ_{WW}}{J_W}\right) \sigma_W{}' \sigma_W + \sum_{j=1}^{K} \left(-\frac{J_{WY_j}}{J_W}\right) \sigma_W{}' \sigma_{Y_j} \tag{33}$$

$$\lambda_{Y_j} = \left(-\frac{WJ_{WW}}{J_W}\right) \sigma_W{}' \sigma_{Y_j} + \sum_{k=1}^{K} \left(-\frac{J_{WY_k}}{J_W}\right) \sigma_{Y_j}{}' \sigma_{Y_k} \tag{34}$$

Proof:

The price at each time t of the discount bond P(t, .) can also be written in a feedback form as P(t,Y(t),W(t)). Applying Ito's lemma yields the following expression for σ_P:

$$\sigma_P = \frac{1}{P} \left(\Sigma_\eta{}' \hat{\alpha} W P_W + \Sigma_Y{}' P_Y\right) \tag{35}$$

where P_Y is the $K \times 1$ vector of partial derivatives of the discount bond price with respect to the state variables. Substituting for σ_P given by (35) into (10) and rearranging terms by using definitions (33) and (34) yields the desired result (31).

The same approach is used to prove (32), using (11) instead of (10). □

Since in equilibrium aggregate wealth W is the value of the market portfolio, (31) and (32) are ICAPM-like equations. However, while result (31) is standard, (32) is not. In addition to the fact that r does not appear, for reasons previously exposed, the various risk premia affecting the forward expected "return" must be *adjusted* for the systematic interest rate risk linked to the presence of the implicit discount bond. This theoretical result has important implications for empirical testing. If a CAPM-like model were applied to forward contracts, the same linear risk-return relationship that is tested for cash assets would implicitly be assumed to hold, namely:

$$\text{Percent change in the forward price} = \text{a constant} + \sum_{j=1}^{K} \beta_j Y_j + \text{a noise.}$$

Since the $\sigma_P' \sigma_{Y_j}$ are actually not constant, the above regression model would be misspecified, and its estimated parameters would be biased.

The multi-beta ICAPM for redundant *spot* (as opposed to forward) *contingent claims* is given in the following proposition. Note that these are replicable using, in particular, the forward contract.

Proposition 3: *The general equilibrium expected return on an attainable spot contingent claim* S^i *is given by:*

$$\mu_{S^i} - r = \frac{W}{S^i} S^i_W \lambda_W + \sum_{j=1}^{K} \frac{W}{S^i} S^i_{Y_j} \lambda_{Y_j} \qquad (36)$$

Proof:

The essence of the proof is to replicate the contingent claim to be priced by means of a portfolio $\overline{F}$ comprising the optimally invested wealth, the forward contract and the riskless asset. Throughout the proof, to ease the notation, we denote the value of the riskless asset at each date t by F^0 and by F^1 the value of the optimally invested wealth. The number of units of each one of the assets held by the investor is written as θ_i. The value of the contingent claim at each time t is equal to the value of the replicating strategy. Therefore, we have:

$$\overline{F} = \theta_0 F^0 + P\int_0^t \theta dF + \theta_1 F^1 \tag{37}$$

Since the strategy is constrained to be self-financing, its dynamics is given by:

$$d\overline{F} = \theta_0 dF^0 + dP\int_0^t \theta dF + P\theta dF + \theta d < F;P > + \theta_1 dF^1 \tag{38}$$

where d <F;P> stands for the instantaneous covariance between the discount bond price changes and the forward price changes.

From (31), the instantaneous expected rate of return on the optimally invested wealth is $(\lambda_W + r)$ and its volatility, from (h), is $\hat{\alpha}'\Sigma_\eta$. Using these and equations (5) and (7), (38) rewrites:

$$d\overline{F} = \begin{bmatrix} \theta_0 F^0 r + \left(\overline{F} - \theta_0 F^0 - \theta_1 F^1\right)\mu_P + P\theta F\mu_F + \theta_1 F^1 r \\ + \lambda_W \theta_1 + P\theta F\sigma_F{}'\sigma_P \end{bmatrix} dt \\ + \left[\left(\overline{F} - \theta_0 F^0 - \theta_1 F^1\right)\sigma_P{}' + P\theta F\sigma_F{}' + \theta_1 F^1\left(\hat{\alpha}'\Sigma_\eta\right)\right] dZ \tag{39}$$

Substituting for (31) and (32) yields the expected return on the contingent claim:

$$\mu_{\overline{F}}\overline{F} = \theta_0 F^0 r + \theta_1 F^1 r + \theta_1 \lambda_W \\ + \left(\overline{F} - \theta_0 F^0 - \theta_1 F^1\right)\left(r + \frac{1}{P}\left[\lambda_W \quad \lambda_{Y_1} \quad . \quad . \quad \lambda_{Y_K}\right]\left[P_W \quad P_{Y_1} \quad . \quad . \quad P_{Y_K}\right]'\right) \\ + P\left[\lambda_W \quad \lambda_{Y_1} \quad . \quad . \quad \lambda_{Y_K}\right]\left[F_W \quad F_{Y_1} \quad . \quad . \quad F_{Y_K}\right]' \tag{40}$$

Rearranging terms, one has:

$$\mu_{\overline{F}} - r = \frac{W}{\overline{F}} \begin{bmatrix} \lambda_W & \lambda_{Y_1} & . & . & \lambda_{Y_K} \end{bmatrix} \begin{bmatrix} F_W & P_W & 1 \\ F_{Y_1} & P_{Y_1} & 0 \\ . & . & . \\ F_{Y_K} & P_{Y_K} & 0 \end{bmatrix} \begin{bmatrix} P\theta \\ \frac{1}{P}\left(\overline{F} - \theta_0 F^0 - \theta_1 F^1\right) \\ \theta_1 \end{bmatrix} \quad (41)$$

Equation (35) relative to the volatility σ_P of the discount bond applies as well to the volatility of the forward contract. Thus:

$$\sigma_F = \frac{1}{F}\left(\Sigma_\eta{}' \hat{\alpha} W F_W + \Sigma_Y{}' F_Y\right) \quad (42)$$

From (39), the instantaneous volatility of the contingent claim price is equal to:

$$\left(\overline{F} - \theta_0 F^0 - \theta_1 F^1\right)\sigma_P + P\theta F \sigma_F + \theta_1 F^1 \left(\Sigma_\eta{}' \hat{\alpha}\right) \quad (43)$$

This can be rewritten as:

$$\begin{aligned} &\left(\overline{F} - \theta_0 F^0 - \theta_1 F^1\right)\sigma_P + P\theta F \sigma_F + \theta_1 F^1 \left(\Sigma_\eta{}' \hat{\alpha}\right) \\ &= \begin{bmatrix} \sigma_P & \sigma_F & \Sigma_\eta{}' \hat{\alpha} \end{bmatrix} \begin{bmatrix} \overline{F} - \theta_0 F^0 - \theta_1 F^1 \\ P\theta F \\ \theta_1 F^1 \end{bmatrix} \end{aligned} \quad (44)$$

Using (35) and (42) yields:

$$\begin{aligned} &\left(\overline{F} - \theta_0 F^0 - \theta_1 F^1\right)\sigma_P + P\theta F \sigma_F + \theta_1 F^1 \left(\Sigma_\eta{}' \hat{\alpha}\right) \\ &= \begin{bmatrix} W\Sigma_\eta{}' \hat{\alpha} & \Sigma_Y{}' \end{bmatrix} \begin{bmatrix} F_W & P_W & 1 \\ F_{Y_1} & P_{Y_1} & 0 \\ . & . & . \\ F_{Y_K} & P_{Y_K} & 0 \end{bmatrix} \begin{bmatrix} P\theta \\ \frac{1}{P}\left(\overline{F} - \theta_0 F^0 - \theta_1 F^1\right) \\ \theta_1 \end{bmatrix} \end{aligned} \quad (45)$$

Applying Ito's lemma to $\overline{F}=\overline{F}(t,W,Y)$ and identifying terms, we have:

$$\begin{bmatrix} \overline{F}_W & \overline{F}_{Y_1} & . & . & \overline{F}_{Y_K} \end{bmatrix}' = \begin{bmatrix} F_W & P_W & 1 \\ F_{Y_1} & P_{Y_1} & 0 \\ . & . & . \\ F_{Y_K} & P_{Y_K} & 0 \end{bmatrix} \begin{bmatrix} P\theta \\ \frac{1}{P}\left(\overline{F} - \theta_0 F^0 - \theta_1 F^1\right) \\ \theta_1 \end{bmatrix} \quad (46)$$

Using (41) and (46) and substituting S^i for $\overline{F}$ yields the desired result.

Since the evaluated financial claim is a spot asset, the multi-beta ICAPM holds in its usual form, without adjustment for the risk premia. However, the replicating strategy is different from the standard one. To the extent that forward contracts are used in the strategy, the latter will involve hedging the implied interest rate risk. It is important to remark that ICAPM (16) holds whether the latter risk can be hedged perfectly (in special cases) or not (in general).

Now, the partial differential equation (PDE) followed by the forward contract is different from the one governing spot assets. It will admit a closed form solution when applied to a well known special case.

Proposition 4: *The price of the forward contract satisfies the following PDE:*

$$\begin{aligned}0 &= \frac{1}{2}W^2\sigma_W{}'\sigma_W F_{WW} + \sum_{j=1}^{K}\sigma_W{}'\sigma_{Y_j}F_{WY_j} + \frac{1}{2}\sum_{j=1}^{K}\sum_{k=1}^{K}\sigma_{Y_k}{}'\sigma_{Y_j}F_{Y_jY_k} \\ &+ \left(\hat{\alpha}'\mu_\eta W - W\lambda_W + W\sigma_W{}'\sigma_P - \hat{C}\right)F_W + \sum_{j=1}^{K}\left(\mu_{Y_j} - W\lambda_{Y_j} + \sigma_P{}'\sigma_{Y_k}\right)F_{Y_j} + F_t\end{aligned} \tag{47}$$

subject to the relevant boundary condition for the forward price as dictated by the terms of the contract.

Proof:

Applying Ito's lemma to F(t,Y,W) yields:

$$\begin{aligned}\mu_F F &= \frac{1}{2}W^2\sigma_{WW}F_{WW} + \sum_{j=1}^{K}\sigma_{WY_j}F_{WY_j} + \frac{1}{2}\sum_{j=1}^{K}\sum_{k=1}^{K}\sigma_{Y_jY_k}F_{Y_jY_k} \\ &+ \left(\hat{\alpha}'\mu_\eta W - \hat{C}\right)F_W + \sum_{j=1}^{K}\mu_{Y_j}F_{Y_j} + F_t\end{aligned} \tag{48}$$

Using (48) and (32) provides the desired result. □

This PDE turns out to possess a unique characteristic, due to the presence of several terms involving the volatility σ_P of the discount bond. To solve this PDE and find the price of the forward contract, a system of two equations must be solved, i.e. the (usual) PDE for the discount bond and the (novel) PDE (47). Fortunately, this can be accomplished in two steps. The price of the discount bond is obtained first, and then the price of the forward contract is derived by substitution. We provide below a specific example that gives the solution without formally resorting to actually solve successively the two PDEs.

10.4. A SPECIAL CELEBRATED CASE

The investor's optimal strategy having been derived and interpreted in all generality, we now analyze a special case where the cash-and-carry relationship will be shown to hold for a standard (linear) forward contract to deliver a predetermined amount $\eta(\tau)$ of the consumption good. We have picked this simple case as it represents the benchmark. We consider the specialized version of our economy pioneered by CIR (1985a).

Thus, there is a single state variable that follows the square root process:

$$dY = \varepsilon_Y (Y + \kappa_Y) dt + \sigma_Y \sqrt{Y} dz \tag{49}$$

and a single available technology, the dynamics of which is given by:

$$\frac{d\eta}{\eta} = \mu_\eta Y dt + \sigma_\eta \sqrt{Y} dz \tag{50}$$

where $\varepsilon_Y, \kappa_Y, \sigma_Y, \mu_\eta,$ and σ_η are constants.

Although this economy is affected by but one source of uncertainty, the market is still incomplete because of the short sale constraint imposed on trading on the technology. This implies that even a simple forward contract written on the technology is not redundant.

Lastly, the representative investor is assumed to have a logarithmic utility:

$$U(t, C(t)) = e^{-\rho t} \mathrm{Ln} C(t) \tag{51}$$

The following proposition sums up the results.

Proposition 5: *The equilibrium aggregate wealth is equal to:*

$$W(t)=\frac{1-e^{-\rho(\tau-t)}}{1-e^{-\rho\tau}}W(0)e^{-\rho t}\eta(t), \tag{52}$$

the equilibrium aggregate consumption is proportional to wealth:

$$\hat{C}(t)=\frac{\rho}{1-e^{-\rho(\tau-t)}}W(t)=\frac{\rho}{1-e^{-\rho\tau}}W(0)e^{-\rho t}\eta(t), \tag{53}$$

and the equilibrium spot rate of interest is given by:

$$r(t)=\left(\mu_\eta-\sigma_\eta^{\,2}\right)Y(t) \tag{54}$$

Proof:

In the special case of a logarithmic utility function, the standard solution for the investor's value function (see Ingersoll (1987) page 274) is:

$$J(t,W)=e^{-\rho t}\frac{1-e^{-\rho(\tau-t)}}{\rho}LnW(t) \tag{55}$$

Using the envelope condition yields equation (53):

$$\hat{C}(t)=\frac{\rho}{1-e^{-\rho(\tau-t)}}W(t)$$

Now, using (53), we have in equilibrium:

$$dW(t)=W(t)\left(\mu_\eta-\frac{\rho}{1-e^{-\rho(\tau-t)}}\right)dt+W(t)\sigma_\eta dZ(t) \tag{56}$$

which yields result (52).

Using (14) and (17) and the fact that all the wealth is invested in the technology in equilibrium, we have:

$$\begin{aligned}(\mu_\eta-\mu_P)J_W+\sigma_\eta(\sigma_\eta-\sigma_P)WJ_{WW}&=0\\(r-\mu_P)J_W-\sigma_P\sigma_\eta WJ_{WW}&=0\end{aligned} \tag{57}$$

Solving this system yields:

$$r = \mu_{\eta} - \sigma_{\eta}^{2} \tag{58}$$

Identifying from (50) yields equation (54). □

Consider now a simple (with linear pay-off) forward contract of maturity τ to deliver an amount $\eta(\tau)$ of the consumption good. Its price is equal to:

$$F(t) = \frac{\eta(t)}{P(t,\tau)} \tag{59}$$

Proof:

The pricing kernel methodology is, in this case, simple to use. The price of the forward contract is such that:

$$0 = E_t[\Lambda(\tau)(\eta(\tau) - F(\tau))] \tag{60}$$

where $\Lambda(\tau)$ is the pricing kernel defined by $\Lambda(t) = U_{\hat{C}}(t, \hat{C})$.
Then (60) can be rewritten as:

$$F(t)E_t[\Lambda(\tau)] = E_t[\Lambda(\tau)\eta(\tau)] \tag{61}$$

The price at time t of a discount bond maturing at time τ is such that:

$$P(t,\tau)\Lambda(t) = E_t[\Lambda(\tau)1] \tag{62}$$

Therefore, we get:

$$F(t)P(t,\tau)\Lambda(t) = E_t[\Lambda(\tau)\eta(\tau)] \tag{63}$$

By definition, and using (51), (52) and (53), we also have:

$$\Lambda(t) = U_{\hat{C}}(t,\hat{C}) = e^{-\rho t}\frac{1}{\hat{C}} = \frac{1}{\frac{\rho}{1-e^{-\rho\tau}}W(0)\eta(t)} \tag{64}$$

Using (63), and (64) twice for t = t and t = τ, then simplifying the integrals involved yields result (59).

We recover, in this special case, the familiar cash-and-carry formula. However, it is worth stressing that the latter is grounded on a general equilibrium model, not on mere absence of arbitrage opportunity. The no arbitrage condition is insufficient to drive the result since the forward contract is not redundant. This important and elegant result was first obtained by Richard and Sundaresan (1981). However, they derived it in a somewhat simpler setting where the representative investor has an infinite horizon and the forward contract has finite maturity. This assumption may be source of confusion and lead to the question as to why the forward contract is not longer-lived.

Now, in Cox-Ingersoll-Ross (1985b), the price of a discount bond with maturity τ is equal to:

$$P(t,\tau) = A(t,\tau)e^{B(t,\tau)r(t)} \tag{65}$$

where $A(t, \tau)$ and $B(t, \tau)$ are deterministic functions.

Applying Ito's lemma yields:

$$\begin{aligned}
\sigma_P &= B(t,\tau)\left(\mu_\eta - \sigma_\eta^2\right)\sigma_Y\sqrt{Y} \\
\sigma_{\hat{C}} &= \sigma_\eta\sqrt{Y} \\
\sigma_F &= \left(\sigma_\eta - B(t,\tau)\left(\mu_\eta - \sigma_\eta^2\right)\sigma_Y\right)\sqrt{Y}
\end{aligned} \tag{66}$$

Using (11) and substituting for (66) leads to:

$$\begin{aligned}
\mu_F &= -\sigma_F\sigma_P + \sigma_F\sigma_{\hat{C}} \\
&= -B(t,\tau)\left(\mu_\eta - \sigma_\eta^2\right)\sigma_Y\sigma_\eta Y \\
&\qquad + B(t,\tau)\left(\mu_\eta - \sigma_\eta^2\right)\sigma_Y B(t,\tau)\left(\mu_\eta - \sigma_\eta^2\right)\sigma_Y^2 Y \\
&\quad - B(t,\tau)\left(\mu_\eta - \sigma_\eta^2\right)\sigma_Y\sigma_\eta Y + \sigma_\eta^2 Y
\end{aligned} \tag{67}$$

Along with the usual risk premium associated with consumption risk, $\sigma_F\sigma_C$, there is an extra risk premium present in the RHS of the first part of equation (67). It should not be ignored, or even downplayed. It may very well be that the compensation for bearing strategy risk is of the same magnitude, or is even larger, than the compensation granted for consumption risk. The pricing of non-redundant forward contracts, as seen in the previous chapter, is different from that of cash assets. Again, it is important to note that the usual cash-and-carry derivation, while applicable in this special case, would not by itself lead to the decomposition of the drift μ_F into the two components present in the first equality (67) nor to its interpretation. A general equilibrium model is indeed required.

10.5. CONCLUSIONS

We have seen how a general equilibrium model of a (one-good) production economy in which the financial market is perfect but possibly incomplete can be derived. In addition to the consumption-related risk premium, the CCAPM for forward contracts is shown to contain a strategy risk premium, not the traditional term relevant for spot assets, namely the riskless interest rate. It compensates the investor for the (systematic) risk that stems from his very portfolio strategy when the latter involves non-redundant forward contracts. Moreover, this result extends to redundant contracts and is valid regardless of whether the cash-and-carry formula holds or not. Also, the multi-beta ICAPM for forward contracts contains *adjusted* risk premia for the market portfolio and each state variable, not the usual risk premia relevant for spot assets. Again, the adjustment is due to the systematic interest rate risk stemming from the trading strategy itself. The traditional ICAPM shows that only the systematic risks associated with the random fluctuations of a spot asset itself are priced. By contrast, the ICAPM that holds for forward contracts indicates that the systematic trading strategy risk is also priced. In the special case of Cox-Ingersoll-Ross (1985a), the magnitude of the strategy risk premium is shown to be possibly as large as that of the traditional risk premium.

The findings of this chapter should help highlight a specific feature of the financial market equilibrium, namely that the expected "return" on a forward asset includes a premium for a risk other than the risk associated with the asset price fluctuations. This result has been derived without the introduction of any exogenous risk (dubbed "background" risk in the literature). None of these results depends on the usual cash-and-carry relationship, which in general does not hold. However, in a specialized version of the economy, it does hold for a linear forward contract to deliver a given amount of the consumption good. Yet this cash-and-carry formula must be grounded on an equilibrium model, not just on the usual no-arbitrage argument.

Endnotes

[1] This chapter, grounded on Lioui and Poncet (2003c), includes futures in addition to forward contracts.

[2] Richard and Sundaresan's (1981) economy contains N consumption goods, thus N forward contracts written on them. Such a generalization would not add any economic insight to the results and, in particular, would not alter the pricing equations.

[3] Alternatively, and equivalently, we can assume as in Richard and Sundaresan (1981) that all investors are identical. Then each individual wealth is a fixed and known fraction of aggregate wealth. See their footnote 3 on page 351, for a brief discussion of this assumption.

[4] The word "return" is written within quotes since no initial payment is involved with a forward contract. The correct phrasing would be "percent change in the forward price".

CHAPTER 11: GENERAL EQUILIBRIUM PRICING OF FUTURES AND FORWARD CONTRACTS WRITTEN ON THE CPI[1]

11.1. INTRODUCTION

This chapter is motivated by the pervasive influence of inflation on many aspects of economic phenomena. As is well known, inflation impinges on investors' behavior (regarding both consumption and portfolio allocations) and welfare and is a major concern of most Central Banks.

First, an investor's optimal portfolio composition depends crucially on the stochastic behavior of changes in the investment opportunity set, of which inflation is a critical element [see, e.g., Campbell and Viceira (2001), Brennan and Xia (2002), Kothari and Shanken (2004) and Roll (2004)]. Moreover, it can be shown in a general equilibrium setting [see Poncet (1983) for an early attempt and Lioui and Poncet (2004a)] that the representative agent's portfolio strategy involves a hedge against inflation risk and that the nominal and real pricing kernels (stochastic discount factors) upon which expected returns on all assets depend are affected by random inflation.

Second, monetary theory and policy emphasize the fundamental role played by the economic agents' expectations regarding inflation in the dynamics of the main aggregate variables and the design of the Central Bank's policy rules. The Phillips curve constitutes the core of most macroeconomic debates and is the cornerstone of the set of equations assumed to represent the economy. The so-called New Keynesian or New Neoclassical Synthesis models focus on the forward looking nature of the equilibrium inflation rate in some monetary version of the real business cycle. In these models, current inflation is a function of inflation expected for the next period (rather than one-period lagged inflation) and of a measure of real activity. As to monetary policy, the widespread use among Central Banks of inflation targeting made expectations of inflation a key variable in policy making. Therefore, the conduct of monetary policy requires accurate estimates of economic agents' expectations of inflation.

These are partly revealed by TIPS (Treasury Inflation Protected Securities, issued for instance by the US Treasury since 1997) markets. However, TIPS do not exist everywhere and when they do, they do not provide a perfect estimator of future inflation for technical reasons. First, and primarily, indexed bonds are not pure real bonds since in general both the coupon and the principal are indexed with a time lag. Such a lag may introduce an important bias in the short run expectations of inflation extracted from the bond prices. Second, a rather involved technical problem arises since only yields to maturity are observed, not spot rates, and the number of available maturity dates is small as compared to the number of points generally desired for the whole term structure. Consequently, either numerical methods must be employed to convert yields into spot rates and then fill in the gaps, or some structural model of the term structure dynamics must be postulated and then calibrated to fit actual bond prices. None of these procedures is completely satisfactory. Third, even though one could get accurate estimates of the nominal and real term structures, the difference between the two does not quite yield the relevant rates of expected inflation. The reason is that, inflation being random, there are inflation risk premia (in addition to expected inflation rates) embedded in the nominal interest rates. The estimation of these premia is difficult and costly and different authors usually propose variously convincing solutions, one of which being simply to assume that they are equal to zero. Finally, markets for indexed bonds suffer from a lack of liquidity, and therefore the quoted prices are likely to incorporate liquidity premia, an issue that has always been ignored. Then such estimates could be of limited practical use. When the inflation rate is a two-digit number, the assumptions necessary to extract the expectations may be relatively innocuous. When inflation is low, however, even small absolute errors in the estimates may be large in relative terms and significantly bias the policy maker's decisions.

Consequently, the creation of derivatives written on the Consumer Price Index (CPI) would provide undoubtedly a close to perfect estimator of inflationary expectations, in addition to revealing useful information as to the inflation risk premium and real interest rates. This information will always be more accurate than the one conveyed by nominal bond and indexed bond prices. It will also be easier to extract from market prices, a very desirable property. Although it might prove difficult to disentangle inflation expectations from inflation risk premia, this direct information will doubtless be superior to any other signal extracted from some market prices. For example, if the inflation risk premium is nil, the futures price yields directly the market expectation of inflation. This is not the case with the approach using bond prices since problems such as those associated with indexation lags and modeling or reconstructing the whole term structure of nominal and real interest rates remain. In brief, standard techniques, such as the comparison of yields on nominal bonds with yields on indexed bonds, rely on too many assumptions to deliver estimates robust and reliable enough for policy purposes or asset allocations. Incidentally, the creation of CPI derivatives is not a new idea. The Coffee, Sugar, & Cocoa Exchange in New York did indeed trade a futures contract on the CPI from 1985 to 1991, date at which the contract was de-listed because inflation was curbed. It may be opportunistic to re-launch such contracts. There is in effect a current concern in most advanced economies, including Japan, that inflation rates are rising.

This requires a model of CPI derivatives pricing similar to what already exists for stocks, currencies and commodities. The standard no arbitrage argument is not sufficient, however, because the CPI is not a traded asset. We need a general equilibrium approach in which the CPI is determined endogenously as part of the solution to all agents' optimization problems. Obtaining a credible endogenous price level thus requires a complete model of a monetary economy affected by both monetary and real shocks.

We will adopt a monetary economy that is a special case of Lioui and Poncet (2003a). The latter is a generalization of the Cox, Ingersoll and Ross (1985a), hereafter CIR, real economy to a monetary economy, which is affected by both real (technological) and monetary shocks. Although this economy is frictionless, money non-neutrality obtains as an inherent feature. Monetary shocks are transmitted to the real sector through changes in real wealth and interest rates. Because money has a positive value at equilibrium, economic agents hold real cash balances from one period to the next. The *effective ex post* cost of holding one unit of real balances between two dates is the real interest rate plus the realized rate of depreciation of the purchasing power of money. In a world of certainty, this cost would be equal to the nominal rate of interest (i.e. Irving Fisher's classic relation would hold). However, under uncertain inflation, the two quantities differ. As of time t, the nominal interest rate represents a deterministic cost from t to t+dt, while the effective cost of holding money from t to t+dt is random if inflation is stochastic. To the extent that either real output or the money supply process, or both as here, are stochastic, so is the inflation rate. Money thus is a risky asset. The volatility of its real rate of return affects the agents' wealth dynamics, and, consequently, all their optimal decisions. Since the volatility of inflation is affected by monetary policy, so will be all endogenous variables: aggregate wealth level and growth rate, inflation, expected real excess returns on technologies and pure financial assets, both real and nominal interest rates and the inflation risk premium.

The remainder of the chapter is articulated as follows. Section 2 provides the main assumptions and the structure underlying our monetary economy. The nominal and real pricing kernels (stochastic discount factors) are obtained and discussed in Section 3. All equilibrium values, and the properties of CPI derivatives prices, are derived and discussed in Section 4.

11.2. THE MONETARY ECONOMY

The structure of the real sector is similar to the one in Cox-Ingersoll-Ross (1985a). We add to it a monetary sector through the introduction of an exogenous money supply process. There is a single physical perishable good that may be allocated to either consumption or investment. When variables are said to be expressed in real terms, it is understood that the implicit numéraire used is this physical good. The latter is produced by a technology (firm) denoted $\eta(t)$, where $\eta(t)$ is the amount (real value) of the good invested at date t in the technology. Production over time through the technology is governed by the following stochastic differential equation (SDE):

$$\frac{d\eta(t)}{\eta(t)} = \mu_\eta dt + \sigma_\eta dZ_\eta(t) \qquad (1)$$

where Z_η is a one-dimensional Wiener process, μ_η and σ_η are positive constants. The Wiener process is defined on the usual complete probability space (Ω, F, P) where P is the true (historical) probability. Like in CIR, equation (1) specifies the growth of an initial investment when the output of the process is continually reinvested in that same process. We impose the normalization $\eta(0) = 1$.

In addition to the technology, agents have access to a money market (savings) account that is in zero net supply. This nominal savings account is denominated in dollars and is riskless in nominal terms, and its instantaneous yield is the nominal interest rate R(t). The latter will be determined as an *endogenous* variable. Trading in the technology and the money market account takes place continuously in frictionless and arbitrage-free markets and at equilibrium prices only. However, short selling the technology, which is a physical investment, not a traded stock, is not admissible. This assumption is made for realism, but has no bearing on the results since our financial market is supposed to be complete.

The Central Bank issues money, and arbitrarily sets its nominal rate of return to zero. On a priori grounds, money thus would be strictly dominated by the nominally riskless money market account yielding R(t). However, since it helps reducing (implicit) transaction costs, it is desired for the liquidity services it provides. The money supply is exogenous to the model. Its dynamics is expressed as:

$$\frac{dM(t)}{M(t)} = \mu_M Y_M(t)dt + \sigma_M Y_M(t)dZ_M(t) + \sigma_{M\eta} Y_M(t)dZ_\eta(t) \tag{2}$$

where Z_M is a one-dimensional Wiener process defined on the probability space (Ω, F, P) and uncorrelated with Z_η, and μ_M , σ_M and $\sigma_{M\eta}$ are positive constants. These are policy parameters and thus exogenous to the model. $Y_M(t)$, the dynamics of which is given by equation (3) below, is a state variable to which the Central Bank presumably reacts and thus influences the evolution of the money supply. We thus call it "nominal". The drift part in (2) is the systematic, thus expected, component of monetary policy while the two diffusion terms reflect its surprise component. In particular, $\sigma_{M\eta}$ depends on the Central Bank's implicit reaction function to shocks affecting the real sector of the economy. It is noteworthy that, since the real sector of the economy is independent of the nominal state variable, the equilibrium *real* prices of financial assets will be affected by monetary factors if and only if money is non neutral.

The state variable is assumed to evolve according to:

$$dY_M(t) = \kappa_{Y_M}\left(\theta_{Y_M} - Y_M(t)\right)dt + \sigma_{Y_M M} dZ_M(t) + \sigma_{Y_M \eta} dZ_\eta(t) \tag{3}$$

where all parameters are constants. The dynamics (3) has been chosen to take into account the considerable amount of evidence on mean reversion in macro variables and financial asset prices. This mean reversion is transmitted to the money supply process and, as money will be shown to be nonneutral at equilibrium, part of it will be transmitted also to equilibrium consumption and thus asset prices. Note also that since the money supply process has been specified so as to exhibit stochastic volatility, imposing a constant volatility for the state variable process is in fact a weak assumption. More general dynamics for the state variable could have been easily assumed, as we have shown in Lioui and Poncet (2003a) in the general framework section. For the issue examined here, no qualitative feature of the economy is impaired by this simplifying assumption.

Since two Brownian motions drive the economy, three assets (with independent payoffs) whose trading is not constrained are needed to span it. The only one we have so far is the money market account since both the technology and money must be held positively. We thus assume that two financial assets (with independent payoffs) are available for trade. These assets are also in zero net supply, and their respective *nominal* prices obey the following SDEs:

$$\frac{dV_i(t)}{V_i(t)} = \mu_i(t)dt + \sigma_{i\eta}(t)dZ_\eta(t) + \sigma_{iM}(t)dZ_M(t) \tag{4}$$

for i = 1, 2. Our market thus is complete and we can safely rely on the existence of a representative agent in this economy.

The general price level, i.e. the money price of one unit of the consumption-investment good, *p*, will be shown to obey the following SDE:

$$\frac{dp(t)}{p(t)} = \mu_p(t)dt + \sigma_{p\eta}(t)dZ_\eta(t) + \sigma_{pM}(t)dZ_M(t) \tag{5}$$

where $\mu_p(t)$, $\sigma_{p\eta}(t)$ and $\sigma_{pM}(t)$ are functions to be found *endogenously* as part of the solution to the equilibrium problem.

To ensure that money is held at equilibrium, several alternatives are available, the main three being the explicit introduction of transaction costs, the cash-in-advance or cash-and-credit goods approach, and the money-in-the-utility-function approach originally developed by Sidrauski (1967). We retain the latter, and will impose a positive constraint on money holdings. In addition, to obtain ultimately closed form solutions we assume the standard log separable utility function for the representative agent:

$$U(t,c(t),m(t)) = e^{-\rho t}\left[\phi \ln c(t) + (1-\phi)\ln m(t)\right]$$

where ρ is a strictly positive constant reflecting the individual's impatience rate, and ϕ respects $0 < \phi < 1$. Consumption is denoted by c(t) and real money holdings by $m(t) = M(t)/p(t)$.

The representative individual, who is infinitely lived, maximizes the expected utility of her intertemporal consumption and real money balances under her budget constraint. Therefore, her consumption and portfolio decisions maximize:

$$E\left[\int_t^\infty e^{-\rho s}\left[\phi \ln c(s) + (1-\phi)\ln m(s)\right]ds \,\middle|\, F_t\right] \tag{6}$$

where $E\left[.\middle|F_t\right]$ is the expectation operator conditional on current endowments and the state of the economy. When maximizing (6), the investor limits her attention to admissible controls only.

Deleting the explicit time dependence of the variables for ease of exposition, the agent's budget constraint writes:

$$\begin{aligned} dw = {} & w\alpha\frac{d\eta}{\eta} + w\lambda\left(\frac{dV_1}{V_1} + \frac{dp^{-1}}{p^{-1}}\right) + w\varphi\left(\frac{dV_2}{V_2} + \frac{dp^{-1}}{p^{-1}}\right) \\ & + w\delta\left(Rdt + \frac{dp^{-1}}{p^{-1}}\right) - cdt + m\frac{dp^{-1}}{p^{-1}} \end{aligned} \tag{7}$$

where w is the *real* wealth, α is the proportion of real wealth invested in the technology, δ is the proportion of real wealth invested in the nominal savings account, and λ (respectively, φ) is the proportion of real wealth invested in the cash asset 1 (respectively, 2).

The last term reflects the opportunity cost of holding real balances, given by the change in the real price of one unit of currency. To see this, note that the change in the agent's real balances is such that:

$$dm = d\left(Mp^{-1}\right) = Mdp^{-1} + p^{-1}dM + dp^{-1}dM$$

or else:

$$dm = m\frac{dp^{-1}}{p^{-1}} + p^{-1}dM + dp^{-1}dM$$

Now, the government budget constraint must be respected. The *real* change in the nominal money supply, *after* prices have cleared, is in fact issued against real goods. Thus the agent's budget constraint writes:

$$\begin{aligned} dw = w\alpha\frac{d\eta}{\eta} - &\underbrace{gdt}_{\text{real government rate of consumption}} + \underbrace{p^{-1}dM + dp^{-1}dM}_{\text{real value of changes in nominal money supply}} \\ &+ w\lambda\left(\frac{dV_1}{V_1} + \frac{dp^{-1}}{p^{-1}}\right) + w\varphi\left(\frac{dV_2}{V_2} + \frac{dp^{-1}}{p^{-1}}\right) + w\delta\left(Rdt + \frac{dp^{-1}}{p^{-1}}\right) - cdt + m\frac{dp^{-1}}{p^{-1}} \end{aligned} \tag{8}$$

For the government budget to be balanced without issuance of Treasury securities, the second and the third term on the RHS of the equation above must cancel out.

Using that $\delta = 1 - \alpha - m/w - \lambda - \varphi$, and adding and subtracting the term rwdt, where r is the instantaneous real interest rate, the wealth dynamics can be rewritten:

$$\begin{aligned} dw = w\alpha\left(\frac{d\eta}{\eta} - rdt\right) &+ w\lambda\left(\frac{dV_1}{V_1} + \frac{dp^{-1}}{p^{-1}} - rdt\right) + w\varphi\left(\frac{dV_2}{V_2} + \frac{dp^{-1}}{p^{-1}} - rdt\right) \\ &+ w\delta\left(Rdt + \frac{dp^{-1}}{p^{-1}} - rdt\right) + m\left(\frac{dp^{-1}}{p^{-1}} - rdt\right) + rwdt - cdt \end{aligned} \tag{9}$$

Notice that r is to be found *endogenously*. Also note that the *ex post real* return on the nominal savings account is equal to Rdt, the nominal interest rate, plus the realized rate of depreciation of the purchasing power of money from t to t + dt, $dp(t)^{-1}/p(t)^{-1}$. In addition, the direct *ex post* cost of holding real balances m(t) between date t and date t + dt is proportional to the decrease in the purchasing power of money. Thus, the exact *ex post* opportunity cost of holding one unit of real cash balances is *not* the (deterministic) interest rate Rdt, but the (stochastic) term $\left[rdt - \frac{dp^{-1}}{p^{-1}}\right]$.

Under inflation uncertainty, these two quantities differ.

11.3. EQUILIBRIUM PRICING KERNELS

In this section, we derive the equilibrium real and nominal pricing kernels and their dynamics. For the economy to be in equilibrium, the following market clearing conditions must be satisfied:

(i): total wealth is equal to the total amount invested in the technologies (equities) plus the real value of money balances held, i.e. $w\alpha + m = w$,

(ii): net holdings in the nominal money market account and the two financial assets are nil, i.e. $\delta = \lambda = \varphi = 0$, and

(iii): money supply equals money demand[2], i.e. $\frac{M}{p} = m = w(1-\alpha)$.

Rather than adopting the customary risk neutral probability (the martingale measure), we use the historical probability. It is well known that in this setting pricing kernels (stochastic discount factors) conveniently summarize the complex stochastic environment in which asset pricing takes place. Recall that if, for instance, an asset yields a stochastic (real) dividend stream x(t) up to infinity, its real price q(t) at date t is such that [see for instance Duffie (2001)]:

$$\Lambda(t)q(t) = E_t\left[\int_t^{\infty} \Lambda(s)x(s)ds\right] \qquad (10)$$

where the *real* pricing kernel, denoted by $\Lambda(t)$, is nothing but the representative investor's marginal utility of consumption. It is given in the following

Proposition 1:

The real pricing kernel is equal to:

$$\Lambda(t) = \frac{\xi_M(t)}{\rho w(0)\eta(t)} \qquad (11)$$

where

$$\frac{d\xi_M(t)}{\xi_M(t)} = \frac{(1-\phi)\rho}{R(t)-(1-\phi)\rho}\left(\sigma_M Y_M(t) + \frac{1}{R(t)}\sigma_{RM}(t)\right)dZ_M(t)$$
$$+\frac{(1-\phi)\rho}{R(t)-(1-\phi)\rho}\left(\sigma_{M\eta} Y_M(t) + \frac{1}{R(t)}\sigma_{R\eta}(t)\right)dZ_\eta(t)$$

and $(\sigma^2_{RM}(t) + \sigma^2_{R\eta}(t))^{0,5}$ *is the instantaneous volatility of the nominal rate of interest.*

Proof: to avoid tedious repetitions, the proofs of Propositions 1 to 4 are provided at the end of Proposition 4.

The main notable feature of this pricing kernel is its dependence on the process $\xi_M(t)$, the dynamics of which is affected by monetary factors. This process, actually a martingale, reflects money non-neutrality in equilibrium. Thus, in addition to the real source of risk in the economy, real prices are affected also by the nominal source of risk. A necessary and sufficient condition for money to be non-neutral is that its dynamics displays a stochastic component, that is $\sigma_{M\eta} \neq 0$ and $\sigma_M \neq 0$. Note that the presence of a nominal state variable is *not* necessary. What drives money nonneutrality here is the effective cost of holding real balances, not the nominal interest rate. The former is equal to the real interest rate plus the rate of depreciation of the value of money, which is stochastic *ex ante* because inflation is random due to both real and monetary uncertainties.

Given (11), the dynamics of the real pricing kernel writes:

$$\frac{d\Lambda(t)}{\Lambda(t)} = -r(t)dt - \lambda_\eta(t)dZ_\eta(t) - \lambda_M(t)dZ_M(t) \tag{12}$$

where

$$\lambda_\eta(t) = \sigma_\eta - \frac{(1-\phi)\rho}{R(t)-(1-\phi)\rho}\left(\sigma_{M\eta} Y_M(t) + \frac{1}{R(t)}\sigma_{R\eta}(t)\right)$$
$$\lambda_M(t) = \frac{(1-\phi)\rho}{(1-\phi)\rho - R(t)}\left(\sigma_M Y_M(t) + \frac{1}{R(t)}\sigma_{RM}(t)\right)$$

As is well known, the volatility of the pricing kernel is equal to the market price of risk. Therefore, $\lambda_\eta(t)$ and $\lambda_M(t)$ are the real market prices of risk for each primary source of risk, Z_M and Z_η. Money nonneutrality regarding the evolution of the real pricing kernel is evidenced by the fact that both lambdas are affected by monetary parameters and, additionally, depend on the nominal interest rate. While in this economy there are two fundamental sources of risk, the volatilities of three macroeconomic variables crucially affect the dynamics of the market prices of risk: real output volatility, money supply volatility and nominal interest rate volatility.

The dynamics of the real pricing kernel depends upon the nominal and real interest rates. These instantaneous rates are given, along with the inflation risk premium, in the following proposition.

Proposition 2:

a) The equilibrium nominal rate of interest is equal to:

$$R(t)=\frac{(1-\phi)\rho}{1-\alpha}=\frac{(1-\phi)\rho}{1-f\left(Y_M(t)\right)} \qquad (13)$$

where $f(Y_M(t)) = \alpha$ is a function given in the proof following Proposition 4;

b) The equilibrium real rate of interest is equal to:

$$r(t)=\mu_\eta-\sigma_\eta^{\ 2}-\frac{(1-\phi)\rho}{R(t)-(1-\phi)\rho}\sigma_\eta\sigma_{M\eta}Y_M(t)-\frac{(1-\phi)\rho}{R(t)^2-(1-\phi)\rho R(t)}\sigma_\eta\sigma_{R\eta}(t) \qquad (14)$$

c) The equilibrium inflation risk premium, defined by $\varepsilon \equiv R+E_t\left[\frac{dp^{-1}}{p^{-1}}\right]-r$, *is equal to:*

$$\begin{aligned}
\varepsilon=\sigma_\eta^{\ 2}&+\frac{(1-\phi)\rho R(t)}{\left(R(t)-(1-\phi)\rho\right)^2}\left(\sigma_{M\eta}^{\ 2}+\sigma_M^{\ 2}\right)Y_M(t)-\frac{R(t)+(1-\phi)\rho}{R(t)-(1-\phi)\rho}\sigma_\eta\sigma_{M\eta}Y_M(t)\\
&+\frac{1}{R(t)-(1-\phi)\rho}\frac{(1-\phi)\rho}{R(t)^2-(1-\phi)\rho R(t)}\left(\sigma_{RM}(t)^2+\sigma_{R\eta}(t)^2\right)\\
&-\frac{R(t)+(1-\phi)\rho}{R(t)^2-(1-\phi)\rho R(t)}\sigma_\eta\sigma_{R\eta}(t)\\
&+\frac{2(1-\phi)\rho}{\left(R(t)-(1-\phi)\rho\right)^2}\left(\sigma_M\sigma_{RM}(t)+\sigma_{M\eta}\sigma_{R\eta}(t)\right)Y_M(t)
\end{aligned} \qquad (15)$$

The real rate is affected by monetary shocks through the nominal state variable and indirectly through the nominal interest rate. The relationship between the nominal and real interest rates is highly non-linear. The spread between the two depends on inflationary expectations and the inflation risk premium. Money nonneutrality compounds the impact of nominal factors on this premium.

Proposition 3:

The equilibrium price level is given by:

$$p(t) = e^{\rho t} \frac{M(t)\xi_M(t)R(t)}{(1-\phi)\rho w(0)\eta(t)} \tag{16}$$

The price level is affected by monetary factors through its dependence upon the money supply process, money non-neutrality and the nominal short rate. We are far from the one-to-one relation between price level changes and money supply changes that characterized the traditional quantity theory of money.

As to the nominal pricing kernel, it is defined, similarly to the real pricing kernel, by:

$$\Pi(t)Q(t) = E_t\left[\int_t^{\infty} \Pi(s)X(s)ds\right] \tag{17}$$

and is to be used when the future dividend stream and the asset current price are defined in nominal terms, so that we recover the *same price* today as the one obtained with the real kernel. This is identical to stating that discounting nominal flows with nominal interest rates is equivalent to discounting real flows with real interest rates. Since then $q(t)\Lambda(t)$ in equation (10) is equal to $Q(t)\Pi(t)$ in equation (17), and $q(t)$ is equal to $Q(t)/p(t)$, we obtain the following relationship between the two kernels:

$$\Lambda(t) = p(t)\Pi(t) \tag{18}$$

Proposition 4:

The nominal pricing kernel thus is given by:

$$\Pi(t)=\frac{(1-\phi)e^{-\rho t}}{M(t)R(t)} \tag{19}$$

and its dynamics is such that:

$$\frac{d\Pi(t)}{\Pi(t)}=-R(t)dt-\pi_M(t)dZ_M(t)-\pi_\eta(t)dZ_\eta(t) \tag{20}$$

where:

$$\pi_M(t)=\sigma_M Y_M(t)+\frac{1}{R(t)}\sigma_{RM}(t)$$
$$\pi_\eta(t)=\sigma_{M\eta} Y_M(t)+\frac{1}{R(t)}\sigma_{R\eta}(t)$$

Proofs of Propositions 1 to 4:

For convenience, we will use the following matrix notation:

$$Z(t)\equiv\begin{bmatrix}Z_\eta(t)\\ Z_M(t)\end{bmatrix};\ \Sigma_\eta(t)\equiv\begin{bmatrix}\sigma_\eta\\ 0\end{bmatrix};\Sigma_{Y_M}(t)\equiv\begin{bmatrix}\sigma_{Y_M\eta}\\ \sigma_{Y_M M}\end{bmatrix};$$
$$\Sigma_M(t)\equiv\begin{bmatrix}\sigma_{M\eta}Y_M(t)\\ \sigma_M Y_M(t)\end{bmatrix}\text{ and }\Sigma_i(t)\equiv\begin{bmatrix}\sigma_{i\eta}(t)\\ \sigma_{iM}(t)\end{bmatrix}$$

where i is any endogenous variable (w, c, α, p, 1 and 2).

Representative investor's first order conditions

Let $J(t,w(t),Y_M(t))$ be the representative agent's value (indirect utility of wealth) function and let LJ be the differential generator of J. We assume that J exists and is an increasing and strictly concave function of w. Define $\psi\equiv LJ+U$. Then deriving the Hamilton-Jacobi-Bellman equation:

$$0=\text{Max}\begin{pmatrix}U+J_w w\mu_w+J_{Y_M}\kappa_{Y_M}\left(\theta_{Y_M}-Y_M\right)+\frac{1}{2}J_{ww}w^2\Sigma_w{}'\Sigma_w\\ +\frac{1}{2}J_{Y_MY_M}\Sigma_{Y_M}\Sigma_{Y_M}{}'+J_{wY_M}w\Sigma_{Y_M}{}'\Sigma_w\end{pmatrix} \tag{21}$$

with respect to the control variables yields the necessary and sufficient conditions for optimality, μ_w and Σ_w denoting the drift and diffusion parameters of the equilibrium wealth dynamics. The value function in the case of a logarithmic investor is known to take the form:

$$J(t, w(t), Y_M(t)) = \frac{1}{\rho} e^{-\rho t} \mathrm{Ln}(Aw(t)) \tag{22}$$

where A could be easily determined (to no effect) using standard calculus and the usual transversality conditions (the investor's horizon being infinite).

We write first the dynamics of the representative investor's wealth at equilibrium, using the market clearing conditions. Substituting for (1) and (5) into (9) yields:

$$\frac{dw}{w} = \mu_w dt + \Sigma_w{}' dZ$$

where:

$$\begin{aligned} \mu_w &= \alpha\mu_\eta - \frac{c}{w} - (1-\alpha)\left(\mu_p - \Sigma_p{}'\Sigma_p\right) \\ \Sigma_w &= \alpha\Sigma_\eta - (1-\alpha)\Sigma_p \end{aligned} \tag{23}$$

Using the usual notations for the partial first and second derivatives of the value function, the optimality conditions read:

$$\psi_c = U_c - J_w \leq 0 \tag{24}$$

$$c\psi_c = 0 \tag{25}$$

$$\begin{aligned} \psi_m &= U_m - \left(r + \mu_p - \Sigma_p{}'\Sigma_p\right)J_w \\ &- \left(w\alpha\Sigma_\eta{}'\Sigma_p + w\lambda\left(\Sigma_1 - \Sigma_p\right)'\Sigma_p + w\varphi\left(\Sigma_2 - \Sigma_p\right)'\Sigma_p - (\delta w + m)\Sigma_p{}'\Sigma_p\right)J_{ww} \leq 0 \end{aligned} \tag{26}$$

$$m\psi_m = 0 \tag{27}$$

$$\begin{aligned} \psi_\alpha &= \left(\mu_\eta - r\right)wJ_w \\ &+ \left(\alpha w^2\Sigma_\eta{}'\Sigma_\eta + \lambda w^2\left(\Sigma_1 - \Sigma_p\right)'\Sigma_\eta + \varphi w^2\left(\Sigma_2 - \Sigma_p\right)'\Sigma_\eta - \left(\delta w^2 + wm\right)\Sigma_p{}'\Sigma_\eta\right)J_{ww} \leq 0 \end{aligned} \tag{28}$$

$$\alpha\psi_{\alpha} = 0 \tag{29}$$

$$\begin{aligned}\psi_{\delta} &= \left(R - r - \mu_p + \Sigma_p{}'\Sigma_p\right)wJ_w \\ &- \left(\alpha w^2\Sigma_\eta{}'\Sigma_p + \lambda w^2(\Sigma_1 - \Sigma_p)'\Sigma_p + \varphi w^2(\Sigma_2 - \Sigma_p)'\Sigma_p - (\delta w^2 + wm)\Sigma_p{}'\Sigma_p\right)J_{ww} = 0\end{aligned} \tag{30}$$

$$\begin{aligned}\psi_{\lambda} &= \left(\mu_1 - r - \mu_p + \Sigma_p{}'\Sigma_p\right)wJ_w \\ &+ \left(\alpha w^2\Sigma_\eta{}'(\Sigma_1 - \Sigma_p) + \lambda w^2(\Sigma_1 - \Sigma_p)'(\Sigma_1 - \Sigma_p) + \varphi w^2(\Sigma_2 - \Sigma_p)'(\Sigma_1 - \Sigma_p)\right. \\ &\left. - (\delta w^2 + wm)\Sigma_p{}'(\Sigma_1 - \Sigma_p)\right)J_{ww} = 0\end{aligned} \tag{31}$$

$$\begin{aligned}\psi_{\varphi} &= \left(\mu_2 - r - \mu_p + \Sigma_p{}'\Sigma_p\right)wJ_w \\ &+ \left(\alpha w^2\Sigma_\eta{}'(\Sigma_2 - \Sigma_p) + \lambda w^2(\Sigma_1 - \Sigma_p)'(\Sigma_2 - \Sigma_p) + \varphi w^2(\Sigma_2 - \Sigma_p)'(\Sigma_2 - \Sigma_p)\right. \\ &\left. - (\delta w^2 + wm)\Sigma_p{}'(\Sigma_2 - \Sigma_p)\right)J_{ww} = 0\end{aligned} \tag{32}$$

Equation (24) is the usual envelope condition. The Kuhn-Tucker conditions (25) and (27) account for the non-negativity constraints the consumption process and the real money balances processes, respectively, must satisfy. Similarly, condition (29) accounts for the impossibility to invest a negative amount of wealth in the real technology.

Aggregate wealth and price level dynamics

Since an interior solution is assumed to exist, the envelope condition (24) can be used with strict equality. Therefore, we have:

$$U_c = J_w \tag{24'}$$

and then, using (22), it follows that:

$$c = \phi\rho w \tag{33}$$

Substituting for (33) into (23) yields:

$$\begin{aligned} \mu_w &= \alpha\mu_\eta - \phi\rho - (1-\alpha)\left(\mu_p - \Sigma_p{}'\Sigma_p\right) \\ \Sigma_w &= \alpha\Sigma_\eta - (1-\alpha)\Sigma_p \end{aligned} \tag{34}$$

To obtain the parameters of the wealth dynamics, we need those of the equilibrium price level. At equilibrium, we have: $m = (1-\alpha)w$. Applying Ito's lemma to

$$p = \frac{M}{m} = \frac{M}{(1-\alpha)w}$$

yields:

$$\begin{aligned} \mu_P &= \mu_M Y_M - \mu_w + \frac{\alpha}{1-\alpha}\mu_\alpha + \frac{\alpha}{1-\alpha}\Sigma_\alpha{}'\Sigma_w \\ &\quad + \left(\Sigma_w - \frac{\alpha}{1-\alpha}\Sigma_\alpha\right)'\left(\Sigma_w - \frac{\alpha}{1-\alpha}\Sigma_\alpha\right) - \Sigma_M{}'\left(\Sigma_w - \frac{\alpha}{1-\alpha}\Sigma_\alpha\right) \\ \Sigma_P &= \Sigma_M - \Sigma_w + \frac{\alpha}{1-\alpha}\Sigma_\alpha \end{aligned} \tag{35}$$

where μ_α and Σ_α stands for the drift and the diffusion coefficient of the relative changes in the proportion of wealth invested in the real technology.

Solving for the system (34) and (35) yields:

$$\begin{aligned} \mu_w &= \mu_\eta - \frac{\phi\rho}{\alpha} - \frac{1-\alpha}{\alpha}\mu_M Y_M - \mu_\alpha \\ &\quad - \Sigma_\alpha{}'\left(\Sigma_\eta - \frac{1-\alpha}{\alpha}\Sigma_M - \Sigma_\alpha\right) + \frac{1-\alpha}{\alpha}\Sigma_M{}'\left(\frac{1}{\alpha}\Sigma_M + \frac{1}{1-\alpha}\Sigma_\alpha - \Sigma_\eta\right) \\ \Sigma_w &= \Sigma_\eta - \frac{1-\alpha}{\alpha}\Sigma_M - \Sigma_\alpha \end{aligned} \tag{36}$$

and

$$\mu_p = \frac{1}{\alpha}\mu_M Y_M - \mu_\eta + \frac{\phi\rho}{\alpha} + \frac{1}{1-\alpha}\mu_\alpha + \Sigma_\alpha{}'\Sigma_w$$
$$-\left(\frac{\alpha}{1-\alpha}\Sigma_\alpha + \frac{1-\alpha}{\alpha}\Sigma_M\right)'\left(\frac{1}{\alpha}\Sigma_M + \frac{1}{1-\alpha}\Sigma_\alpha - \Sigma_\eta\right)$$
$$+\left(\Sigma_\eta - \frac{1}{\alpha}\Sigma_M - \frac{1}{1-\alpha}\Sigma_\alpha\right)'\left(\Sigma_\eta - \frac{1-\alpha}{\alpha}\Sigma_M - \frac{1}{1-\alpha}\Sigma_\alpha\right) \tag{37}$$
$$\Sigma_p = \frac{1}{\alpha}\Sigma_M + \frac{1}{1-\alpha}\Sigma_\alpha - \Sigma_\eta$$

Optimal proportion of real wealth invested in the technology (α)

The next step consists in computing the equilibrium value of α. This is achieved as follows. On the one hand, the nominal rate R is related to the ratio of the marginal utilities of consumption and real balances; on the other hand, it is the return on a financial asset (the nominal savings account). Identifying the two expressions yields the expression for α. What follows provides the detailed derivation.

Since an interior solution is assumed to exist, the envelope conditions (26) can also be used with strict equality. Therefore, at equilibrium, we have:

$$U_m = \left(r + \mu_p - \Sigma_p{}'\Sigma_p\right)J_w + \left(w\alpha\Sigma_\eta{}'\Sigma_p - m\Sigma_p{}'\Sigma_p\right)J_{ww} \tag{38}$$

(30) implies:

$$RJ_w = \left(r + \mu_p - \Sigma_p{}'\Sigma_p\right)J_w + \left(w\alpha\Sigma_p{}'\Sigma_\eta - m\Sigma_p{}'\Sigma_p\right)J_{ww} \tag{39}$$

Substituting for (38) into (39) and using (24') yields the equilibrium nominal rate:

$$R = \frac{U_m}{U_c} = \frac{1-\phi}{\phi}\frac{c}{m} = \frac{(1-\phi)\rho}{1-\alpha} \tag{40}$$

On the other hand, from (39) above, we have:

$$R = r + \mu_p - \Sigma_p{}'\Sigma_p - \Sigma_p{}'\left(-w\alpha\Sigma_\eta + m\Sigma_p\right)\frac{J_{ww}}{J_w} \tag{41}$$

which is the Fisher relation under uncertainty. Using (22) and (37), we obtain:

$$\left(-\alpha\Sigma_{\eta}+(1-\alpha)\Sigma_{p}\right)\frac{wJ_{ww}}{J_{w}}=\Sigma_{\eta}-\frac{1-\alpha}{\alpha}\Sigma_{M}-\Sigma_{\alpha} \tag{42}$$

Moreover, using the three market-clearing conditions provided in the text and (28)-(29), we have:

$$r=\mu_{\eta}+\Sigma_{\eta}'\left(\alpha w\Sigma_{\eta}-m\Sigma_{p}\right)\frac{J_{ww}}{J_{w}} \tag{43}$$

and therefore:

$$r=\mu_{\eta}-\Sigma_{\eta}'\left(\Sigma_{\eta}-\frac{1-\alpha}{\alpha}\Sigma_{M}-\Sigma_{\alpha}\right) \tag{44}$$

Finally, using (37), (42) and (44), and substituting into (41) yields:

$$R=\frac{1}{\alpha}\mu_{M}Y_{M}+\frac{\phi\rho}{\alpha}+\frac{1}{1-\alpha}\mu_{\alpha}-\frac{1}{\alpha}\Sigma_{M}'\left(\Sigma_{M}+\frac{\alpha}{1-\alpha}\Sigma_{\alpha}\right) \tag{45}$$

Identifying (40) and (45) yields:

$$\frac{(1-\phi)\rho}{1-\alpha}=\frac{1}{\alpha}\mu_{M}Y_{M}+\frac{\phi\rho}{\alpha}+\frac{1}{1-\alpha}\mu_{\alpha}-\frac{1}{\alpha}\Sigma_{M}'\Sigma_{M}-\frac{1}{1-\alpha}\Sigma_{M}'\Sigma_{\alpha} \tag{46}$$

Rearranging terms in (46) now gives:

$$\left(\phi\rho+\mu_{M}Y_{M}-\Sigma_{M}'\Sigma_{M}\right)+\alpha\left(\mu_{\alpha}-\Sigma_{M}'\Sigma_{\alpha}-\rho-\mu_{M}Y_{M}+\Sigma_{M}'\Sigma_{M}\right)=0 \tag{47}$$

Clearly, it follows from (47) that:

$$\alpha=f(Y_{M}) \tag{48}$$

Applying Ito's lemma to (48) and using (3), we obtain:

$$\frac{df}{f}=\left(\frac{f'}{f}\kappa_{Y_{M}}\left(\theta_{Y_{M}}-Y_{M}\right)+\frac{1}{2}\frac{f''}{f}\Sigma_{Y_{M}}'\Sigma_{Y_{M}}\right)dt+\frac{f'}{f}\Sigma_{Y_{M}}'dZ \tag{49}$$

Substituting into (47) yields:

$$\frac{1}{2}\Sigma_{Y_M}{}'\Sigma_{Y_M}f'' + \left(\kappa_{Y_M}\left(\theta_{Y_M} - Y_M\right) - \Sigma_M{}'\Sigma_{Y_M}\right)f' - \left(\rho + \mu_M Y_M - \Sigma_M{}'\Sigma_M\right)f \\ + \left(\phi\rho + \mu_M Y_M - \Sigma_M{}'\Sigma_M\right) = 0 \qquad (50)$$

Using the definitions given at the outset of the proof yields:

$$\frac{1}{2}\left(\sigma_{Y_M\eta}{}^2 + \sigma_{Y_M M}{}^2\right)f'' + \left(\kappa_{Y_M}\theta_{Y_M} - \left(\kappa_{Y_M} + \sigma_{Y_M\eta}\sigma_{M\eta} + \sigma_{Y_M M}\sigma_M\right)Y_M\right)f' \\ - \left(\rho + \mu_M Y_M - \left(\sigma_{M\eta}{}^2 + \sigma_M{}^2\right)Y_M{}^2\right)f + \left(\phi\rho + \mu_M Y_M - \left(\sigma_{M\eta}{}^2 + \sigma_M{}^2\right)Y_M{}^2\right) = 0 \qquad (51)$$

Nominal interest rate

From (40) and (48) we have:

$$R(t) = \frac{(1-\phi)\rho}{1 - f(Y_M(t))} \qquad (52)$$

Applying Ito's lemma then yields:

$$dR(t) = \frac{(1-\phi)\rho}{(1-f)^2} \\ \times\left(\kappa_{Y_M}\left(\theta_{Y_M} - Y_M(t)\right)f' + \frac{1}{2}\left(\sigma_{Y_M M}{}^2 + \sigma_{Y_M\eta}{}^2\right)f'' + \left(\sigma_{Y_M M}{}^2 + \sigma_{Y_M\eta}{}^2\right)\frac{(f')^2}{(1-f)}\right)dt \\ + \frac{(1-\phi)\rho}{(1-f)^2}\sigma_{Y_M M}f'dZ_M(t) + \frac{(1-\phi)\rho}{(1-f)^2}\sigma_{Y_M\eta}f'dZ_\eta(t) \qquad (53)$$

From (52), it follows that:

$$\frac{1}{1 - f(Y_M(t))} = \frac{R(t)}{(1-\phi)\rho} \quad \text{and} \quad \frac{1}{(1 - f(Y_M(t)))^2} = \frac{R(t)^2}{(1-\phi)^2\rho^2} \qquad (54)$$

Substituting into (53) yields:

$$dR(t) = \mu_R(t)dt + \sigma_{RM}(t)dZ_M(t) + \sigma_{R\eta}(t)dZ_\eta(t) \qquad (55)$$

where

$$\mu_R(t) = \frac{R(t)^2}{(1-\phi)\rho}$$
$$\left(\kappa_{Y_M}\left(\theta_{Y_M} - Y_M(t)\right)f' + \frac{1}{2}\left(\sigma_{Y_M M}{}^2 + \sigma_{Y_M \eta}{}^2\right)f'' + \left(\sigma_{Y_M M}{}^2 + \sigma_{Y_M \eta}{}^2\right)\frac{R(t)}{(1-\phi)\rho}\left(f'\right)^2 \right) \tag{56}$$
$$\sigma_{RM}(t) = \frac{R(t)^2}{(1-\phi)\rho}\sigma_{Y_M M} f'$$
$$\sigma_{R\eta}(t) = \frac{R(t)^2}{(1-\phi)\rho}\sigma_{Y_M \eta} f'$$

Dynamics of optimal α

From (52) we have:

$$\alpha(t) = f\left(Y_M(t)\right) = 1 - \frac{(1-\phi)\rho}{R(t)} \tag{57}$$

Applying Ito's lemma yields:

$$\begin{aligned} \frac{d\alpha(t)}{\alpha(t)} &= \frac{(1-\phi)\rho}{R(t)^2 - (1-\phi)\rho R(t)}\left(\mu_R(t) - \frac{1}{R(t)}\left(\sigma_{RM}(t)^2 + \sigma_{R\eta}(t)^2\right)\right)dt \\ &+ \frac{(1-\phi)\rho}{R(t)^2 - (1-\phi)\rho R(t)}\sigma_{RM}(t)dZ_M(t) \\ &+ \frac{(1-\phi)\rho}{R(t)^2 - (1-\phi)\rho R(t)}\sigma_{R\eta}(t)dZ_\eta(t) \end{aligned} \tag{58}$$

Real interest rate

From (44) and the notations at the outset of the proof, we have:

$$\begin{aligned} r(t) = \mu_\eta - \sigma_\eta{}^2 &- \frac{(1-\phi)\rho}{R(t) - (1-\phi)\rho}\sigma_\eta \sigma_{M\eta} Y_M(t) \\ &- \frac{(1-\phi)\rho}{R(t)^2 - (1-\phi)\rho R(t)}\sigma_\eta \sigma_{R\eta}(t) \end{aligned} \tag{59}$$

Aggregate wealth and price level

Integrating (36) yields:

$$w(t) = w(0)e^{-\rho t}\eta(t)\xi_M(t)^{-1} \tag{60}$$

where:

$$\begin{aligned}\frac{d\xi_M(t)}{\xi_M(t)} &= \frac{(1-\phi)\rho}{R(t)-(1-\phi)\rho}\left(\sigma_M Y_M(t) + \frac{1}{R(t)}\sigma_{RM}(t)\right)dZ_M(t)\\ &+ \frac{(1-\phi)\rho}{R(t)-(1-\phi)\rho}\left(\sigma_{M\eta} Y_M(t) + \frac{1}{R(t)}\sigma_{R\eta}(t)\right)dZ_\eta(t)\end{aligned} \tag{61}$$

Since

$$p(t) = \frac{M(t)}{m(t)} \text{ and } m(t) = (1-\alpha(t))w(t) \tag{62}$$

substituting for (57) and (60) yields:

$$p(t) = e^{\rho t}\frac{M(t)\xi_M(t)R(t)}{(1-\phi)\rho w(0)\eta(t)} \tag{63}$$

Applying Ito's lemma to (63) yields the diffusion parameter of the price level dynamics:

$$\Sigma_p = \frac{1}{\alpha}\Sigma_M - \Sigma_\eta + \frac{1}{1-\alpha}\Sigma_\alpha \tag{64}$$

Inflation risk premium

From (41) we have:

$$\varepsilon = -\Sigma_p{}'\left(-w\alpha\Sigma_\eta + m\Sigma_p\right)\frac{J_{ww}}{J_w} \tag{65}$$

Substituting for (42) yields:

$$\varepsilon = -\left(\frac{1}{\alpha}\Sigma_M - \Sigma_\eta + \frac{1}{1-\alpha}\Sigma_\alpha\right)'\left(\Sigma_\eta - \frac{1-\alpha}{\alpha}\Sigma_M - \Sigma_\alpha\right) \tag{66}$$

and therefore,

$$\begin{aligned}\varepsilon = {} & \sigma_\eta{}^2 + \frac{(1-\phi)\rho R(t)}{(R(t)-(1-\phi)\rho)^2}\left(\sigma_{M\eta}{}^2 + \sigma_M{}^2\right)Y_M(t) \\ & - \frac{R(t)+(1-\phi)\rho}{R(t)-(1-\phi)\rho}\sigma_\eta \sigma_{M\eta} Y_M(t) \\ & + \frac{1}{R(t)-(1-\phi)\rho}\frac{(1-\phi)\rho}{R(t)^2-(1-\phi)\rho R(t)}\left(\sigma_{RM}(t)^2 + \sigma_{R\eta}(t)^2\right) \\ & - \frac{R(t)+(1-\phi)\rho}{R(t)^2-(1-\phi)\rho R(t)}\sigma_\eta \sigma_{R\eta}(t) \\ & + \frac{2(1-\phi)\rho}{(R(t)-(1-\phi)\rho)^2}\left(\sigma_M \sigma_{RM}(t) + \sigma_{M\eta}\sigma_{R\eta}(t)\right)Y_M(t)\end{aligned} \quad (67)$$

Real pricing kernel

Since $\Lambda(t) = U_c(t, c(t), m(t))$, we have $\Lambda(t) = \phi e^{-\rho t}/c(t)$. Given (33), it follows that:

$$\Lambda(t) = \frac{e^{-\rho t}}{\rho w(t)} = \frac{\xi_M(t)}{\rho w(0)\eta(t)} \quad (68)$$

Applying Ito's lemma to (68) yields:

$$\begin{aligned}\frac{d\Lambda(t)}{\Lambda(t)} = {} & -r(t)dt - \frac{(1-\phi)\rho}{(1-\phi)\rho - R(t)}\left(\sigma_M Y_M(t) + \frac{1}{R(t)}\sigma_{RM}(t)\right)dZ_M(t) \\ & -\left(\sigma_\eta - \frac{(1-\phi)\rho}{R(t)-(1-\phi)\rho}\left(\sigma_{M\eta} Y_M(t) + \frac{1}{R(t)}\sigma_{R\eta}(t)\right)\right)dZ_\eta(t)\end{aligned} \quad (69)$$

Nominal pricing kernel

The nominal pricing kernel is such that:

$$\Pi(t) = \frac{\Lambda(t)}{p(t)} = \frac{e^{-\rho t}}{\rho p(t) w(t)} \quad (70)$$

and therefore:

$$\Pi(t) = \frac{(1-\phi)e^{-\rho t}}{M(t)R(t)} \tag{71}$$

Its dynamics is given by:

$$\begin{aligned}\frac{d\Pi(t)}{\Pi(t)} = -R(t)dt &- \left(\sigma_M Y_M(t) + \frac{1}{R(t)}\sigma_{RM}(t)\right)dZ_M(t) \\ &- \left(\sigma_{M\eta} Y_M(t) + \frac{1}{R(t)}\sigma_{R\eta}(t)\right)dZ_\eta(t)\end{aligned} \tag{72}$$

which is result (20), given the definitions of $\pi_M(t)$ and $\pi_\eta(t)$.

To summarize up to this point, the preceding analysis shows that random money is inherently non-neutral, although the economy is frictionless and void of any nominal rigidities and/or credit constraints. This feature makes the model both realistic and tractable, in particular with respect to the pricing of derivatives.

11.4. PRICING CPI DERIVATIVES

In this section we use the equilibrium results of the previous section to derive the general valuation equation for CPI derivatives in general and then particular solutions for forward and futures contracts.

11.4.1. General Valuation Equation:

Consider a contingent claim whose terminal path-independent real cash flow is a well-behaved function of the price level p(T), say $\gamma(p(T))$, where T is the maturity of the contingent claim. We can state the following

Proposition 5:

The real price of any contingent claim written on the CPI, whose nominal payoff at maturity T is $\gamma(p(T))$, writes $\gamma(t, r(t), R(t))$ and solves:

$$\frac{1}{2}\left(\sigma_{rM}{}^{2}+\sigma_{r\eta}{}^{2}\right)\gamma_{rr}+\frac{1}{2}\left(\sigma_{RM}{}^{2}+\sigma_{R\eta}{}^{2}\right)\gamma_{RR}$$
$$+\left(\mu_{r}-\lambda_{M}\sigma_{rM}-\lambda_{\eta}\sigma_{r\eta}\right)\gamma_{r}+\left(\mu_{R}-\lambda_{M}\sigma_{RM}-\lambda_{\eta}\sigma_{R\eta}\right)\gamma_{R} \quad (73)$$
$$+\left(\sigma_{RM}\sigma_{rM}+\sigma_{r\eta}\sigma_{R\eta}\right)\gamma_{rR}+\gamma_{t}=r\gamma$$

Proof:

The real price of any contingent claim writes as:

$$\Lambda(t)\gamma(t,T)=E\left[\Lambda(T)\gamma(p(T))\middle|F_{t}\right] \quad (74)$$

R(t) and r(t) play the role of state variables in this economy. This is because from (59), we have:

$$0=-r(t)+\mu_{\eta}-\sigma_{\eta}{}^{2}-\frac{(1-\phi)\rho}{R(t)-(1-\phi)\rho}\sigma_{\eta}\sigma_{M\eta}Y_{M}(t)$$
$$-\frac{(1-\phi)\rho}{R(t)^{2}-(1-\phi)\rho R(t)}\sigma_{\eta}\sigma_{R\eta}(t) \quad (75)$$

And then one can write:

$$Y_{M}(t)=\psi(r(t),R(t)) \quad (76)$$

where, using (56),

$$0=-r(t)+\mu_{\eta}-\sigma_{\eta}{}^{2}-\frac{(1-\phi)\rho}{R(t)-(1-\phi)\rho}\sigma_{\eta}\sigma_{M\eta}\psi(r(t),R(t))$$
$$-\frac{(1-\phi)\rho}{R(t)^{2}-(1-\phi)\rho R(t)}\sigma_{\eta}\frac{R(t)^{2}}{(1-\phi)\rho}\sigma_{Y_{M}\eta}f'(\psi(r(t),R(t))) \quad (77)$$

Thus:

$$\gamma(t,T)=\gamma(t,T,r(t),R(t)) \quad (78)$$

Applying Ito's lemma to $\Lambda(t)\gamma(t,T)$ and setting the drift equal to 0 yields the PDE for the real price.

Although this equation presents features similar to the standard CIR's one, the presence of money leads to additional terms. In particular, both the real and nominal interest rates play a role in the valuation of any CPI contingent claim. This is so because the price of the underlying, i.e. the price level, is not taken as exogenous as in the standard Black-Scholes model, but is found endogenously as part of the equilibrium and turns out to depend upon these two rates.

Straightforward computation shows that the nominal price of any contingent claim may be written too as a function of the two rates. And indeed the nominal price of any contingent claim written on the CPI, whose nominal payoff at maturity T is $\Gamma(p(T))$, solves:

$$\begin{aligned}&\frac{1}{2}\left(\sigma_{rM}^{\ 2}+\sigma_{r\eta}^{\ 2}\right)\Gamma_{rr}+\frac{1}{2}\left(\sigma_{RM}^{\ 2}+\sigma_{R\eta}^{\ 2}\right)\Gamma_{RR}\\&\quad+\left(\mu_r-\pi_M\sigma_{rM}-\pi_\eta\sigma_{r\eta}\right)\Gamma_r+\left(\mu_R-\pi_M\sigma_{RM}-\pi_\eta\sigma_{R\eta}\right)\Gamma_R\\&\quad\quad+\left(\sigma_{RM}\sigma_{rM}+\sigma_{r\eta}\sigma_{R\eta}\right)\Gamma_{rR}+\Gamma_t=r\Gamma\end{aligned}\tag{79}$$

These partial differential equations are also valid for pricing nominal and indexed bonds since these are particular cases of CPI contingent claims.

11.4.2. Prices of CPI Forwards and Futures

Consider at time t a forward contract written on the price level with maturity T (T > t). Denote by G(t,T) the (nominal) price of the forward contract at time t[3]. Since initial investment in the contract is zero, the forward price solves, at each date t,

$$0=E\left[\Pi(T)(p(T)-G(t,T))\middle|F_t\right]\tag{80}$$

where F_t is the information available at t and $E\left[.\middle|F_t\right]$ is the conditional expectation under the true (historical) probability measure. This can be rewritten:

$$G(t,T)E\left[\Pi(T)\middle|F_t\right]=E\left[\Pi(T)p(T)\middle|F_t\right]\tag{81}$$

Using equation (17), the price Q(t, T) at time t of a nominal discount bond yielding one dollar at date T is such that:

$$\Pi(t)Q(t,T)=E\left[\Pi(T)1\middle|F_t\right]$$

Thus, substituting into equation (81) and using equation (18) yields:

$$G(t,T)\Pi(t)Q(t,T) = E[\Lambda(T)|F_t] \tag{82}$$

Also, the time t price q(t, T) of a real discount bond yielding 1 unit of the good at time T is such that:

$$\Lambda(t)q(t,T) = E[\Lambda(T)1|F_t]$$

Thus, substituting into equation (82) yields:

$$G(t,T)\Pi(t)Q(t,T) = \Lambda(t)q(t,T) \tag{83}$$

Using equation (18) again, we can state the following

Proposition 6:

The price at time t of a forward contract on the CPI maturing at time T is equal to:

$$G(t,T) = \frac{p(t)q(t,T)}{Q(t,T)} \tag{84}$$

This result has an intuitive interpretation, as it is equal to the ratio of the nominal price today of a real discount bond maturing at the maturity of the forward contract over the nominal price of a nominal discount bond maturing at the same date. This formula recovers formally the standard cash-and-carry relationship, although the underlying of the contract is the non-traded variable p(t). To obtain one unit of the good at date T, it suffices to buy today an indexed discount bond maturing at the forward contract maturity and to hold it until the contract maturity. The cost of carry is, as usual, the nominal interest rate paid on the loan that financed the real bond purchase. This result is similar to that of Richard and Sunderasan (1981) who has shown that in a general equilibrium framework, the equilibrium prices of (even non-redundant) forward contracts is given by the standard cash-and-carry. This result is not general since it is not valid for assets that generate intermediate random cash-flows such as dividends. However, in the case of the CPI it does hold, even in economies where the exogenous processes are slightly more general than the present ones [see for instance Lioui and Poncet (2003b)].

The forward price, to be obtained explicitly, requires explicit computation of the prices of nominal and perfectly indexed bonds. Of course, the valuation equations (73) and (79) could be used since the discount bonds are particular cases of contingent claims where the terminal cash flow is simply one unit of the consumption good in the case of the perfectly indexed bond and one unit of currency in the case of the nominal bond.

Finally, the CPI futures price can be computed from the following

Proposition 7:

The price at time t of a futures contract on the CPI maturing at time T is given by:

$$\frac{H(t,T)}{G(t,T)} = E\left[\exp\left\{\int_t^T (R(s)-f(t,s))ds\right\}\middle| F_t\right] + \mathrm{Cov}\left[\frac{\Lambda(T)}{\Lambda(t)}\frac{1}{q(t,T)};\exp\left\{\int_t^T (R(s)-f(t,s))ds\right\}\middle| F_t\right] \tag{85}$$

Proof:

From Duffie and Stanton (1992), theorem 1, the futures contract nominal settlement price is the same as the price of an asset that yields $p(T)\exp\left\{\int_t^T R(s)ds\right\}$ at T. Hence,

$$\Pi(t)H(t,T) = E\left[\Pi(T)p(T)\exp\left\{\int_t^T R(s)ds\right\}\middle| F_t\right] \tag{86}$$

Using (84), it follows that:

$$\frac{H(t,T)}{G(t,T)} = E\left[\frac{\Pi(T)}{\Pi(t)}\frac{Q(t,T)}{p(t)q(t,T)}p(T)\exp\left\{\int_t^T R(s)ds\right\}\middle| F_t\right] \tag{87}$$

and thus:

$$\frac{H(t,T)}{G(t,T)} = E\left[\frac{\Lambda(T)}{\Lambda(t)}\frac{Q(t,T)}{q(t,T)}\exp\left\{\int_t^T R(s)ds\right\}\middle| F_t\right] \tag{88}$$

The price of a discount bond yielding one dollar at maturity can be written as:

$$Q(t,T) = \exp\left\{-\int_t^T f(t,s)ds\right\} \tag{89}$$

where f is the instantaneous forward rate. Thus (88) becomes:

$$\frac{H(t,T)}{G(t,T)} = E\left[\frac{\Lambda(T)}{\Lambda(t)}\frac{1}{q(t,T)}\exp\left\{\int_t^T (R(s)-f(t,s))ds\right\}\middle| F_t\right] \tag{90}$$

and then:

$$\begin{aligned}\frac{H(t,T)}{G(t,T)} = {} & E\left[\frac{\Lambda(T)}{\Lambda(t)}\frac{1}{q(t,T)}\middle| F_t\right]E\left[\exp\left\{\int_t^T (R(s)-f(t,s))ds\right\}\middle| F_t\right] \\ & +\mathrm{Cov}\left[\frac{\Lambda(T)}{\Lambda(t)}\frac{1}{q(t,T)};\exp\left\{\int_t^T (R(s)-f(t,s))ds\right\}\middle| F_t\right]\end{aligned} \tag{91}$$

Finally, noting that:

$$E\left[\frac{\Lambda(T)}{\Lambda(t)}\frac{1}{q(t,T)}\middle| F_t\right] = 1$$

result (85) follows.

As always, the futures and forward prices differ in as much as interest rates are stochastic and would be equal if rates were deterministic. For instance, for R and r constant, we would have from (84) and (85): G(t,T) = H(t,T) = p(t) exp((R-r)(T-t)).

One merit of our general equilibrium approach is that all the solutions, including the ones for contingent claim prices, can be expressed as functions of the fundamental economic parameters. This cannot be the case in the arbitrage approach. This is the positive compensation for having to introduce more restrictive assumptions as to the underlying stochastic processes. As previously stated, money nonneutrality transpires in the behavior of the interest rates, upon which all option prices depend. The nominal rate is affected in all cases and the real rate is in general affected unless $\sigma_{M\eta}$ is zero, i.e. when monetary shocks and real shocks happen not to be correlated.

In a continuous time monetary economy that is affected by both real and nominal shocks and in which money is inherently not neutral, a cash-and-carry type relationship has been shown to hold at equilibrium for forward contracts on the CPI but not for futures. Numerical methods or Monte Carlo simulations (now routinely applied and mastered) are then required and the practitioners are left with the usual tradeoff between realism and tractability. Since the CPI index itself is not traded, the derivations could not rely on standard arbitrage arguments but necessitate, and justify, the general equilibrium approach adopted in this chapter. Since inflation impinges on economic agents' behavior (in terms of both consumption and portfolio allocation) and welfare, and present TIPS are imperfect hedges against uncertain inflation, the introduction of such CPI derivatives should be Pareto-improving. If the gain might be minimal in countries experiencing low and stable inflation rates, in other countries it could be substantial and worth the effort to design such new instruments.

Endnotes

[1] This chapter, except for its introduction, is an adaptation of Lioui and Poncet (2004b) in which the interested reader will also find the pricing of a European option written on the CPI.

[2] Note that one of these conditions is redundant when the others (along with condition (i)) are satisfied.

[3] Like any contingent claim, this price will depend upon the implicit state variables in the economy. Thus the notation G(t,T) is a shortcut for G(t, r(t), R(t); T).

REFERENCES

Adler, M. and J. Detemple, 1988a, On the optimal hedge of a non-traded cash position, *Journal of Finance* 43, 143-153.

Adler, M. and J. Detemple, 1988b, Hedging with futures in an intertemporal portfolio context, *Journal of Futures Markets* 8, 249-269.

Amin, K. and R. Jarrow, 1991, Pricing foreign currency options under stochastic interest rates, *Journal of International Money and Finance* 10, 310-329.

Amin, K., and A. Morton, 1994, Implied volatility functions in arbitrage-free term structure models, *Journal of Financial Economics* 35, 141-180.

Anderson, R. and J.P. Danthine, 1983, The time pattern of hedging and the volatility of futures prices, *Review of Economic Studies* 50, 249-266.

Ang, J., and Y. Cheng, 2004, Financial Innovations and Market Efficiency: The Case of Single Stock Futures, Florida State University, Working Paper.

Athanasoulis, S., R. Shiller and E. van Wincoop, 1999, Macro Markets and Financial Security, *FRBNY Economic Policy Review* 5, 21-39.

Bajeux-Besnainou, I., Portait, R., 1997, The Numeraire Portfolio: A New Perspective on Financial Theory, *European Journal of Finance* 3, 291-309.

Bartram, S., G. Brown and F. Fehle, 2003, International Evidence on Financial Derivative Usage, Working Paper.

Benninga, S. and A. Protopapadakis, 1994, Forward and Futures prices with markovian interest rates processes, *Journal of Business* 67, 401-421.

Benninga, S., A. Protopapadakis and Z. Wiener, 2000, Limiting Differences between Forward and Futures Prices in a Lucas Consumption Model, *Journal of International Financial Markets, Institutions and Money* 10, 151-61.

Black, F., and M. Scholes, 1973, The Pricing of Options and Corporate Liabilities, *Journal of Political Economy* 81, 637-654.

Brealey, R. and E. Kaplanis, 1995, Discrete exchange rate hedging strategies, *Journal of Banking and Finance* 19, 765-784.

Breeden, D., 1979, An Intertemporal Asset Pricing Model with Stochastic Consumption and investment Opportunities, *Journal of Financial Economics* 7, 265-296.

Breeden, D., 1984, Futures Markets and Commodity Options Hedging and Optimality in Incomplete Markets, *Journal of Economic Theory* 32, 275-300.

Brennan, M. and J. Xia, 2002, Dynamic Asset Allocation Under Inflation, *Journal of Finance* 57, 1201-1238.

Briys, E. and B. Solnik, 1992, Optimal currency hedge ratios and interest rates risk, *Journal of International Money and Finance* 11, 431-445.

Campbell, J. and L. Viceira, 2001, Who Should Buy long – term bonds ? *American Economic Review* 91, 99-127.

Cassassus, J. and P. Collin-Dufresne, 2003, `Maximal' Affine Model of Convenience Yields Implied From Interest Rates and Commodity Futures , Working paper.

Chatrath, A., B. Adrangi and M. Alleder, 2001, The impact of margins in futures markets: Evidence from the gold and silver markets, *The Quarterly Review of Economics and Finance* 41, 279–294.

Chen, N., R. Roll and S. Ross, 1986, Economic Forces and the Stock Market, *Journal of Business* 59, 383-403.

Chernenko, S., K. Schwarz and J. Wright, 2004, The Information Content of Forward and Futures Prices: Market Expectations and the Price of Risk, Working Paper.

Chow, Y., M. McAleer and J. Michael, 2000, Pricing of Forward and Futures Contracts, *Journal of Economic Surveys* 14, 215-53.

Clerc, N. and R. Gibson, 2000, Do Newly Listed Derivatives Affect the Market Risk Premium in a Thin Stock Market?, *European Finance Review* 4, 97-127.

Cochrane, J., 1997, Where is the Market Going? Uncertain Facts and Novel Theories, *Economic Perspectives XXI: 6, Federal Reserve Bank of Chicago.*

Cotter, J., 2001, Margin Exceedences for European Stock Index Futures Using Extreme Value Theory, *Journal of Banking and Finance* 25, 1475-1502.

Cowen, T., 1997, Should Central Banks Target CPI Futures?, *Journal of Money, Credit, and Banking* 29, 275-85.

Cox, J. and C.F. Huang, 1989, Optimal consumption and portfolio policies when asset prices follow a diffusion process, *Journal of Economic Theory* 49, 33-83.

Cox, J. and C.F. Huang, 1991, A variational problem arising in financial economics, *Journal of Mathematical Economics* 20, 465-487.

Cox, J. , J. Ingersoll and S. Ross, 1981, The relation between forward and futures prices, *Journal of Financial Economics* 9, 321-346.

Cox, J. , J. Ingersoll and S. Ross, 1985a, An Intertemporal General Equilibrium Model of Asset Prices, *Econometrica* 51, 363-383.

Cox, J. , J. Ingersoll and S. Ross, 1985b, A Theory of the Term Structure of Interest Rates, *Econometrica* 51, 385-407.

Cuny, C., 2002, Spread Futures: Why Derivatives on Derivatives?, Working Paper.

Da-Hsiang-Donald, L., 1992, Optimal hedging and spreading in cointegrated markets, *Economics Letters* 40, 91-95.

Dai, Q. and K. Singleton, 2000, Specification Analysis of Affine Term Structure Models, *Journal of Finance* 55, 1943-78.

Day, T. and C. Lewis, 2004, Margin Adequacy and Standards: An Analysis of the Crude Oil Futures Market, *Journal of Business* 77, 101-135.

De Jong, F. and P. Santa Clara, 1999, The dynamics of the forward interest rate curve: a formulation with state variables, *Journal of Financial and Quantitative Analysis* 34, 131-157.

Detemple, J. and A. Serrat, 2003, Dynamic Equilibrium with Liquidity Constraints, *Review of Financial Studies* 16, 597-629.

Dezhbakhsh, H., 1994. Foreign exchange forward and futures prices: are they equal ? *Journal of Financial and Quantitative Analysis* 29, 75-87.

Dowd, K., 1994, A Proposal to End Inflation, *Economic Journal* 104, 828-40.

Duffie, D., 1989, *Futures Markets*, Englewood Cliffs, New Jersey: Prentice-Hall.

Duffie, D., 2001, *Dynamic Asset Pricing Theory*, Princeton University Press, Third Edition.

Duffie, D. and M. Jackson, 1990, Optimal hedging and equilibrium in a dynamic futures market, *Journal of Economic Dynamics and Control* 14, 21-33.

Duffie, D. and R. Stanton, 1992, Pricing continuously resettled contingent claims, *Journal of Economic Dynamics and Control* 16, 561-573.

Dutt, H. and I. Wein, 2003, On the adequacy of single-stock futures margining requirements, *Journal of Futures Markets* 23, 989–1002.

El Karoui, N. and J.C. Rochet, 1989, A Pricing Formula for Options on Coupon Bonds, Working Paper, Modeles Mathematiques en Finance, INRIA.

Fama, E., 1996, Multifactor Portfolio Efficiency and Multifactor Asset Pricing, *Journal of Financial and Quantitative Analysis* 31, 441-65.

Fama, E. and K. French, 1996. Multifactor Explanations of Asset Pricing Anomalies, *Journal of Finance* 51, 55-84.

Figlewski, S., Y. Landskroner and W. Silber, 1991, Tailing the hedge: Why and How, *Journal of Futures Markets* 11, 201-212.

Flesaker, B., 1993, Arbitrage free pricing of interest rate futures and forward contracts, *Journal of Futures Markets* 13, 77-91.

Follmer, H. and M. Schweitzer, 1986, Hedging non redundant contingent claims, In Contributions to Mathematical Economics, In Honor of Gerard Debreu, North Holland.

Follmer, H. and M. Schweitzer, 1991, Hedging of Contingent Cliams under Incomplete Information, In Applied Stochastic Analysis, Stochastic Monographs 5, Gordon and Breach, 389-414.

French, K., 1983, A Comparison of Futures and Forward Prices, *Journal of Financial Economics* 12, 311-342.

Glen, J. and P. Jorion, 1993, Currency hedging for international portfolios, *Journal of Finance* XLVIII, 1865-1886.

Gorton, G. and G. Rouwenhorst, 2004, Facts and Fantasies about commodity futures, Yale ICF Working Paper No. 04-20.

Graham, J. and C. Smith, 1999, Tax Incentives to Hedge, *Journal of Finance* 54, 2241-2262

Grinblatt, M. and N. Jegadeesh, 1996, The relative pricing of eurodollar futures and forward contracts, *Journal of Finance* 51, 1499-1522.

Hakansson, N., 1971, On Optimal Myopic Portfolio Policies With and Without Serial Correlation of Yields, *Journal of Business* 44, 324-334.

Harrison, M. and D. Kreps, 1979, Martingales and arbitrage in multiperiod securities markets, *Journal of Economic Theory* 20, 381-408.

Harrison, M. and S. Pliska, 1981, Martingales and stochastic integrals in the theory of continuous trading, *Stochastic Processes and Their Applications* 11, 215-260.

He, H. and N. Pearson, 1991, Consumption and portfolio policies with incomplete markets and short sale constraints, *Journal of Economic Theory* 54, 259-304.

Heath, D., R. Jarrow and A. Morton, 1992, Bond Pricing and the Term Structure of Interest Rates: a New Methodology for Contingent Claims Valuation, *Econometrica* 60, 77-105.

Hicks, 1939, *Value and Capital*, Oxford, Clarendon Press.

Hilliard, J. and J. Reis, 1998, Valuation of Commodity Futures and Options under Stochastic Convenience Yields, Interest Rates and Jump Diffusions in the Spot, *Journal of Financial and Quantitative Analysis* 33, 61-86.

Ho, T., 1984, Intertemporal Commodity Futures Hedging and the Production Decision, *Journal of Finance* 34, 351-375.

Huang, C.F., Litzenberger, R., 1988, *Foundations for Financial Economics*, North Holland.

Hull, J., 2003, *Options, Futures and Other Derivative Securities*, Prentice Hall, Englewood Cliffs.

Ingersoll, J., 1987, *Theory of financial decision making*, Rowman and Littlefield Studies in Financial Economics, Totowa, N.J.

Jamshidian, F., 1987, The Multifactor Gaussian Interest Rate Model and Implementation, Preprint, World Finance Center, Merrill Lynch, New York.

Jamshidian, F., 1989, An Exact Bond Option Formula, *Journal of Finance* 44, 205-209.

Jarrow, R. and G. Oldfield, 1981, Forward Contracts and Futures Contracts, *Journal of Financial Economics* 9, 373-382.

Jarrow, R. and G. Oldfield, 1988, Forward Options and Futures Options, *Advances in futures and options research* 3, 15-28.

Jegadeesh, N. and S. Titman, 1993, Returns to Buying Winners and Selling Losers: Implications for Stock Market Efficiency, *Journal of Finance* 48, 65-91

Kandel, S., Stambaugh, R., 1995, Portfolio Inefficiency and the Cross-Section of Expected Returns, *Journal of Finance* 50, 157-84.

Karatzas, I., J. Lehoczky and S. Shreve, 1987, Optimal portfolio and consumption decisions for a small investor on a finite horizon, *SIAM Journal Control and Optimization* 25, 1557-1586.

Karatzas, I., J. Lehoczky, S. Shreve and G. Xu, 1991, Martingale and duality methods for utility maximization in an incomplete market, *SIAM Journal Control and Optimization* 29, 702-730.

Karatzas, I. and S. Shreve, 1991, *Brownian Motion and Stochastic Calculus*, Springer Verlag, Second edition.

Keynes, J. M., 1930, *A Treatise on Money,* London: Harcourt, Brace, and World.

Kim, T.S., and Omberg, E., 1996, Dynamic Nonmyopic Portfolio Behavior, *Review of Financial Studies* 9, 141-161.

Kolb, R., 2002, *Futures, Options & Swaps*, Blackwell Publishing.

Korn, O., 2004, Drift Matters: An Analysis of Commodity Derivatives, *Journal of Futures Markets*, Forthcoming.

Korn, R. and H. Kraft, 2004, On the stability of continuous-time portfolios problems with stochastic opportunity set, *Mathematical Finance* 14, 403-414.

Kothari, S.P. and J. Shanken, 2004, Asset Allocation with Inflation-Protected Bonds, *Financial Analyst Journal* 60.

Kraus, A., and Litzenberger, R.H., 1975, Market Equilibrium in a Multiperiod State Preference Model with Logarithmic Utility, *Journal of Finance* 30, 1213-1227.

Lettau, M. and S. Ludvigson, 2004, Expected Returns and Expected Dividend Growth, *Journal of Financial Economics*, Forthoming.

Lintner, J., 1965, The valuation of risky assets and the selection of risky investment in stock portfolios and capital budgets, *Review of Economics and Statistics* 47, 13-37.

Lioui, A., 1997, Marking-to-Market and the Demand for Interest Rates Futures, *Journal of Futures Markets* 17, 303-316.

Lioui, A. and R. Eldor, 1998, Optimal Spreading When Spreading Is Optimal, *Journal of Economic Dynamics and Control* 23, 277-301.

Lioui, A. and P. Poncet, 1996a, Optimal hedging in a dynamic futures market with a non-negativity constraint on wealth, *Journal of Economic Dynamics and Control* 20, 1101-1113.

Lioui, A. and P. Poncet, 1996b, Optimal hedging in a dynamic incomplete futures market, *Geneva Papers on Risk and Insurance Theory* 21, 103-122.

Lioui, A. and P. Poncet, 2000a, The Minimum Variance Hedge Ratio Under Stochastic Interest Rates, *Management Science* 46, 658-668.

Lioui, A. and P. Poncet, 2000b, Bernoulli speculator and trading strategy risk, *Journal of Futures Markets* 20, 507 - 523.

Lioui, A. and P. Poncet, 2001a, Mean Variance Efficiency of The Market Portfolio and Futures Trading, *Journal of Futures Markets* 21, 329 - 346.

Lioui, A. and P. Poncet, 2001b, On The Optimal Portfolio Choice Under Stochastic Interest Rates, *Journal of Economic Dynamics and Control* 25, 1841-1865.

Lioui, A. and P. Poncet, 2002, Optimal Currency Risk Hedging, *Journal of International Money and Finance* 21(2), 241 – 264.

Lioui, A. and P. Poncet, 2003a, Monetary Analysis In Continuous Time, Working Paper.

Lioui, A. and P. Poncet, 2003b, Dynamic Asset Pricing with Non Redundant Forward Contracts, *Journal of Economic Dynamics and Control* 27, 1163-1180.

Lioui, A. and P. Poncet, 2003c, General Equilibrium Pricing of Non Redundant forward contracts, *Journal of Futures Markets* 23, 817-840.

Lioui, A. and P. Poncet, 2004a, General Equilibrium Real and Nominal Interest Rates, *Journal of Banking and Finance* 28, 1569-1595.

Lioui, A. and P. Poncet, 2004b, General Equilibrium Pricing of CPI's Derivatives, *Journal of Banking and Finance*, Forthcoming.

Long, J. B., 1990, The Numeraire Portfolio, *Journal of Financial Economics* 26, 29-69.

Lucas, R., 1978, Asset Prices in an Exchange Economy, *Econometrica* 46, 1429-1445.

Mckenzie, M., T. Brailsford and R. Faff, 2001, New Insights into the Impact of the Introduction of Futures Trading on Stock Price Volatility, *Journal of Futures Markets* 21, 237–255.

Merton, R., 1971, Optimum Consumption and Portfolio Rules in a Continuous-Time Model, *Journal of Economic Theory* 3, 373-413.

Merton, R.C., 1973, An Intertemporal Capital Asset Pricing Model, *Econometrica* 41, 867-887.

Meulbroek, L., 1992, A comparison of forward and futures prices of an interest rate sensitive financial asset, *Journal of Finance* XLVII, 381-396.

Murawski, C., 2003, On the Forward-Futures Spread and Default Risk, Working Paper.

Neuberger, A., 1999, Hedging Long-Term Exposures with Multiple Short-Term Futures Contracts, *Review of Financial Studies* 12, 429-459.

Ohashi, K., 1995, Endogenous determination of the degree of market incompleteness in futures innovation, *Journal of Economic Theory* 65, 198-217.

Ohashi, K., 1997, Optimal Futures Innovation in a Dynamic Economy: The Discrete-Time Case, *Journal of Economic Theory* 74, 448-65.

Pennings, J. And R. Leuthold, 2001, Introducing New Futures Contracts: Reinforcement versus Cannibalism, *Journal of International Money and Finance* 20, 659-675.

Poitras, G., 1989, Optimal futures spreads positions, *Journal of Futures Markets* 9, 123-133.

Polakoff, M., and P. Grier, 1991, A Comparison of Foreign Exchange Forward and Futures Prices, *Journal of Banking and Finance* 15, 1057-80.

Poncet, P., 1983, Optimum Consumption and Portfolio Rules with Money as an Asset, *Journal of Banking and Finance* 7, 231-52.

Poncet, P. and R. Portait, 1993, Investment and Hedging Under a Stochastic Yield Curve, *European Economic Review* 37, 1127-1147.

Rendleman, R., 2002, *Applied Derivatives: Options, Futures and Swaps*, Blackwell Publishers.

Ribeiro, D. and S. Hodges, 2004, A Two-Factor Model for Commodity Prices and Futures Valuation, Working Paper.

Richard, S.F., and Sundaresan, S., 1981, A continuous time equilibrium model of forward prices and futures prices in a multigood economy, *Journal of Financial Economics* 9, 347-371.

Roll, R., 1977, A Critique of the Asset Pricing Theory's tests' Part I: On Past and Potential Testability of the Theory,' *Journal of Financial Economics* 4, 129-176.

Roll, R., 2004, Empirical TIPs, *Financial Analyst Journal* 60.

Ross, S., 1997, Hedging Long Run Commitments: Exercises in Incomplete Market Pricing, *Economic Notes* 26, 385-419.

Rubinstein, M., 1976, The strong case for the generalized logarithmic utility model as the premier model of financial markets, *Journal of Finance* 31, 551-571.

Schrock, N., 1971, The theory of asset choice: simultaneous holding of short and long positions in the futures market, *Journal of Political Economy* 79, 270-293.

Schroder, M., 1999, Changes of Numeraire for Pricing Futures, Forwards, and Options, *Review of Financial Studies* 12, 1143 – 63.

Schwartz, E., 1997, The Stochastic Behavior of Commodity Prices: Implications for Valuation and Hedging, *Journal of Finance* 52, 923-73.

Schwartz, E.S. and J.E. Smith, 2000, Short-term Variations and Long-term Dynamics in Commodity Prices, *Management Science* 46, 893-911.

Sharpe, W., 1964, Capital Asset Prices: A Theory of Market Equilibrium Under Conditions of Risk, *Journal of Finance* 19, 425-442.

Shiller, R., 1993, Macro markets: Creating institutions for managing society's largest economic risks, Clarendon Lectures in Economics. Oxford and New York: Oxford University Press, Clarendon Press.

Siddique, A., 2003, Common asset pricing factors in volatilities and returns in futures markets, *Journal of Banking and Finance* 27, 2347–2368.

Sidrauski, M., 1967, Rational Choice and Patterns of Growth in a Monetary Economy, *American Economic Review* 57, 534-544.

Smith, C., 1995, Corporate Risk Management: Theory and Practice, *Journal of Derivatives* 2, 21-30.

Solnik, B., 1991, *International Investments*, Reading, Mass.: Addison-Wesley.

Stulz, R., 1984, Optimal Hedging Policies, *Journal of Financial and Quantitative Analysis* 19, 127-40.

Subrahmanyam, M., 1996, The term structure of Interest rates: Alternative Paradigms and Implications for Financial Risk Management, *Geneva papers on risk and insurance theory* 21, 7-28.

Sumner, S., 1995, The Impact of Futures Price Targeting on the Precision and Credibility of Monetary Policy, *Journal of Money, Credit, and Banking* 27, 89-106.

Sumner, S., 1997, Can Monetary Stabilization Policy Be Improved by CPI Futures Targeting? Reply, *Journal of Money, Credit, and Banking* 29, 542-45.

Svensson, L. and I. Werner, 1993, Nontraded Assets in Incomplete Markets: Pricing and Portfolio Choice, *European Economic Review* 37, 1149-68.

Telser, L., 2000, *Classic Futures: Lessons from the Past for the Electronic Age,* Risk Books.

Tong, W., 1996, An examination of dynamic hedging, *Journal of International Money and Finance* 15, 19-35.

Tse, Y. and T. Zabotina, 2004, Do designated market makers improve liquidity in open-outcry futures markets ?, *Journal of Futures Markets* 24, 479–502.

Wahab, M., 1995, Conditional dynamics and optimal spreading in the precious metals futures markets, *Journal of Futures Markets* 15, 131-166.

SUBJECT INDEX